Reginald Charles Oldknow

The Mechanism of Men-of-War

Being a Description of the Machinery to be Found in Modern Fighting Ships

Reginald Charles Oldknow

The Mechanism of Men-of-War
Being a Description of the Machinery to be Found in Modern Fighting Ships

ISBN/EAN: 9783337132866

Printed in Europe, USA, Canada, Australia, Japan

Cover: Foto ©ninafisch / pixelio.de

More available books at **www.hansebooks.com**

THE MECHANISM OF MEN-OF-WAR

BEING A DESCRIPTION OF THE MACHINERY
TO BE FOUND IN MODERN
FIGHTING SHIPS

BY

REGINALD C. OLDKNOW

FLEET ENGINEER R.N. (RETIRED)

WITH NUMEROUS ILLUSTRATIONS

LONDON
GEORGE BELL AND SONS
1896

CHISWICK PRESS:—CHARLES WHITTINGHAM AND CO.
TOOKS COURT, CHANCERY LANE, LONDON,

PREFACE.

A BOOK of this description must necessarily be more or less of a compilation, and I have to express my gratitude to the numerous authorities who have so kindly given me permission to make free use of the information derived from them.

Among these I would mention the United States Government, who, through their Naval Attaché, Lieut.-Commander Cowles, gave me permission to quote as I pleased from their invaluable "Naval Progress." To "The Times," "Engineering," "Engineer," and Lord Brassey, my thanks are also due; while the engineering firms of Humphrys, Maudslay, Penn, Earle's, Naval Construction and Armaments Company, Yarrow, Thornycroft, and many others, have most kindly supplied me with material both for text and illustrations.

I am in hopes that the book may be of interest not only to the professional engineer, but also to such of the general public as concern themselves with naval matters. I have tried to write in as popular a style as I could, but it must be confessed that treatises on technical subjects have to remain, in a great measure, technical still.

REGINALD C. OLDKNOW.

139, SHOOTER'S HILL ROAD,
BLACKHEATH.

ERRATUM.

Page 111, under illustration. For *Archer*, read *Barham*.

CONTENTS.

LIST OF ILLUSTRATIONS.

THE MECHANISM OF MEN-OF-WAR.

CHAPTER I.

As a matter of course, when steam had turned out a successful means of propulsion in the mercantile marine, it was not long before it was adopted in the British Navy. After an interval of more than seventy years, it is difficult very often to get at the exact truth, but I think it is pretty well established that the first, or at all events the second, vessel for his Majesty's Sea Service to be fitted with a steam-engine was the *Comet*, a paddle-wheel ship of small size, which was introduced in 1821, and was certainly running about Portsmouth Harbour forty years later, fulfilling the humble, but useful, duties of a tug. Her engines were undoubtedly side-lever, and, I think, were built by Messrs. Boulton and Watt, of Soho, Birmingham, but there is at this date no easily attainable record, and she must indubitably be regarded as an historical ship. Two years later, in 1823, Messrs. Maudslay, of Lambeth, supplied the *Lightning* with engines, and in 1827 they engined the *Echo*, *Confiance*, and *Columbia* with machinery of 200 and 240 horse-power, and the *Dee* received from them engines of 400 horse-power. Of these, the *Echo* and *Dee* were distinguished for their longevity, the last-named being employed as a storeship till some twenty years ago.

B

The speed of these elderly vessels was, as may be supposed, extremely moderate, averaging at their best some seven knots per hour. The pressure of steam in the boilers did not exceed from 4 lb. to 6 lb. above that of the atmosphere, and the stopping and reversing of the engines was a matter of some time and difficulty, excepting to engineers who had long been acquainted with their peculiarities.

I do not purpose in this chapter to give anything like a history of the advance and progress of steam in the Navy, which would fully occupy a much larger volume than this is intended to be, but simply to indicate the most important changes that have occurred, changes which of themselves mark epochs in the narrative of naval engineering.

By 1840 the *Cyclops*, 1,195 tons and 300 horse-power, and the *Gorgon*, 1,108 tons and 320 horse-power, were engaged at the bombardment of Acre, when the *Princess Charlotte* was flagship, on board of which was serving, as a boy of fourteen, the late lamented Sir Geoffrey Hornby, G.C.B. The *Salamander*, a smaller vessel of 220 horse-power, was at this time employed on the coast of Spain, during the Carlist War, under the command of the late Sir Sydney Colpoys Dacres, then a commander. Out of the thirty steamers then on the official "Navy List," all but three were fitted with what were called "side-lever" engines. Side-lever engines are now as obsolete as the ships they used to be placed in, but this form had, in its day, certain solid and undeniable, although old-fashioned, advantages which long enabled it to maintain a successful opposition to its more modern competitors.

In the year 1843 two remarkable events occurred regarding the development of steam propulsion in the Navy. The *Penelope*, a paddle-wheel frigate, afterwards flagship at the Cape, was fitted with tubular boilers, being the first man-of-war that was supplied with any but those of the antiquated "flue" variety; and about the same time the *Black Eagle*, Admiralty yacht, was ordered to be fitted with oscillating cylinders. She had previously side-lever engines, but these were ordered to be removed and replaced by others on the oscillating principle by Messrs. John Penn and Sons. I do not attempt here to describe either the side-lever or oscillating type of marine engine, but the latter is to this day the favourite when on rare occasions the paddle is preferred to the screw as a means of propulsion. I am aware that diagonal cylinders, fixed to the ship's side, have been used lately with success for paddles, particularly in Scotland, but I imagine the oscillating cylinder is hard to beat.

The last paddle engines built for the Royal Navy were those for the Royal yacht *Osborne*, built for the use of H.R.H. the Prince of Wales, which went for her first cruise in the autumn of 1874, and afterwards did the whole of the Indian trip, accompanying her Majesty's ship *Serapis*. These engines were of the oscillating variety, and were supplied by Messrs. Maudslay; they are working in the *Osborne* at the present time, and are as good as ever they were, having outlasted no less than three sets of boilers. In 1827 Mr. Joseph Maudslay invented and patented the oscillating engine, which was first employed for marine purposes in 1828. Mr. John Penn subsequently improved upon it, but its original invention and introduction were due to the firm of Maudslay.

Merely noticing *en passant* the *Terrible*, which was the most powerful steam fighting ship in the world of her date, 1846, and the *Inflexible*, which was the first steam man-of-war to make a voyage round the world, which she did between August, 1846, and September, 1849, at a consumption of 8,121 tons of coal, we come next to the most important invention of the age, the screw-propeller. In 1841 Messrs.

Maudslay engined the first screw vessel in the English Navy, named the *Rattler*, of 888 tons and 518 horse-power. And here I may pause for a moment to bring to the reader's notice the fact that neither tons nor horse-power were then as they are now. The tonnage of a ship in those days was calculated by a somewhat intricate rule, which resulted in giving considerably less than that in vogue universally nowadays, whereby the weight of water displaced by a vessel is considered as her exact tonnage.

The horse-power then was always " nominal," of which the real, or " indicated " power, was about two and a half times the nominal in the case of the *Gorgon* in 1837, till it reached more than seven times the nominal in the case of the *Inconstant* in 1869. The Admiralty at length saw the absurdity of retaining any mention of the nominal horse-power, which has now for almost a quarter of a century become entirely obsolete and forgotten. Of course, in the " Navy List," the powers given are the indicated or real ones.

The *Rattler* was tied to the *Alecto*, paddle vessel, of the same horse-power, by a strong hawser between the sterns of both ships. Both went full speed ahead, and the *Rattler* towed the *Alecto* stern foremost at a speed of 2·8 knots per hour, contrary to the expectations of most of the experts of that period, who had many wise reasons why such an event must be impossible. In 1849 a second experiment was carried out with the *Basilisk*, a powerful paddle-steamer engined by Messrs. Miller, Ravenhill, and Co., of exactly the same horse-power as the *Niger*, *i.e.*, 400, engined by Messrs. Maudslay. Here again the screw towed the paddler at the rate of 1·5 knots per hour. As the result of these experiments the screw-propeller was finally decided on as the most suitable for fighting ships.

Who invented the screw-propeller is to this day a vexed question, on which America, France, and England are never likely to agree. "An early example of a successful screw vessel was the Royal yacht *Fairy*, built of iron in 1845, and engined by Messrs. Penn. She had oscillating cylinders driving a cogged wheel geared into a pinion on the screw-shaft, so that the screw made five revolutions for every one of the engines. She was kept running for many years between Gosport and Cowes, till at last her plating was worn so thin that a bluejacket alongside sent his boat-hook right through it. She was then replaced by the *Alberta*," which was a paddle yacht, as are now all the vessels intended for the personal service of her Majesty.

There is no doubt that, considered solely from a passenger's point of view, there can be no question but that a paddle-ship is in every way preferable to one propelled by a screw. Naturally, the paddles act as a sort of outriggers, which prevent rolling, and the perpetual throb, throb, of the one or possibly two screws is unknown. Nevertheless, in a fighting ship, paddles are as impossible as sails. Sir Charles Napier, when Commander-in-Chief in the Baltic during the Russian War, had for his flagship, the *Duke of Wellington*, what are probably about the last example of geared engines ever used in the Navy for screw propulsion. By "geared" engines, I mean such as working themselves at a low speed, say of twenty revolutions a minute, drive a large cogged wheel, which geared into a small wheel of about one-third of its diameter, which is fixed on the screw-shaft, causes the screw to revolve at sixty revolutions per minute.

About this time a change came over the design of engines for the propulsion of war vessels so complete and radical as to mark a distinct epoch in their history. "When once the fact had been grasped that all men-of-war for the future would be propelled by the screw, the immense advantage realized by the low position of the main shaft, far below the water-line, became apparent, as the engines, being in those

days horizontal, would be in a great measure protected from
the enemy's fire, instead of being, as in paddle-wheel ships,
dangerously and invariably exposed to it.   It was also soon
seen what great benefit would be derived if the engines
were coupled directly to the main shaft, without the inter-
vention of cogged wheels, to obtain the required number of
revolutions of the screw.   To insure this result much
higher speed of crank-shaft was necessary, but the engineering skill of the country proved quite equal to the
occasion.

Messrs. Maudslay and Field, and Messrs. John Penn and
Sons, now began to almost monopolize the Government
orders, as I find that of twenty-six sets of screw engines
completed for the Government between the years 1852 and
1860 twenty-one are credited to these two firms. The workmanship of both was admirable, but at that time Messrs.
Maudslay erred, if anything, on the side of strength, and
Messrs. Penn on the side of lightness.   The number,
"twenty-six," given above is exclusive of a large fleet of
high-pressure steam gunboats that were built and engined
with unexampled rapidity at the beginning of the Russian
War.

High-pressure steam was first tried in the Navy in
September, 1853, on board the corvette *Malacca*.   She
was fitted with engines working with steam at 60 lb.
pressure by Messrs. Penn, but she was not a success;
engineers had not yet been educated up to so vast an
innovation.

"In 1860 was completed for sea a ship remarkable from
an historical point of view as the last three-decker in commission on active service in the British Navy.   This was the
Victoria, of 120 guns and 4,403 indicated horse-power.
She was fitted by Messrs. Maudslay with horizontal double
piston-rod return connecting-rod engines, a type they had

made peculiarly their own, and from which for a great many years they never varied. The *Victoria* relieved the *Marlborough*, a ship of a similar kind, but of only 3,054 indicated horse-power, as flagship of the Commander-in-Chief on the Mediterranean station. Her engine-room, as compared with the cramped chambers of modern vessels, was of palatial dimensions. The pressure of steam in the boilers was 22 lb., and at full power the ship attained a speed of over twelve knots. With sail set on her enormous yards, and her progress perhaps helped by her screw, she was a magnificent sight as she made her way in or out of the harbours of Malta or Corfu. But her day had come, she was the last of her race; for it was recognized that in a combat with even an ironclad of her day she could have been nothing but a floating shambles. She is, however, worthy of mention here as being probably the finest specimen of a wooden steam man-of-war the world has ever seen. She had but that one commission, and has quite lately been sold to be broken up."[1]

About this time various causes were combining to bring about the substitution of iron for wood as a shipbuilding material. There is no doubt the necessity of employing a stronger material to resist the increasing vibration set up by increased speeds had a great deal to do with it. The *Mersey*, *Doris*, and *Orlando*, all built as answers to the defiance of the American *Niagara*, had, I think, only one commission each, in consequence of their wooden sterns being unable to withstand the enormous shaking of their propellers at full speed. Iron had been used before in the Navy, but had not been much approved of. The frigate *Vulcan* was finished in 1849, and the troopships *Megæra* and *Simoom* in the following year; but it was not till June,

---

[1] Captain Eardley Wilmot's " Development of Navies."

1859, that *La Gloire*, the magnificent conception of M. Dupuys de Lôme, forced us to attempt a still more magnificent counterblast in the shape of the *Warrior*, a splendid ship when she was designed and constructed, and a useful vessel to this day.

The construction of the *Warrior*, however, though a landmark in naval history, had no direct effect on naval engineering. If higher speeds or greater powers were demanded, engines were made bigger, and that was all. There were no alterations in design, excepting, of course, some improvements in details, but boiler pressure had by this time reached 25 lb. per square inch, and consumption of coal had to a slight extent diminished in consequence, though the general principle and arrangement of the machinery remained unaltered. "The engines of the *Warrior*, however, when she was first commissioned, were considered to involve so vast a responsibility, and to require such effective supervision, that it was decided to take the unprecedented step of appointing *two* chief engineers to her, whereas to-day the post would unhesitatingly be given to the junior chief-engineer in the fleet, if it happened to be vacant, and he to be unemployed. Messrs. Penn and Sons obtained the contract for these engines, as also for those of the sister ship *Black Prince*.

"Here a most curious fact may be mentioned which excited a good deal of speculation at the time. The designs for the two ironclads were got out at the Admiralty by Mr. Watts, Chief Constructor of the Navy, in consultation with Mr. Scott Russell, and identical drawings were sent to the contractors, the Thames Iron Shipbuilding Company, and Messrs. R. Napier and Sons, of Glasgow, for their information and guidance. The engines were in every way duplicates, of course. And yet the *Warrior* was, and is to this day, appreciably superior both in steaming and sailing to the *Black Prince*. Many ingenious explanations for this difference were proposed, but none that could in any way be called convincing." [1]

It may seem to my readers that I am dwelling to an unnecessary length on the early history of steam in the Navy, but I imagine that anybody who feels any interest in its present condition will likewise be glad to learn something of its past. How from the ponderous side-lever engine of the *Comet* in 1821 have arisen the triple-expansion engines of the torpedo-boat destroyers of the present year is surely a bit of history worth tracing and knowing.

By 1860 the consumption of coal in the Royal Navy had increased to so great an extent as compared with that of the mercantile marine under similar circumstances, that the Admiralty determined to give *carte blanche* to three eminent engineering firms to design and construct machinery for three crack sailing frigates, with the one single object of economy of fuel. The firms were Messrs. Maudslay, Messrs. Penn, and Messrs. Randolph and Elder. The ships were the *Octavia*, *Arethusa*, and *Constance*. The results were not very satisfactory, for not one of the three ever saw a second commission, and all the machinery which cost such a lot of money has long ago gone to the scrap-heap.

The engines of Messrs. Maudslay and Messrs. Penn were, except in detail, much the same as had been previously supplied, but the Scotch firm entered the lists with six cylinders, which was the first introduction of the compound engine into her Majesty's Navy. So little, however, was at that time known on the subject that the *Constance* did little, if at all, better than her sisters.

The next event of importance in marine engineering was the advent of a small ironclad, the *Pallas*, in 1866, designed

<hr />

[1] Captain Eardley Wilmot's "Development of Navies."

by Sir E. J. Reed and engined by Messrs. Humphrys with
the first efficient compound engines used in the service, for
the machinery of the *Constance* gave never-ending worry
and anxiety to all who were responsible for its working,
while that of the *Pallas* gave no trouble at all.

"The *Pallas* had only two cylinders instead of six, of un-
equal volume, one being four times the size of the other. The
steam was admitted at high pressure, 60 lb., into the small
cylinder, and thence passed into the larger one, which it of
course filled by its expansion. This is the whole principle
of compound engines; she had surface condensers, and
there is no doubt that for the horse-power developed,
and for those days, she was very economical in fuel. The
boilers were fitted with superheaters, a series of tubes at the
base of the funnel through which the steam passed, with the
object of drying it and surcharging it with heat—a contrivance that was always looked upon with distrust by
naval engineers, and has long ago passed into oblivion.
Her speed was 13·4 knots, and she was a handy and essentially comfortable little ship." [1]

The success of the *Pallas* induced the Admiralty, but not
until after a considerable interval, to order compound
engines for nearly all their new ships, which necessitated
surface condensers and the employment of steam of not
less than 60 lb. pressure. The change in the character of
boilers consequent on this alteration was remarkable. Instead of the square box type which had up to now been exclusively used, a form was introduced resembling in shape
a Gloucester cheese set on edge, with the furnaces on one
of its flat sides. This shape, except where water-tube
boilers have been introduced, has maintained its position
to the present day; only, whereas it formerly was, for

---

[1] Captain Eardley Wilmot's "Development of Navies."

convenience sake, oval, it is now, for strength's sake, universally circular.

With increased pressure came increased thickness of plates, and, as a natural consequence, increased difficulty of manufacture. Holes for rivets that used to be punched, leaving rough and torn edges, were now drilled, insuring much better workmanship, but not eventually costing much more, on account of the improvements effected in machine tools.

The *Penelope*, completed in 1868, is noteworthy as being the first ironclad fitted with twin screws, but, although this principle is now adopted for all ships above the size of a gunboat, when the five vessels of the *Audacious* class were built, two of them, the *Triumph* and *Swiftsure*, only had one propeller each, indicating a hesitation on the part of the Admiralty to pledge themselves too deeply to a new principle—a reproach which certainly cannot be levelled at their successors of to-day, who have adopted the Belleville boilers for the two largest and most powerful cruisers the world has as yet seen.

Just after the *Penelope*, in August, 1869, there was commissioned a simple-engines, surface-condenser, single-screw frigate which certainly excited the wonder and admiration of the world. This was the *Inconstant*, designed by Sir E. J. Reed and engined by Messrs. Penn. She was the first ship to be sheathed outside with two layers of wood, teak and fir, on which copper could be fastened as on to a wooden hull. Her engines worked up to 7,360 horse-power, nominally 1,000, at her trial trip in Stokes Bay, which gave her a mean speed of 16·51 knots, which had never up to that time been approached by a fighting ship. She happened to be the next vessel in line to the *Captain*, when that unfortunate ship capsized on the night of October 6th, 1870, and the next day was dispatched to Plymouth with the sad news.

She averaged 15¾ knots, with one boiler out of her ten kept in reserve. Twenty-five years ago this was considered a very fine performance, but she is now quite obsolete.

The next important event was the completion of the *Iris* and *Mercury*, both engined by Messrs. Maudslay. They were sister ships in every particular, built side by side in Pembroke Dockyard, the hulls constructed of soft Landore steel, and the shafting of Whitworth's compressed steel, and, for the first time in the Navy, tubular, but the experience gained in the elder ship, the *Iris*, led to the magnificent result on trial of 18·87 knots per hour by the *Mercury*, and this in 1879. It is hardly to be wondered at that the fame of such unparalleled achievements spread all over Europe and excited the emulation of foreign powers, but at that time they had neither engineers nor shipwrights who could pretend to rival ours.

These two vessels, splendid as they were, and useful as they are to this day, have two very grave defects; they are totally unprotected and their supply of coal is so small that at full speed they would soon become *hors de combat*. They, however, formed a distinct epoch in naval engineering. Perhaps in consequence of the first defect mentioned, which was minimised as far as practicable by water-tight subdivision and coal protection, it was somewhere about this date that Rear-Admiral Robert Scott conceived the idea of protecting the engine-rooms of comparatively light cruisers by the working in to the ship of a steel-armoured deck, up to three or four inches thickness. This was indeed a boon to the engineers, who had long known that the proper and normal position of the cylinder and piston of a steam-engine is the vertical, but, having to keep themselves and their machinery in safety below the water-line, had been fain to put up with the horizontal.

Now, however, all that is changed. The *Shannon* and

Dreadnought, both built at Pembroke, and engined, the one by Laird, the other by Humphrys, were the first ironclads to be fitted with vertical engines, which are now of universal occurrence in the fighting ships of the Navy.

The *Rattlesnake*, a first-class gunboat of 550 tons, built and engined by Messrs. Laird, was launched in September, 1886, and was the first instance of triple-expansion engines being supplied to the Admiralty. Every care was taken with the manufacture of her machinery, but it was sufficiently over the stipulated weight for the Admiralty to inflict a smart fine on the contractors. The performances of the ship were, however, so good that, I am happy to say, the money was returned to them. I have now completed my brief historical sketch, and must pass on to subjects more modern.

CHAPTER II.

To an outsider, ignorant of machinery and unacquainted with the methods of making it, the various processes through which it passes after being evolved from the brain of its designer in the drawing office till it is actually fitted in position in its own engine-room on board ship, cannot fail to be deeply interesting, that is, supposing him to care anything about the matter at all.

When the Admiralty have made known to a certain number of selected firms their desire to receive tenders for the construction of a set of engines of, say, 10,000 horse-power natural draught, and 13,000 horse-power forced or induced draught, accompanying their notice by a severely strict specification, the firms, each one for itself, consider at what price they can afford to undertake the work. And this is, in these days of competition and labour disputes, too often ruinously low. Time was when the Government orders given to Maudslay, Humphrys, and Penn meant such a percentage of profit as to enable large fortunes to be amassed, but now that Glasgow, Barrow-in-Furness, Birkenhead, Jarrow, and Hull have joined in the scramble for employment, I have been assured that contracts are often undertaken with no idea of any present profit, but simply to keep the factory occupied and the staff of workmen together. The Admiralty, I believe, almost always, but not invariably, accept the lowest tender made, and when once this point has been settled work begins with the favoured firm.

It is often made a ground of complaint against the British Admiralty that they interfere too much with their contractors. That while foreign governments are content to leave details to the manufacturers, and are perfectly satisfied so long as they get good workmanship and the satisfactory performance of the conditions demanded, our naval authorities insist on having their not always successful finger in the pie ; and for their mistakes they have often had to pay pretty smartly. I believe, however, that this grievance of undue interference is nowadays gradually being reduced.

In these days the marine engine has so nearly approached perfection that all makers have almost the same designs, and there is little room left for originality. With boilers it is of course very different, as we shall see further on. At the same time every firm has its own traditions and peculiarities, and, to their credit be it said, almost all firms have a constant desire towards improvements, which of small importance though they be, perhaps, still tend towards the unattainable goal of perfection.

The member, or employé, of the firm that has undertaken for so many thousand pounds to construct the machinery for one of her Majesty's battleships, or, say, first-class cruisers, to whom is intrusted the work of designing it, first makes a rough sketch embodying his principal ideas, from which, after it has been submitted to the criticism of all concerned, a finished drawing is made which is sent to the Admiralty, who are not difficult to please with large engines, but who are apt sometimes to be very troublesome with small ones, as the builders of torpedo-boats and "destroyers" can testify.

The number of drawings required for a first-class set of engines at the present time is enormous. Every portion of the work must be represented on separate sheets of paper for the use of the artisans in the shops, who are thus responsible to their employers for the accuracy of their work. It stands to reason that a large staff of draughtsmen forms an important part of every engineering establishment. It might be thought from the clean and gentlemanly nature of their employment, and the sub-scientific character of their acquirements that they would command high pay, but this is not the case ; and there are many instances where a blacksmith earns double the pay of a highly skilled draughtsman, while the draughtsman has always to be decently dressed, and, except on Sundays, the forgeman is clothed in blue serge.

In earlier times, often much more than this, before machinery had intervened to disturb the lordly earnings of the forgemen, the contrast between the remuneration of the mere manual labour and skill of the smith and the scientific attainments of the draughtsman was greater than it is at present.

It can easily be understood that before the detail drawings for the production of a huge set of engines could be got out, delicate and difficult calculations as to the weight and strength of the different portions of the machinery were of old time absolutely necessary. But, excepting in the case of a quite new departure, it is not so now. Almost every firm that contracts for the manufacture of engines and boilers for the Royal Navy has a vast store of previous experience to draw upon, which renders new calculations generally not needful. Nevertheless, the good and efficient draughtsman must be prepared to make such calculations when they are asked for. Be this as it may, a detail drawing of every part of the machinery to be constructed is a necessity. As a general rule these drawings are kept in store, to be referred to when occasion requires; but tracings, as they are called, executed on thin paper, are now largely made by women and girls, and, after being mounted on stout calico, are sent into the shops for the use of the workmen.

Every workman in every department of a large engineering establishment works from a drawing, or, at least, almost everyone. In the "pattern shop," where wooden models of all parts of the machinery that are destined to be cast are made of fir or plane-tree, for the use of the moulders, the drawing is of paramount importance.

Pattern-making is a trade, almost an art, of itself. Patterns must not only be made slightly larger than the drawings indicate, to allow for a certain inevitable shrinkage in the metal when it cools, but they must also possess a little taper, that is, be ever so little larger at the top than the bottom, so that they may be drawn out of the loam or sand, of which the mould is composed, without injury to it. An expert pattern-maker can generally command high wages, and it is a very cleanly and pleasant trade, in which, however, there is not so much competition as might be expected, for it demands not only a capacity for understanding drawings easily, but also a certain delicacy of touch, neither of which are universal among artisans.

The pattern, having been completed, and passed by the foreman, is now sent to the foundry. Years ago very few of the large engineering firms did their own casting, but put out their work to adjacent iron or brassfounders, who made a more than comfortable living by undertaking it. Nowadays this is largely altered. Except for heavy steel work, very few firms go outside their own establishments for castings connected with the main propelling machinery. Of course, I say nothing here of sub-contracts for auxiliary

C

engines, which are, perhaps, more frequent than they should be.

When the pattern arrives at the foundry, it is, if large, such as the blade of a screw-propeller, imbedded in loam, the mould being strengthened outside sometimes with bricks and iron to withstand the interior pressure of the molten metal ; if small, such as, say, a stuffing-box gland, it is imbedded in sand, but in each case the principle involved is the same. The pattern is withdrawn from the mould, which is filled up with the melted steel, brass, or what not.

The drawings of those parts of the machinery that cannot be cast in this way are sent to the forge, whence their representatives return, it may generally be said, in a far rougher state than the portions that have been cast from patterns. This, however, by the introduction of machinery, has greatly improved of late years.

Another most important department is that which has to do with the supply of the numberless copper pipes, so necessary in a modern marine engine. Unlike the castings and forgings, these come out of the coppersmiths' shop fit and ready for use. For high-pressure steam it is now a very common practice to "serve" the copper pipe all over with fine wire, which adds enormously to its power to resist explosion, as also, in a less degree, to its cost. In the most modern engines it is also the practice to substitute strongly welded and lap-jointed steel pipes for copper pipes, especially when, as in the case of main steam-pipes, they are of large diameter. Like pattern-making, and all the other trades which go to make up the various professions of an engineering workman, a coppersmith has a trade to himself. Only premium apprentices are initiated into all the trades, and they too often but scantily.

A "handy man," who can do anything that comes in his

FIG. 2.—VIEW OF A TURNERY. MESSRS. MAUDSLAY, SONS, AND FIELD.

way, is hampered by the laws of trade unionism in Great
Britain, but can often pick up a monstrous good living in
Australia or New Zealand. Hence the number of desertions
that used, formerly more often than now, to take place
among the blacksmiths, carpenters, and shipwrights, from
her Majesty's ships in those parts. Frequently the fugitives
found out their mistake. Somebody discovered their
identity, and they had to part with half their wages to
prevent his " splitting " on them.

From the foundry and the forge the articles produced in
each of these departments find their way to the turnery
and fitting-shop. It is here that they are finished with all
the exactitude that machinery and the highest variety of
skilled manual labour permit. Sliding surfaces, such as
guides, are frequently fitted to the one-hundredth part of
an inch. Steel is now almost universally used wherever
practicable, on account of the saving in weight, which is
accentuated in the case of large shafts by their being
tubular and made of Whitworth's compressed metal, the
strength of which is unsurpassed.

In the fitting-shop all kinds of labour-saving contrivances
are now in vogue, more particularly in the more modern
engineering establishments. Ribbon saws, such as are in
use at Messrs. Penn's, and small hydraulic lifts, like those
introduced by Messrs. J. and G. Thomson at Clydebank
some years ago, have been found of the greatest value in
expediting the work. Lathes, planing and slotting, and
screw-cutting machines, of different types and for different
purposes, are all in use, in innumerable varieties, in every
fitting-shop in the United Kingdom. To fully and accurately describe one of these would require more space than
that afforded by the whole of this volume, and to those of
my readers who are anxious to gain some knowledge of its
interior I can only say, Go and see for yourselves.

When the various parts of a set of marine engines have been made as fit as possible for the work they have to do, they are straightway conveyed to the erecting-shop, where they are put together, exactly as they will be later in the engine-room of the ship to which they are destined. All the photographs of machinery that appear in this book, or indeed any other, have been taken in the erecting-shop, where only sufficient light can be obtained. Occasionally, but very rarely, when the engines are thus put together, some trifling error is discovered, which is, of course, rectified before they are pulled to pieces and sent on board ship. I am not here speaking of the boilers, of which I shall have much to say further on, but of the engines themselves which form the propelling machinery of the vessel.

The art of putting engines into a ship is one of the most difficult known to the profession, but in these days of steel, now the all but universal material for shipbuilding, it is of less difficulty than it used to be when wood was so largely employed. Out of the seven or eight corvettes of the "gem" class that were built twenty years ago, the machinery of only one of them, the *Emerald*, never gave any trouble at all, principally because such pains were taken to see that her screw-shaft was truly laid. The chief engineer of one of them never went to bed while the engines were running, and the chief engineer of another committed suicide at the Cape, doubtless from intense mental worry and anxiety.

Naturally, the most experienced and capable men are employed by the different firms on this important part of the business. Each firm has an employé, who is styled an outdoor foreman, who with a competent staff is as nearly as may be continuously engaged in putting machinery into new vessels. When this work has been satisfactorily performed, and everything is ready, preparations are made for

the trial trip of the engines, on the results of which will
depend, to a certain extent, the future speed of the ship,
and her reception from the contractors by the Admiralty.

During the whole time of the construction of the engines,
the chief engineer who is hereafter to have charge of them
has superintended, on behalf of the Government, the various
stages of their development. Unless he or the contractors
are very cantankerous, he is usually on excellent terms
with them. If he desires some small improvement he
is generally met more than halfway by the builders, but
if they and he persistently differ, the matter is, of course,
referred to the Engineering Department of the Admiralty,
who decide it. Of a necessity, the wider awake this officer
is while he is in the contractors' shops the less occasion
will he have to find fault, and the smoother will be the
course of things, but he must endeavour to steer as nearly
as he can between officiousness and negligence.

In these later days an engineering inspector is usually
appointed to look after the construction of the machinery
of all the small craft—torpedo-boats, destroyers, and the
like—being built in a certain district, such as the Thames,
the Tyne, or the Mersey, on account of the terrible scarcity
in the Navy of engineer officers; but of this I shall have
more to say by-and-by.

There is hardly any large firm of marine engineers that
does all the work of an important contract by itself—in
fact, I may say, none. But they differ among themselves
very largely as to how far they are dependent on outside
establishments for help—particularly in the case of auxiliary
engines.

The sub-contracts of some firms are very extensive, while
others do nearly all their work themselves. Of course it is
of no concern to the Admiralty who does the work so long
as it is well done. Certain firms have made to themselves

a specialty of certain forms of manufacture, say, distilling apparatus, dynamos, steering-engines, and the like, and doubtless those builders of engines are wise who buy these things from their makers instead of making them themselves; and the argument that they thus employ fewer hands is nonsense, for if fewer hands are employed in London, more are at work in Ipswich, or elsewhere.

The most serious point to be considered in the making of engines, whether for the Royal Navy or the mercantile marine, is the excessive competition, which has cut down prices to such a low ebb. There is no doubt that foreign governments are now the most valued customers of English manufacturers, for they pay higher prices than our own Admiralty, without the red tape or official interference, and there can be no doubt foreigners who have vessels built by English first-class firms get quite as well, and often better, served, than our own Government; but this state of affairs cannot be expected to last very long. Sooner or later other nations will arrive at such a pitch of excellence in the making of engines that they will no longer come to us for them, who are indeed rapidly losing the great superiority we formerly undoubtedly possessed. We once possessed this to such an extent that it was rare to find a big firm that had not some foreign students sent by their governments, who sometimes paid considerable premiums for their education, but that was long ago. I was myself, during my five years' apprenticeship, shopmate with four Italians, one South American, three Swedes, two Germans, and a Dane, all of whom, excepting one of the Germans, were sent over and paid for by their respective governments.

These governments have adopted a different plan nowadays. An English firm is invited to set up an engineering establishment under its own direct supervision, but employing only foreign labour, and it would be odd indeed if under these circumstances no capable engineers were turned out among the foreigners. At Pozzuoli, at Barcelona, and at Bilboa, this arrangement has had surprisingly good results for the Italian and Spanish authorities.

The French have for a long period of time held on their own way, with such success that we have borrowed from them from time to time many improvements, and, of late, Belleville boilers. But they have only won their way to the front at the expense of many failures, some of which remain to them, and various fatal accidents. The same might have been said of us years ago, but not lately.

Perhaps the most striking change in the manufacture of marine engines is the comparatively recent substitution of steel, almost universally, for the cast and wrought-iron of twenty years ago. I know of more than one large establishment in the north that in the days of iron was flourishing like a green bay tree, and that now, because its proprietors neglected or declined to recognize the coming supremacy of steel, can nowhere be found. Some day, possibly, steel will be superseded by aluminium. Who knows? Orders have been given that in future in the German Navy no more wooden furniture is to be carried, after the teachings of the Chino-Japanese War, but aluminium ware is to be employed instead. Torpedo gear is already being made of aluminium.

CHAPTER III.

Now, assuming the engines to have been safely erected in their own engine-room on board the ship they are eventually to propel, to the satisfaction of the contractors, the chief engineer of the vessel, and the dockyard officials, the machinery will be subjected to a preliminary trial by the contractors, which affords them a good gauge as to what its behaviour and the speed of the vessel will be when it comes to the official trial by the naval authorities. The necessity for such a trial is of course disputed by nobody, and the results are nowadays seldom anything but satisfactory to all concerned. Nevertheless, it has to take place.

There is a clever article in "Harper's Magazine" for March, 1895, by William Floyd Sicard, on the "Trial Trip of a Cruiser," which is very interesting as showing how far American customs differ from ours on occasions of this kind. He tells us that the "official" trial is "under the direction of a board of naval officers appointed for the purpose by the Secretary of the Navy, and is generally held off the coast of New England, at a point designated by the contractors, where the water is deep and the conditions are favourable for a fair test. If a speed trial is contemplated, the run is made over a measured course, and all steps are taken to secure exhaustive data of the vessel's performance, for upon this depends"—strange as it may sound to us—

" the premium that the contractor shall gain, or penalty that he shall pay, as the vessel comes above or below her contract requirements. On account of the large sum of money involved, a trial trip is never entered upon until the contractor feels reasonably sure that his vessel will come up to the requirements, and in order to be certain of this it is customary to have one or more preliminary trials.

" These are entirely affairs of the company building the vessel, held by them at their own expense and for their own purposes, the Government having nothing whatever to do with them. . . . In the builder's, or preliminary trial, the ship is seldom pushed to do her best, for from her general behaviour then an opinion can be formed whether she will develop the horse-power necessary to drive her over the course at the required speed. As a rule the engines are speeded up to nearly the required number of revolutions, but the steam pressure is not constantly at the maximum ; the boilers not being pushed to their utmost, and the air-pressure in the fire-rooms is not held as high as when the vessel is doing her best. Nor is it necessary or advisable to require the machinery to work at its highest power, for it is new, and should be driven slowly at first, and after-wards gradually speeded up to its limit. So if the engines run smoothly and well, developing somewhere near the necessary power, with a good reserve, and the bearings and moving parts do not become heated and ' seize,' there will generally be but little trouble in getting the required speed out of the ship when the final or official test comes. If the preliminary trial is a success, as it usually is, the official trial follows soon after."

The article from which I quote is a description, not of an official but of a contractor's trial, for the purpose of satis-fying the builders that they are prepared to ask the Govern-ment for the official series of runs to take place. " There

are on board almost as many men as the ship will carry
when she finally goes into commission. The director of the
trial, one of the engineering members of the firm, is a man
of large experience, and a veteran in all that pertains to the
running of vessels at high speed. All on board are under
his orders, and with him in a great measure rests the responsibility of the trip. The captain, who has charge of
the practical navigation of the ship, is also under his orders,
and is assisted by a pilot who is familiar with the locality
where the run is to be made. The engine and boiler-rooms
are under the general supervision of one of the firm's staff
of engineers, and under his direction are the men who
actually run the engines—men tried and seasoned by many
a trial trip, and who can be depended on to do all that can
be done to make the trial a success. . . . By far the greater
part of those on board belong to the engine and boiler-
room forces, for on a trial that is essentially for speed, and
depending therefore entirely on the propelling machinery,
every precaution must be taken to insure that each detail
of the machinery has proper attention, and this of course
requires a great number of men. Engineers, wipers and
oilers, machinists, water-tenders, firemen, coal-passers, and
skilled mechanics of every kind, are the men who make up
the crew of a large vessel." In our Navy they are simply
known as engineer officers, artificers, and stokers.

"Early in the afternoon the vessel is headed out to sea for
a run in deep water under forced draught. Now the decks
are virtually deserted, all the men are below at their stations,
attending to their various engineering duties, and leaving
only the navigating officers and the visitors on the bridge.
. . . On the bridge is also a telegraphic indicator for signalling to the engine-room. This apparatus is so arranged
that by simply pushing a handle to different marked posi-
tions on a dial it immediately strikes a large gong in the

engine-room, thus calling the engineer's attention to a dial placed there, on which he can read the order transmitted from the bridge, as ' Stop,' ' Ahead,' or ' Astern,' etc., the order being indicated by means of a pointer on the dial. As soon as the engineer reads this order he pushes the handle of his instrument to a corresponding position, and this movement being transmitted back to the bridge shows the officer in charge that the order is understood.

" There are also two dials on the bridge showing, by means of pointers, which way the screws are turning, so the captain can tell at a glance whether the engines are running ahead or astern." And here it seems a proper time to discuss at short length the important question of engine-room telegraphs.

In a number of the " Army and Navy Gazette," published a few years ago, was a leading article on engine-room telegraphs which is as true now as when it was first written. The writer says that the question how to establish a means of communication between the officers of the upper deck and the engine-room, which shall combine the greatest simplicity and speed with the least liability to failure or error, is always one of great importance to naval tacticians.

The methods at present in use are three—viz., vocal, mechanical, and electric. In the dark ages of steam navigation the first of these only was in vogue, and that in its most primitive form. The shrill-voiced, smutty-faced call-boy, with his " Ease 'er," " Back 'er," " Stop 'er," was familiar enough to those who patronized the river steamboats of a generation or two ago, but the call-boy is almost as extinct now on the Thames as the " rat in the fore-chains."

It must be a very old-world steamer nowadays that does not boast an engine-room telegraph of some sort. The voice-tube, however, is still in very general use as an auxiliary to the telegraph on board nearly all men-of-war, and probably will never be altogether superseded, especially as a means of communication with magazines and shell-rooms. It is, nevertheless, open to several objections. Its maximum length for efficiency, taking a pipe of one inch in diameter, is about 300 feet if straight, but for every bend at right angles, or nearly so, 15 feet must be deducted.

It requires, moreover, a certain amount of practice. A man who shouts into the mouthpiece who is hoarse with hailing the foretop, or who speaks through a thick moustache, will probably only succeed in conveying a confused rumbling to the other end. But supposing his accents to be ever so clear and distinct, if the engines are working at a moderately high rate of speed, the odds are that the clack of the feed-valves, the hum of the fans, or some similar noises, will render him unintelligible to his listener on the platform.

No one who has not experienced it can imagine the irritation caused, at perhaps an anxious moment when the telegraph has broken down, by the frequent whistle of the voice-tube, followed by the inevitable, " *What* did you say ?" All the same when things are quiet in the engine-room, or the ship is in harbour, the speaking-tube will always be useful for brief orders from above and reports from below, such as relate to ashes, water-tight doors, and the like, and thus save a good deal of running up and down ladders. This is its legitimate use.

It is strange, considering the number of years the mechanical telegraph has been in use, not in the British Navy only, but in steamships all over the world, that, although there are of course many makers, it still remains, to all intents and purposes, the same as when it was first introduced some half a century ago. As long as the distance to be covered was short, and the number of changes in the direction of rods was few, its working was quite satisfactory, or nearly so; but when steam was applied to line-of-battle ships difficulties began to arise.

The workmanship might be good in the first instance, the shafting truly in line, and the bevel-wheels accurately fitted, but in a short time the natural straining and yielding of wooden beams in a seaway did their work, and the index in the engine-room as often pointed to the line between two orders as anywhere else. To overhaul and attempt to adjust the telegraph on coming into harbour came as natural as drawing fires and sweeping tubes.

The inherent rigidity of steel ships might be supposed to have got rid of this evil—it has materially diminished it, that is all. Whether it be that the workmanship is not as good as it might be, or the metal of which the wheels are made is inferior and easily grinds away, or, what is more probable, the strain caused by the transmission of power through such long distances is too much for the rods and connections, the fact remains that the engine-room telegraph of to-day is a far from perfect implement.

A manifest step in the direction of improvement would be a judicious wedding of electrical with mechanical power. As things are at present, in the majority of instances, the hand that works the telegraph on the bridge has not only to cause the index to move below, but also to sound a gong at each shift of position. For this there is no necessity. All engine-room gongs should be electric, and each movement of the handle on deck should simply make contact, and sound a note of warning below. In like manner the answering gong from the engine-room, showing the order is understood, should be electric also. By this alteration a good deal of mechanism that throws extra strain on the shafting, and is constantly getting out of order, might be done away with,

Various small improvements have from time to time been introduced, but in its main features the telegraph remains what it was when first invented.

Such as it is, the captain of the ship now reaches over and moves the handle. "Instantly from far down in the engine-room is heard a faint clanging; it is the gong warning the engineer that we will shortly begin the run. The tremble and vibration increase somewhat as the ship rushes on with a long heavy roll, now to starboard, now to port. The brown smoke that was lazily rising from the funnels turns darker and increases in volume." Further on, the writer tells us, "Now smoke, thick and black, is pouring from the funnels in great clouds, showing that the boiler fires are being urged fiercely."

In an English trial trip, happily, there is a very small display of smoke, for only from South Wales can almost smokeless fuel be obtained. At one time it was seldom used except on board the Royal yachts, now, when it can be obtained, it is the common property of the whole service.

Formerly, political requirements induced the Admiralty to order the use of "Baxter's mixture" (so called from its secretary, the then member for Dundee), which was composed of two-thirds Welsh and one-third North-country coal. In vain commanders-in-chief protested, pointing out that the smoke produced by it rendered steam evolutions difficult and dangerous.

"The captain again pushes the handle of the telegraph, this time to full speed ahead. The wind is blowing strongly, and now and then a white-cap appears on the water. Some great white sea-gulls sweep round us, picking up pieces of bread thrown overboard, and a 'Mother Cary's chicken' flutters here and there in the wake of the ship." Not on a British trial would it flutter. Stormy petrels are not so common in England.

A peculiarity of high-speed trials is the enormous wave that is developed near the bow and travels along with the ship. Some ships make a much larger bow wave than others, as can be seen from the photographs of various ships at full speed. Abaft all, at the stern of the ship, says Mr. Sicard, "is the rudder, and a little forward of it and on either side are the propellers, or screws, which propel the ship. The water seems to fall away from the stern, and a great following wave stretches out on either side. Directly below is a huge pile of white foam, seething, boiling, swirling here and there, like the rapids of Niagara, while far behind a broad path of smooth water, covered with foam and bubbles, stretches towards the horizon, easily distinguished from the ordinary sea waves, and looking like some great smooth road surrounded by rough ground."

The depth of water has considerable effect upon a vessel's speed, shoal water retarding her. In some ships running at a high rate of speed in shoal water, the stern or afterpart is drawn down very considerably. This is caused by the water not filling with sufficient quickness the cavity at the stern caused by the forward movement of the vessel. This lack of water at the stern causes the ship to settle there and be pursued by a huge wave. In one of the American small, swift ships, this settling was so marked that the crest of the following wave actually boiled over at the stern and broke upon the deck. In other words, she was what old-fashioned sailors used to call "pooped."

But to follow Mr. Sicard a little further, "Just above our heads are two immense blowers, forcing fresh air down the ventilator-pipes into the engine-rooms. A long narrow ladder stretches down from the door just mentioned to the engine-room floor; below us lie the engines, and, further forward, the boilers, the seat of power. A strange grinding roar, accentuated at regular intervals, reaches us; as we start down the ladder the air becomes hot and sickly, reeking with the smell of oil and steam. Going down a short distance we come to the 'first platform,' a light iron grating around the upper part of the engines, near the cylinders. Here men are stationed at the indicators—instruments which trace upon small slips of paper diagrams showing at a glance the action of the steam in the cylinders to which they are attached, and from these cards the horse-power developed by the engines will be calculated when the run is over.

"Continuing down the slippery steps, we soon reach the engine-room floor. The engineer stands near us at the hand-wheel of the throttle, now and then opening or closing it slightly, guided by the indications of the steam-gauge. Above tower the great engines, one on each side of the ship, separated by a water-tight bulkhead. The cranks set at different angles seem to fly in every direction, and the cylinders tremble and shake with every stroke of the pistons and the force of the mighty energy imprisoned within.

"The 'engineer's force' is everywhere; men with great syringes for squirting oil on the flying cross-heads; men with oil-cups for the smaller gear; men reaching down and feeling crank-pins; men climbing up and feeling cross-heads; men at the pumps, the bearings, everywhere. The engine-room is a perfect maze of copper pipes and machinery. Pumps seem to be all about, some working constantly, others standing idle at the moment, but in case of emergency ready to be run at an instant's notice." Besides the main engines, there are in large ships a vast number of separate engines for various auxiliary purposes—the *Vulcan* has ninety-eight—but to them I must devote a separate chapter later on.

Mr. Sicard proceeds, "The slightest carelessness or inattention might have the most serious results. Occasionally, though, no amount of care can prevent a bearing or cross-head from heating, particularly if the machinery is new, has not sufficiently worn itself to perform its duties, and is being run at a high rate of speed."

All of which conditions, I may remark, generally obtain on steam trials. If a bearing has become heated excitement runs high in the engine-rooms. "The engines are probably working almost at full power and moving rapidly, so if the heated part cannot be cooled sufficiently they will have to be shut down and the run will be lost. The rush and roar of the machinery, the tremble of the ship as she is forced ahead by the immense horse-power transmitted by each shaft, the hurry of the engineer's force, each one of whom has constant and important duties to perform, all add to the excitement. Water pours in torrents on the heated parts, and as it strikes the flying engines is thrown in all directions. The engine-room floor swims with oil and water, and the oil thus thrown upon the cold-water pipes congeals and completely covers them, looking like snow upon the trees after a heavy storm."

From hence the writer takes us into the "fire-room," or stokehold, as we call it. He says, with truth, that the fireman's task is no easy one, and it requires considerable skill to fire a boiler properly, keeping the fuel well and evenly distributed over the grates. "The huge furnaces fairly devour coal; and when for the purpose of feeding in more the furnace doors are opened, throwing a red glare through the room, we can see the white-hot fuel heaped clear to the crown of the furnace, and the flames that leap halfway up to the smoke-stack rush wildly out, impelled by the 10,000 cubic feet of air per minute furnished by the blowers, which we hear spinning overhead with a steady whir. The amount of coal burned by a large vessel running at full speed is almost incredible. Some of the great Atlantic liners burn from 350 to 400 tons a day, and some of the large cruisers, were they run constantly at full speed, would burn nearly as much."

I never remember reading, from a literary point of view, so excellent an article on so prosaic a subject as the one from which I have been so largely quoting. It is only in matters of small importance that this paper would not answer equally well as a description of a trial trip in the British Navy. English contractors are generally surer of their work than Americans seem to be. They seldom or never have such a severe preliminary trial as the one described above, unless it be for the torpedo-boat destroyers, which have sometimes been driven by Messrs. Yarrow and Messrs. Thornycroft at an even higher rate of speed than that intended to be gained on the official trial. The system of pecuniary rewards and punishments which almost universally obtains in America is to us unknown, of late years, with the result that if the contract horse-power is obtained the manufacturer gets his money, if it is exceeded he gets no more. As to its being under the mark, such a thing never happens nowadays.

Some years ago, when a trial trip was to take place at one of the only three places ever used then, Stokes Bay for Portsmouth, the Maplin Sands for Chatham, or outside Plymouth Breakwater for Devonport, at each of which places there is a " measured mile," a large number of naval engineers would be ordered from the Steam Reserve to attend, but nothing of the kind happens now, because there are no engineers left in Reserve, almost every one is on active service, whence he cannot be spared to go on trial trips.

The contractors' people run, and are responsible for the

working of, the machinery, and dockyard factory officials take diagrams, notes, and the like. There are always two trials of men-of-war, or nearly always, of which the first is called the " natural draught " trial, and is an index of what the ship will do on ordinary service, the other, two or three days later, is called the " forced draught " trial, and shows what it may be hoped will possibly be got out of a ship when she is pressed to the very utmost.

These two trials are of different lengths for different classes of ships, but are usually of from four to eight hours' duration. But besides these trials which determine the acceptance by the Government of the machinery from the contractors, there are frequently other trials during the time the ship is in commission. And it is a noteworthy fact that in many cases when the engine-room staff has got used to the machinery under its charge, often after one or two years' experience of it, better results are actually sometimes obtained than on the official trial.

Thus, a few months ago, the *Vulcan*, a description of whose machinery will appear later on, a torpedo depôt ship of 6,620 tons, with engines of natural draught horse-power of 7,200, was ordered to proceed at full speed, natural draught, from Volo to Malta, for forty-eight hours by the way. She was commissioned at Portsmouth in June, 1893, so she had been at work for one year and nine months. She had to go round Cape Matapan and proceed north as far as Corfu to fill up the time, and even then had to make one turn round the islands of Malta and Gozo. She put in 850 miles in the forty-eight hours, which is an average of 17·75 knots per hour. The *Royal Arthur*, flagship in the Pacific, I am told, did quite as well as this for a similar period.

Now it is quite safe to say that speeds such as these had never previously been attained by any fighting ships in the

world for a run of two whole days. The power in the
Vulcan averaged 7,230, which is thirty more than what is
reckoned as the official natural draught speed, which is a
very good result indeed. In the beginning of the *Vulcan's*
career her boilers were something of a disappointment till
ferrules were fitted in her tubes, but they are now as good
as ever and capable of steaming any distance so long as
the coal, of which there is 1,000 tons, holds out. Probably
no greater speed than seventeen knots could be maintained
for several days on account of the small allowance of grate-
surface, which is really only equal to that of the second-
class cruisers. No assistance was asked for or obtained from
the deck, though on a more prolonged voyage this would
be found necessary. The stokers, engineers, and artificers
were in three watches, with the exception of the chief and
senior engineers, who followed the old familiar routine of
" watch and stop on." The engines worked splendidly, no
water on any bearings, except a very little on the guides,
just sufficient to raise a lather; even this was not necessary
but was a useful precaution. The average number of
revolutions was eighty-five. The total consumption of coal
was 288 tons, or exactly 120 cwts. per hour, being a mean
of 1·865 lb. per indicated horse-power per hour, which is
indeed an excellent result for full speed. The steam pressure was 145 lb., and the links were set to cut off at
$26\frac{1}{2}$ inches, the stroke being 51 inches. At that cut-off
the engines were working practically with the stop-valves
wide open, and eighty revolutions was all that could be
done without running out the links further. The fires
were cleansed every six hours, and the work was very hard,
as the stokers trimmed their own coal and hoisted the ashes
by steam, the only assistance rendered by the deck authorities being the removal of the ashes from the top of the
hoist to the shoot.

It is sometimes assumed that our present system of eight hours' trial under natural and four hours under forced draught is bad and unsatisfactory. It is said that the whole thing is too much of a spurt, and untrustworthy as a guide to the subsequent speed of the ship. The speeds obtained under forced draught on trials, with picked coal, picked men, and every bearing running with oil and water, are quite deceptive, and would never be reached under service conditions. This was no doubt only too true in the past, but here we have examples of certainly two ships—and there are plenty more like them—that for forty-eight hours have actually exceeded the maximum horse-power and speed obtained at their official trials, without any special coal or any distress to their stokers. It is true they were only tried under natural draught.

Forced draught, however, it must be remembered, is only intended to be used on active service in a case of great emergency, there is always a chance of the boilers being injured, and therefore the Admiralty consider it would be unwise to order sea trials of it which could be no profit to any one. The official trials used to be considered valuable as affording a means of comparison between different ships, now they fulfil the much more serviceable duty of indicating what the real speed of the ship will be when the machinery has worn itself into shape and the people are getting used to handling it.

It will be found in most of the new vessels that under such circumstances the speed will be little, if at all, inferior to that of the official trials. Of course, for the first year or so the results obtained at full power will not be so satisfactory, if for no other reason, because a large proportion of the stokers are necessarily green and untrained; but once these men have learned to do their work, all will go well.

I am here speaking of ships and machinery with whose

design and manufacture there is no fault to be found, not of such failures as the *Barham* and *Bellona*, where the old attempt to put a quart of peas into a pint pot was tried once again with the usual lack of success. At the time when things seemed the worst with the Engineering Department of the Admiralty, when even a lethargic public was beginning to grumble, Government engineers were vying with each other in their efforts to get enormous horse-power by the aid of excessive forced draught—not inaptly termed by the late Admiral Mayne, M.P., "an invention of the Evil One"—out of tiny boilers, only fit for half their duty, and by ruthlessly cutting down the weights of the engines were getting perilously near the line that separates danger from security.

Then arose a reaction. Forced draught became moderate and is now superseded, in one or two vessels, by "induced" draught, of which an account will be given by-and-by; boilers were made very much larger, with more heating and grate surface, and, in short, common sense was allowed a little fair play.

Since then, there has been comparatively no trouble with large ships, and but little with small craft. With regard to the *Barham*, however, a correspondent of the *Globe* wrote, on July 28th, 1893, when she had been commissioned on the Mediterranean station for about three months: "I learn from Malta that the machinery of the *Barham* is in a very bad way. It will be remembered that while this ship was at Portsmouth she was the bugbear both of engineers and shipwrights. Originally entered in the 'Navy List' as of 1,830 tons and 6,000 horse-power, she now appears as of N.D.—*i.e.*, Natural Draught—3,200, and F.D. 'not yet settled,' nor ever likely to be. There is hardly a tube in her boilers or condensers but leaks, and her chief engineer has had a lively time of it lately."

Her boiler tubes are so small in diameter that when it was attempted to strengthen their ends by applying the Admiralty ferrule, the soot quickly accumulated in them to such an extent that very soon there were practically no tubes at all. The *Bellona* is nearly as bad, but not quite such violent attempts to force her were made as in the case of her sister, the *Barham*. Both these ships are now in commission, and both have proved comparative failures. They can only serve as lessons of warning to future designers who are tempted to endeavour after extreme and unnatural lightness of material at the expense of stability and efficiency.

CHAPTER IV.

IN the early days of ironclads the propelling machinery was always horizontal so that it could lie well below the waterline and thus be unlikely to be injured by hostile projectiles. Of these old vessels not more than a score still remain on the "Navy List," among which are such almost obsolete craft as the *Warrior*, the first iron ironclad, and the *Hector*, now condemned to be sold. Every ship above the size of a gunboat, and, in the case of the torpedo-boats and their "destroyers," often below it, is now fitted with vertical engines, to which the protective deck of, say, four inches of steel affords a refuge. Even more than in the days of horizontal engines, when there were at least two types, differing completely from one another, namely, Penn's trunks and Maudslay's return connecting-rods, about neither of which need we concern ourselves nowadays, are the vertical engines we at present use in all our battleships and cruisers destitute of any attempt at originality in design.

In the details of construction each maker tends to certain peculiarities, but it may safely be said that their adoption makes scarcely the slightest difference to the working of the machinery. That, in the case of battleships, has with one exception, been always most efficient.

Beginning with the engines of the *Dreadnought* and

Shannon and coming down to the *Resolution* and *Magnificent*,
the trials have been in all instances in all respects satisfactory. One cause that has tended to this has undoubtedly
been the strength and power to resist vibration of the
engine-room foundation beams in a modern battleship:
the extreme care taken nowadays to see that the bearings
for the screw-shafts are always mathematically level and
true has had a great deal to do with the abolition of much
of the trouble of former years, when the precautions taken
to this end were very much less severe and strict. The
improvements in machine-tools for use in engineering shops
has also, no doubt, had something to do with the increased
accuracy of fitting the different parts of a marine engine,
tending naturally to increased smoothness of working and
consequent effectiveness.

Remembering that I am writing not so much for the
engineer as for the general individual of the public, who
pays his taxes and takes a certain amount of intelligent
interest in what becomes of the money, it occurs to me that
this may be perhaps a convenient opportunity for explaining
a few technical terms that must necessarily be used in the
course of this volume, the main object of which is to be as
nearly as possible up to date.

To begin with the boilers, which are, indeed, the beginning of motive power in the ship, " natural draught " means
that no method of forcing the combustion of the fires on
the grates is permitted other than that due to the ascending
column of heated air in the funnel. The fires burn as
naturally as in the kitchen fireplace at home, and this condition is by far the most important in the stokehold. Probably never in peace time, and possibly only once or twice
if war should unhappily come upon us, would " forced " or
" induced " draught be employed. Men who have made
this subject their study have arrived at the conclusion that,

under certain circumstances, the possession of the power by forcing the fires to obtain another one or two knots of speed might make all the difference between success and ruin, hence we continually go on, at the expense of many thousands of pounds per vessel, providing the necessary means for obtaining this extra force in our warships. As I have said before, it is never used on ordinary occasions but it is in reserve, and could be used without difficulty in case of need.

When forced draught is used the stokehold is hermetically closed and made air-tight, the only vent being through the ash-pits, furnaces, combustion chambers, tubes, and out through the funnels. As Mr. Harry Williams, in his excellent book on the " Steam Navy of England," says, " Air is pumped into the stokeholds by large fans until the required pressure is obtained, this pressure being measured by water-gauges, indexed by inches and parts of inches. When the boilers are put under forced draught it is obvious that, as the only vent for the compressed air is through the fires, the velocity of the air depends upon the pressure in the stokehold. As this pressure increases, the velocity of the air currents through the fires increases; the heat generated in the furnaces is more intense, the evaporation of the water more rapid, and the generation of steam quicker. There is, in fact, no limit to this except the ability of boilers to bear the strain. Unfortunately this limit exists, and the fixing of this is of primary importance; for allowing for a safe margin under this limit there is no reason why the boilers should suffer injury, but over it there is great probability of their breaking down under the strain."

Although Mr. Williams's book was only published at the end of 1892, things have altered so much in the interval that the importance of his remarks has sensibly diminished. Once the trial trip is over and the promised horse-power has been realized, no persons trouble their head any more about forced draught, which, they know, is never likely to be used again, although its readiness for possible employment is universally recognized as an absolute necessity.

With regard to " induced " draught, a system introduced mainly by Mr. Martin, of Blackfriars, which is now being applied by Messrs. Penn to the boilers of the battleships *Magnificent* and *Illustrious,* for which they are providing the machinery, Mr. Williams says :—" It is understood that the induced draught is obtained by placing at the bottom of the funnels a fan, by the working of which the air is partially exhausted from the uptakes and lower parts of the funnels. This exhaustion of the air causes the air in the boiler-room to be forced in through the ash-pits, furnaces, combustion-chambers, tubes, and smoke-boxes, into the uptakes, and so up through the funnel. The exhaustion of the air from the uptakes causes a fall in the pressure of the air at this point, and the denser air in the boiler-rooms rushes through the fires, etc , to fill the void, and thus establishes equilibrium. But in consequence of the air-exhausting process being continuous, the indraught of air from the boiler-room is also continuous. Thus there is a continuous current of air passing through and stimulating and forcing the fires, causing intense heat and generation of steam more or less rapid in proportion to the velocity of the air currents passing through the boilers. . . . But in what does this differ from forced draught? It is forced draught called by another name. In both cases air fans are used ; in forced draught at the stokehold end of the boilers, in this induced draught at the funnel end of the boilers. In both cases the object aimed at is exactly the same, viz., to cause so much difference in the air pressures

in the stokeholds and funnels as to make the air rush
through the line of fire in the boilers and out through the
funnels."

Now this sounds all right and true, and he would have
been a bold man who should have attempted to answer
Mr. Williams till after the trials of the *Magnificent*, which
have so successfully taken place. Meanwhile, I hope I
have said enough about the different kinds of draught to
satisfy the general reader.

It may be some comfort to him to know that the extra
pressure in the atmosphere of an inch or two of water in
no way inconveniences the stokers. They do not like forced
draught because their work is naturally heavier, and because,
in case of accident, they could not so readily escape to the
upper air; but those who are constantly employed in
torpedo-boats, catchers, and destroyers, get so accustomed
to their peculiar circumstances of work as not to mind it
in the least.

Another subject of grave importance with which it is
necessary that the everyday man should be acquainted, if
he aspires to take any interest in, or know anything about,
naval engineering, is the different varieties of engines now
in use on board men-of-war. I mean compound and triple-
expansion.

Of these the compound engine is now considered as
antique and obsolete as its predecessor, the simple variety.
There are, however, some examples left in ships that were
considered notable in their day—the *Benbow*, for instance,
has compound engines, and many more ships of about her
date—but the general type of engines of modern construction, both in the Royal Navy and the mercantile marine, is,
at present, the triple-expansion. There are, however, many
good judges who consider the use of triple-expansion
engines, however valuable they may be in a merchant ship

on account of the undeniable economy in the coal they con-
sume, to be indefensible in a fighting ship, which probably
goes through a commission without deriving any benefit
from the economy of her engines more than once or twice
in the whole period.

The fact is, triple-expansion engines are not economical
in a man-of-war, where the usual rate of steaming is with
one-fourth the maximum horse-power, or even much less.
Mr. Williams on this subject says : " Let us suppose the case
of a large cruiser, which, with twin-screw triple-expansion
engines and boilers worked with a safe forced draught, de-
velops an engine-power of 12,000 horses, and attains a speed
of twenty-one knots.   At this speed, and with the development of this power, the engines are, we will suppose, fairly
well balanced, each of the three engines developing nearly
the same power, and therefore causing an equality of strain
along the crank-shaft.   Now, when the power is reduced
this balance is lost ; and though it can, to some extent, be
retained by a judicious use of the link motions, yet a limit
will be soon reached when this can be no longer done.
Also, with a further reduction of power, there will soon be
a point reached when the balance will be so entirely lost as
to cause the low-pressure engine to do nothing ; and beyond
this point, this engine will not only do nothing, but will
actually be dragged round by the other two engines. . . .
It may be remarked here that in the case of a ship of the
Edgar class, a first-class cruiser having a maximum speed,
in round numbers, of twenty-one knots per hour, the varia-
tion of the indicated horse-power at lower speed is very
remarkable."

In the following statement the power is shown opposite
the rates of speed obtained by the development of the
various degrees of engine power.   These were the results
of actual trials as reported in the Press :

"Speed of ship in knots.	Gross indicated horse-power.
20·97	12,550
18·83	8,524
16·50	5,206
14·00	3,023
13·40	2,511
11·87	1,756
9·60	890

.   .   .   .

" It is considered in this connection that it should be easy for our engine makers to make and fit such arrangements as would make the disconnections and re-connections of the high-pressure engine a work of a very few minutes; and this itself is a great reason why it should be done. Of course, if the necessary disconnections occupied a day, or even half a day, it would, perhaps, be well not to make the change ; but if, as stated, it could be done in a few minutes, it would be advantageous, for it would prevent a wasteful expenditure of power, and so improve the coal endurance of the ship.

" As to the way in which this change would affect speed, on a pinch a twenty-one knot ship could easily get sixteen knots with the suggested compound arrangement, and that is all that would be wanted for ordinary fleet service. Of course, in a time of war it would be better to work with all three cylinders, so as to be able to put on full speed at the shortest notice. But when at peace there is no doubt that the present triple-expansion engines, converted into pairs of compound engines as suggested, would give all the engine power that could possibly be required for fleet service, and would cause a considerable saving of coal, which in these days is a matter of the very greatest importance, affecting as it does the duration of the efficiency of ships of war at sea. The foregoing suggestions are commended to the consideration of the engineering firms who contract to make engines for the Navy."

They may well be commended to the consideration of all people who are in any way interested in naval engineering. I have the very highest respect for Mr. Williams's opinion, he is certainly the most able example of the naval engineer of old times now left to us; but still, with some diffidence and doubt, I am reluctantly compelled to think that in the above profession of his faith he has committed two errors. He does not give adequate reasons, in the first place, for disconnecting the high-pressure in preference to the low-pressure engine. Of course, the parts of the former are very much lighter and smaller than those of the latter, which of itself would be a great advantage towards securing the rapidity of operation Mr. Williams thinks is so important. But would it be important?

Surely, moreover, to obtain a given power, steam of a higher pressure would be required for the two smaller than the two larger cylinders, and this should tend to economy.

In the second place, though I know that the power to cut off at will one of the cylinders of a triple-expansion engine has long been desired and sought for by manufacturing engineers, I am inclined to believe that, in battleships at all events, the best results would be obtained by a return to the compound engine. How often in the course of a three years' commission will the *Magnificent*, say, gain any advantage from her engines being triple-expansion?

As Mr. Williams very justly points out, at a speed of twelve knots they are absolutely wasteful. In swift cruisers, by all means, retain this type of machinery, but it is in them that I should be inclined to say Mr. Williams's idea of laying by one cylinder—I do not say which—would be most useful. Even in war I do not believe that an extra speed of one knot would be likely to be of any strong advantage to a battleship. Battleships will generally be called upon to fight in company, and the speed of the squadron will of course be that of its slowest ship.

As I have said before, there is little of interest to report of battleships' trials. They invariably attain a little more than the expected speed, and it may be said that they never have any accident or mishap. Occasional differences occur in their steaming, as for instance when the *Centurion*, which was originally described as a second-class battleship, but is now the flagship of the commander-in-chief on the China station, with little wind and no sea, attained an average deep-sea speed of 18·51 knots, which, though believed to be below her actual performance, is the greatest speed hitherto attained by an ironclad, and superior by one knot to that of her sister ship the *Barfleur*.

In this case the *Centurion* was built at Portsmouth and the *Barfleur* at Chatham. The engines of both ships, constructed by the Greenock Foundry Company, were identical, and the ships themselves were built from the same drawings, so the difference in speed is as inexplicable as that of the *Warrior* and *Black Prince*, which occurred under precisely similar circumstances.

Whatever the battleship of these days may be, whether built and engined at Jarrow by Messrs. Palmer, or at Clydebank by Messrs. Thomson, or at any other establishment, or built at Portsmouth or Chatham and engined by Messrs. Humphrys or Messrs. Maudslay, they always give perfect satisfaction on trial in their engine-room department, which, as I observed above, may be partly accounted for by the extra firmness and solidity of the foundations they are able to afford for their machinery. And what machinery it is may be guessed at by the reproductions of photographs I am enabled to offer to the notice of my readers.

As this is not intended to be an historical treatise, but

E

rather a plain statement of the present condition of steam
in the Royal Navy, I do not think it necessary to go
further back for battleships' machinery than 1882, when
Messrs. Maudslay, Sons, and Field, of Lambeth, engined
the ironclad *Benbow*, one of the three ships that were designed to carry 111-ton guns. Of the other two, the loss
of the *Victoria* in the Mediterranean, when the commander-
in-chief, Sir George Tryon, K.C.B., perished in company
with so many of his officers and men, is still fresh in the
memory of most of us; the *Sans Pareil* has lately returned
from the Mediterranean to take up the duties of port guard-
ship at Sheerness.

The *Benbow* is now the coastguard ship at Greenock. In
her engines one high-pressure and two low-pressure cylinders
are adopted for each of her twin propellers, the high-pressure being placed forward, and all three coupled direct to
one crank-shaft, with three cranks placed at angles of 120
degrees, thereby balancing the engine and giving steadiness
of running. She has twelve boilers of the oval, single-
ended type, with three furnaces in each boiler. The principal dimensions of these engines are as follows:

High-pressure cylinder	52 inches diameter.
Two low-pressure cylinders	74 inches diameter.
Stroke	3 feet 9 inches.
Boiler pressure	90 lb.
Revolutions at full speed	101·7.
Pitch of propellers	18 feet 6 inches.
Diameter of propellers	16 feet.
Indicated horse-power	10,852.
Speed	17·495 knots.

Besides the main engines, the *Benbow*, like all big
steamers of modern type, carries a large number of
auxiliary engines—forty in fact, which is considerably

fewer than those found necessary in ships of a more modern type—which are thus made up:

2 starting engines; 2 turning engines; 6 feed engines; 1 capstan engine; 1 steering engine; 2 hydraulic engines; 4 ash-raising engines; 4 centrifugal engines; 2 air-compressing engines; 2 electric light engines; 4 fire-pump engines; 2 boat-hoisting engines; 8 fan engines.

I never heard of the slightest difficulty with the *Benbow's* machinery under way; and this may be ascribed not so much to the simplicity of its design as to the excellence of its construction, and the ability of the engineer officers who have superintended its working.

In 1890 the battleship *Nile*, also engined by Messrs. Maudslay, completed a most successful series of trials. Her machinery is of the triple-expansion type, and is very similar to that of the first-class cruiser *Royal Arthur*, supplied by the same firm. It differs chiefly in the arrangement adopted for the crossheads, the *Nile* having slipper-blocks working on slides suspended from a bracket cast on the bases of the cylinders, and supported at the lower end by a tie-bar between two adjacent columns, while in the *Royal Arthur* there are two guide-blocks to each crosshead, these working between slides bolted to the insides of the columns. The cylinders of the *Nile* are supported on four cast-steel columns, and the engines of this vessel are one of the first examples of the employment of cast steel for this purpose. The principal dimensions of these engines are as follows:

High-pressure cylinder .	43 inches diameter.
Intermediate cylinder .	62 inches diameter.
Low-pressure cylinder .	96 inches diameter.
Stroke	4 feet 3 inches.
Boiler pressure . . .	135 lb. per sq. inch.

Revolutions at full speed . 93·35.
Air pressure . 1·825 inch of water.
Pitch of propellers . 21 feet 3 inches.
Diameter of propellers . 16 feet 6 inches.
Indicated horse-power . 12,109.
Speed on measured mile . 16·883 knots.

Of course it will be understood that there are two sets of these triple-expansion engines, of three cylinders each, one to each of the twin screws. The number and duties of the auxiliary engines differ somewhat from those of the *Benbow*, as is shown by the following list :

2 reversing engines; 2 turning engines; 4 centrifugal engines; 4 feed engines; 2 hydraulic engines; 2 dynamo engines; 10 fan engines; 2 boat-hoisting engines; 4 fire-pump engines; 1 workshop engine; 1 steering engine; 2 ash-raising engines; 1 capstan engine; 2 air-compressing engines; 2 distilling engines; 2 air-pumps and circulating engines.

To this vast number of auxiliary engines I shall refer at length in a future chapter; I may here, however, remark that they often give a chief engineer more trouble and anxiety than his main propelling machinery.

Coming now to one of our latest battleships, one that at the time I write has not yet run her trials, the *Magnificent*, a correspondent of the "Globe" wrote November, 1894: "I had an opportunity the other day, through the courtesy of Messrs. John Penn and Sons, of inspecting one set of the engines out of two that they are building for the first-class battleship *Magnificent*, now in course of construction at Chatham. A better idea can be got of the merits of machinery when it is complete in the erecting-shop than when it has been removed to the ship, for access to every part of it is so much easier. There is no particular novelty

Fig. 3. Engines of the "Royal Arthur," 12,000 Horse-Power.

about these engines, but I noticed what I had never observed before, that some of the lubricating pipes were of steel and made to do duty as handrails.

"The cylinders are carried on cast-iron columns at the back, to which the motion-bars are attached, and round forged steel columns at the front. The piston-rods are of Siemens-Martin steel, and are fitted with combination metallic packing. The crank-shafts are hollow, of forged steel, in three separate pieces, and the cranks are set, as usual, at 120 degrees apart. The surface condensers are entirely of brass, the cooling surface being 13,500 square feet. The circulating water is supplied by four 16-inch centrifugal pumps, made by Messrs. Penn.

"The reversing gear is of the ordinary link-motion type, with solid bar-links and adjustable working parts. It is, of course, available for use by hand should the steam gear give out. A Weir's evaporator and Kirkaldy's distiller is fitted to each engine-room. As a matter of course, the usual electric light, air-compressing, and boat-hoisting engines are supplied to the ship. The boilers, all of steel, are designed for a working pressure of 155 lb. per square inch. The heating surface is 25,248, and the grate 855 square feet. All copper pipes of six inches and over are wound with copper wire for greater security."

A picture of the *Magnificent's* engines, taken from a splendid photograph produced for Messrs. Penn by Mr. Parry, of South Shields, is given on the opposite page. The very greatest interest is being felt in her trials, because undoubtedly by their result the system of induced draught must stand or fall. Messrs. Penn, however, appear so confident of its efficacy, that I understand they purpose fitting it also in the *Illustrious*, a sister ship to the *Magnificent*.

Of the *Majestic*, a sister to the *Magnificent*, the propel-

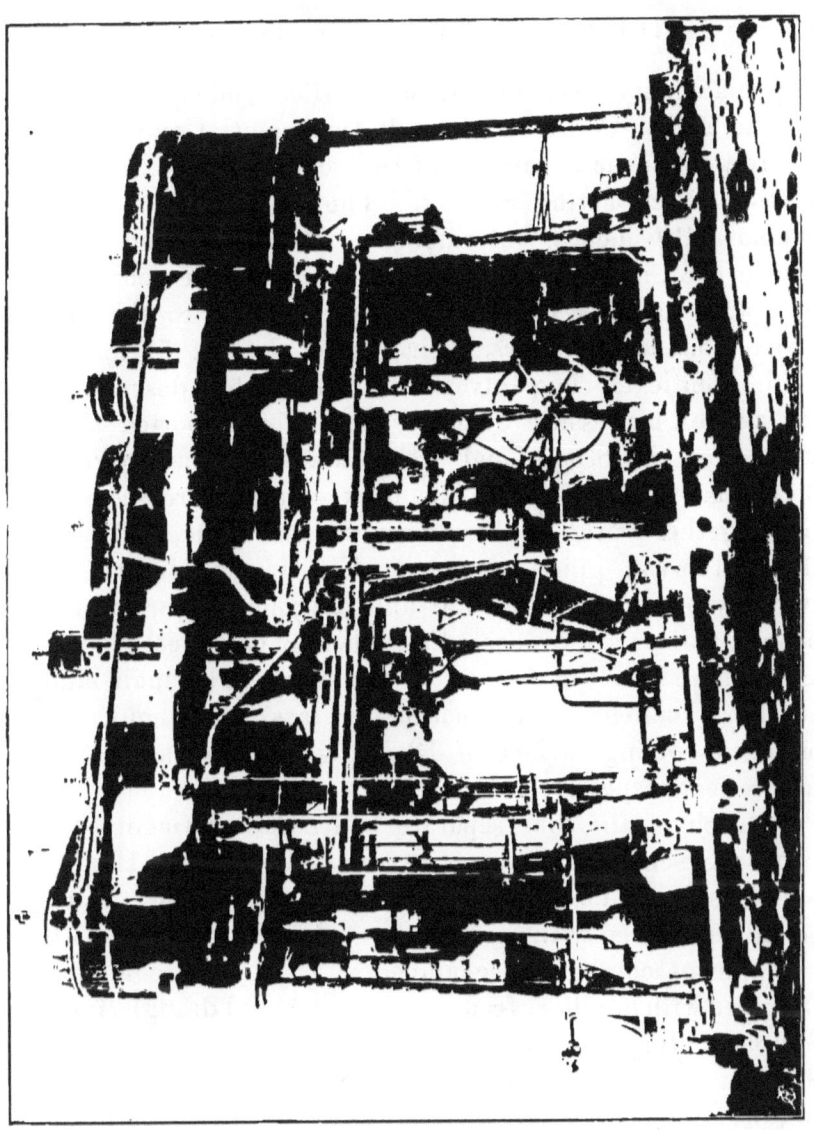

FIG. 4.—ENGINES OF THE "MAGNIFICENT," 12,000 HORSE-POWER.

ling machinery, designed by Mr. A Blechynden, and built by the Naval Construction and Armaments Company, of Barrow-in-Furness, consists of two sets of triple-expansion vertical direct-acting engines. The cylinders are high-pressure 40 inches, intermediate 59 inches, and low-pressure 88 inches, thus showing a remarkable consensus of opinion among constructive engineers as to the best proportions of cylinders, their stroke also, of 51 inches, being identical. The valves are of the piston description for the high-pressure cylinders, and double-ported slide valves for the others, and are actuated by the ordinary double-bar link motion. The back columns are securely tied together at the top by a wrought-steel plate, and form the piston-rod guide supports. The front columns are strongly braced by horizontal and diagonal stays, and the bottom frames are connected together by cast-steel girders and secured to the frames of the ship. The main and auxiliary condensers are formed of brass throughout, and possess a cooling surface of 13,500 square feet and 1,800 square feet respectively.

In each of the four separate boiler compartments are two single-ended cylindrical return tube boilers, 16 feet 4 inches in diameter, and 10 feet 3 inches long. Each boiler is provided with four corrugated furnaces, fitted with a couple of combustion chambers. The boiler-rooms are equipped with auxiliary feed pumps and forced draught fans. Supplementary machinery rooms are placed at the sides of the ship, containing dynamos, air-compressors, ventilating fans, and workshop appliances. The ship will carry eighteen boats, of which four will be steamboats capable of acting independently of the ship for purposes of torpedo attack, and there will be six search-light projectors, worked by three dynamos of 600 ampères each. Her complement will consist of 757 officers and men.

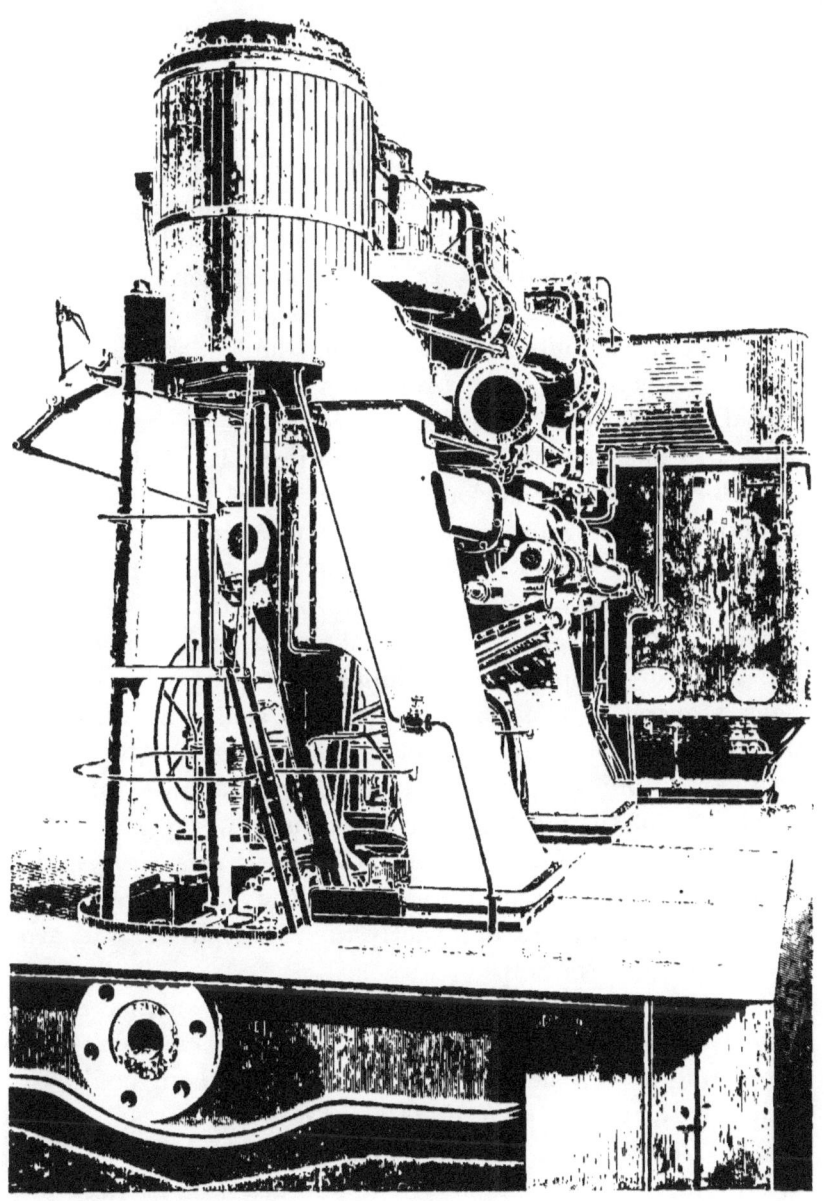

FIG. 5.—ENGINES OF THE "PRINCE GEORGE," 12,000 HORSE-POWER.

In the " Globe " of October 10th, 1893, I read, " The full speed trial of the *Centurion*, which was built at Portsmouth, and engined by the Greenock Foundry Company, took place on Friday last between the Warner Light Ship and Beachy Head. The highest speed ever attained by a battle-ship was reached, namely, 18·51 knots per hour, and even this is believed to be below the actual performance of the vessel, as it was obtained solely from the log, which rarely flatters. There was little wind and a smooth sea. The trial lasted for four hours, and the mean results were—boiler pressure, 146 lb.; vacuum, 27·35; revolutions, 104·7 starboard, and 104·8 port, a remarkable indication of the uniformity of action in the two sets of engines; total indicated horse-power, 13,174, or 174 beyond what had been stipulated for. Some effective alterations had been made in the slide valves; and the leakages in the stokeholds, which prevented the fans for compressed air doing their proper work, had been stopped. The consumption of coal was 2·24 lb. per indicated horse-power per hour. Altogether, the trial was a grand success." As further examples of the machinery of the most modern battleships I here give additional sketches of the engines of the *Prince George*, by Messrs. Humphrys and Tennant, and the *Cæsar*, by Messrs. Maudslay. They are of exactly the same power, and are intended for sister ships.

Now, there are only two battleships of a smaller class, 10,500 tons and 13,000 horse-power, but most people think there might well be more, when three of them could be built for the cost of two *Magnificent's*.

The *Renown*, just built at Pembroke, is of 12,350 tons only, and therefore smaller than our heaviest battleships, and her horse-power has been increased for natural draught, by far the more important of the two, from the 9,000 of the *Centurion* and *Barfleur* to 10,000, the forced draught

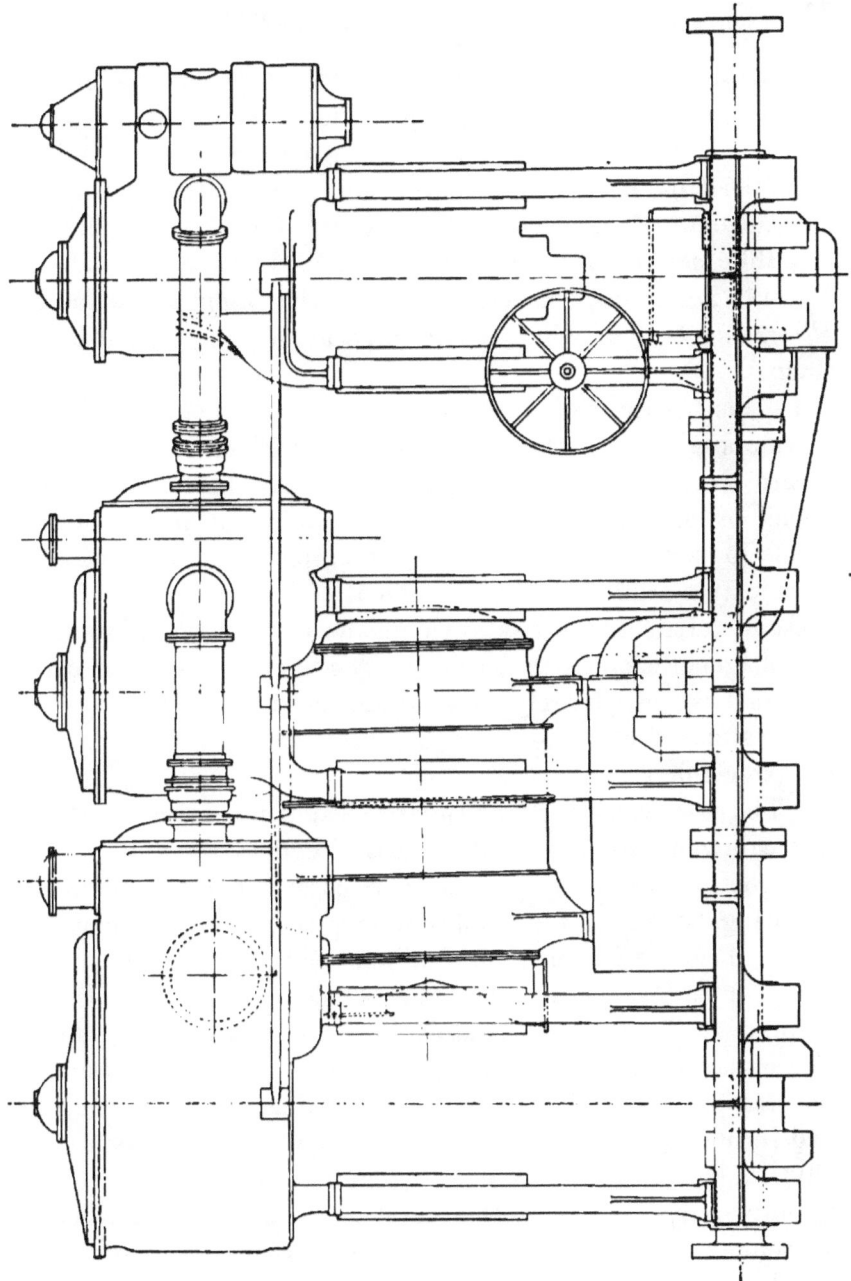

FIG. 6.—Elevation of the Engines of the "Cæsar," 12,000 Horse-Power.

power having been diminished to 12,000, which is undoubtedly a step in the right direction, and one that will
give the ship a practical increase of sea-going speed.   And
here, perhaps, it is as well that I should give Mr. Martin's
own account of his invention, or, at any rate, introduction
to public notice, of his system of induced draught, which
Messrs. Penn are about to apply to the *Magnificent* and
Illustrious, both of which battleships are to be engined by
them.

In his paper on "Induced Draught as a Means for
Developing the Power of Marine Boilers," read in April
before the Institution of Naval Architects, he says, "Induced or exhaust draught has been adopted in various
forms for many years, and has been employed especially on
locomotives from the commencement of railways up to the
present.   It is the best-known means of promoting rapid
steam generation with safety.   The locomotive type of
boilers has been largely adapted for marine purposes, but
the system of working them has been reversed, with very
unfavourable results.

"The author, having made a large number of experiments
in steam generation, with all classes of boilers, is enabled to
place before the meeting some particulars that may be interesting, both on forcing and inducing draught.   Although
it has been sometimes maintained that so long as you
create a difference in pressure between the air in the
chimney and that in the stokehold, it matters not whether
you exhaust from, or blow to, the fire; yet it will be seen,
on closer examination, that the characteristics of forcing
and inducing are widely different.   The forcing system is
advantageously used for blasting down ores, and for iron
foundry purposes, where the metal can fall below the blast
as soon as melted; but it is an unsuitable process for
puddling, reverberatory, and re-heating furnaces, such as

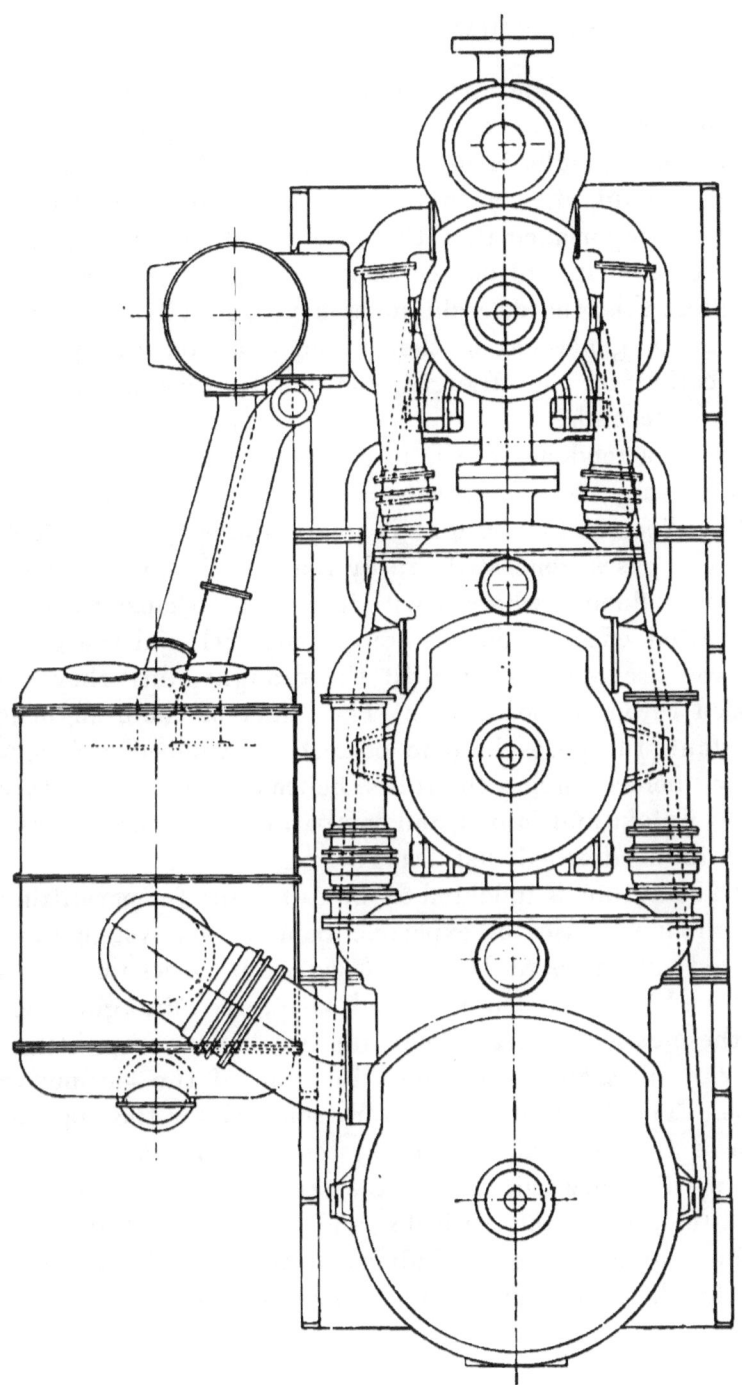

FIG. 7.—PLAN OF THE ENGINES OF THE "CÆSAR."

are used in iron and armour-plate making, where volume
and steady heat are required. For these purposes exhaust
or induced draught is used. The marine boiler exposes a
large amount of surface to be acted upon, and it is of
primary importance that the heat should be evenly distributed over it, and not concentrated on particular parts.
To effect this, the draught must have perfect control over
the gases generated in the furnaces, as on the proper
application of the draught the whole working of the
furnace depends.

"It is a tendency of the forced draught system, as used
in the Navy, to concentrate and localize the heat. The
initial effect of the draught is under the body of the fuel,
and the gases generated are driven on without any controlling influence, whereas, with induced or exhaust draught,
the initial effect is on the top of the fuel, and the gases
evolved are under control of the draught until they are
passed through the funnel. The effect of the draught is
constant, the gases become perfectly developed and consumed before leaving the tubes, hence a lower temperature
in the uptake and funnel, and comparative absence of smoke
with induced or exhaust draught.

"The author is indebted to the Admiralty for permitting
an extensive series of experiments upon his system to be
carried out on board H.M.S. *Gossamer* at Chatham. This
ship had been fitted and worked with forced draught prior
to these experiments. There are two boiler-rooms identi-
cally similar, and two boilers in each, of the locomotive
type. The forward boilers were selected for the application of the induced draught system, which was fitted in
the uptake forward, leaving the stokehold in its original
condition, with the air-locks and other forced draught
fittings, unnecessary for induced draught. The air-locks
and hatches, however, were left open during the trials, and

in this respect only was there any difference in the working of the two systems.

"The following table gives a summary of the trials that were carried out. It will be noticed that the power produced by the boilers with the induced draught system was far in excess of that developed under forced draught; also, that in point of economy induced draught was greatly superior. The table is by no means exhaustive, as there are other points not noticed, such as the greatly lessened temperature both in stokehold and funnel, the immunity from dust, and the freedom of ingress and egress in the stokehold.

"Experiments at Chatham with boilers on board H.M.S. *Gossamer*:

Date of Trials.	Description of Trials.	Hours.	Indicated horse-power.		I. H. P. per foot of grate.	Lb. of coal per I. H. P.	Lb. of coal per sq. ft. of grate.
			Intended.	Actual.			
1893. March 6th and 7th	Induced draught	30	1,250	1,288·11	16·3	1·92	31·3
May 1st to 5th	Forced draught	96	750	710·69	8·99	2·32	20·87
1894. February 7th, 8th, and 9th	Forced draught	48	750	772·64	9·77	1·87	18·29
February 14th, 15th, and 16th	Induced draught	48	750	825·81	10·45	1·68	17·56
February 22nd and 23rd	Induced draught	24	1,000	1,004·04	12·709	1·60	20·36

Grate surface, 143·32 sq. ft. ; tube surface, 5,772 sq. ft. ; number of tubes, 1,728 ; length, 7 ft. 1½ in. ; diameter, 1½ in."

Mr. Martin goes on to say that another important point in favour of induced draught is the saving in weight in comparison with forced draught. The ironwork involved by the latter for casing and air-locks in a first-class battleship is about nineteen tons. "It should also be observed that the principle of induced draught renders it quite independent of the length of funnel. In fact, the funnel may be dispensed with altogether, so that in the case of a war-vessel, if the funnel were shot away in action, it would not in any way affect the facility of steaming." These remarks would also apply equally well to forced draught. With artificial draught of any kind the intensity of the draught depends very little on the height of the funnel.

It must be distinctly understood that all that has been said here touching the efficacy of induced draught, is given on Mr. Martin's authority—I vouch for none of it—but if it has to be taken *cum grano salis*, I am, nevertheless, of opinion that such engineers as Messrs. Penn are not likely to have made a mistake, and that their adoption of the system will probably make its fortune.

CHAPTER V.

THE torpedo dépot ship *Vulcan* is not properly a cruiser, but her duties come closer to those of that type of vessel than of any other, so I have thought fit to begin this chapter with a description of her, written by one who has good reason to know her peculiarities.[1] She is at present unique in the world. No navy but ours has as yet produced a ship a bit like her.

The *Vulcan* is intended to accompany a fleet to sea, to form a depôt for supplying mining and countermining stores, electrical gear, Whitehead torpedoes, etc., to assist in the work of laying out mines or fishing them up, as occasion may require, as well as forming a school of instruction for this kind of work in time of peace. She is also fitted with a factory for executing repairs to torpedo gear and boats, and to such ships of war as are not provided with the means of performing their own repairs. In addition to this, she was designed on such lines as, with the large engine power provided, to have sufficient speed to act as a cruiser or to perform scouting work for the fleet.

She was built in Portsmouth Dockyard, the first keel plate having been laid down on June 18th, 1888, and the ship launched on June 13th of the following year, less than

---

[1] "Engineer," 1892.

F

twelve months after her commencement, a feat which was considered remarkable at that time, but has since become an affair of ordinary occurrence. She is built of steel throughout, unarmoured at the sides, but provided with a protective deck varying in thickness from 5 inches in the most exposed parts to $2\frac{1}{4}$ inches below the water-line, the shape being the ordinary turtle-back pattern usual in cruisers of this type. This deck forms the protection for the magazines, engines, and boilers, and the vital parts of the ship generally, the coal-boxes also being so arranged as to materially assist in protecting these parts when they are full of coal.

The principal dimensions are, 350 feet between perpendiculars, and 58 feet beam, the displacement being 6,630 tons at 23 feet, mean draught. Her bunkers, 21 in number, stow 1,000 tons of coal, but 300 tons more can be stowed, if necessary, in the wing compartments adjoining the bunkers, these compartments having been so fitted that coal can easily be stowed in them or got out to the fires when required. It was considered by her designers that this amount of coal would have sufficed to give the ship a cruising range of 10,000 miles at ten knots, but sufficient allowance has not been made for the auxiliary machinery, lighting the ship, etc., and a range of 7,000 miles is as much as she is ever likely to be able to traverse at ten knots without replenishing her bunkers.

A highly interesting feature of the ship is the hydraulic boat-hoisting machinery. The most striking portion of this machinery is a pair of enormous goose-necked cranes placed on each side of the ship, almost amidships. They have a total height of 65 feet, and an overhang, or rake, of 38 feet, which will allow of her boats being hoisted in or out without disarranging her torpedo net defence, a most important item in a ship of this class, the nature of the work she is designed generally to perform rendering her specially liable to sudden torpedo attack. To provide support and security for these cranes about 30 feet of the pillar lies buried, passing down through the upper, main, and protective decks to the bottom of the ship, which is specially strengthened and fitted to support the weight and allow rotation. The upper deck, which takes the canting strain, is specially strengthened and fitted with a heavy steel ring in which the crane rotates. Rollers are not provided to reduce the friction at this point, the crane being simply fitted with a plain disc, $5\frac{1}{4}$ inches in thickness, fitting easily in the deck socket.

The lifting machinery, which is placed inside the pillar of the crane, and therefore being well down in the hold is fairly protected from gun fire, consists mainly of two hydraulic rams; the larger one $17\frac{1}{2}$ inches in diameter, the smaller one $5\frac{1}{2}$ inches, having a vertical stroke of 10 feet, giving a lift of 40 feet at the purchase, through the multiplying power of the fourfold pulleys, which the rams are constructed to operate in the usual manner. At the ordinary working pressure of 1,000 lb. on the square inch, the thrust on the crosshead carrying the pulleys is about 118 tons, which gives a lifting power at the gib of 20 tons, moving at the rate of 90 feet per minute. The small cylinder plays an important part in this mechanism, being designed to mitigate the danger which always attends the hoisting boats in or out in a seaway, and is the subject of a patent. Its special duty is to keep taut the slings after they have been hooked on to the boat until a favourable moment for hoisting presents itself. The valves are so arranged that the main lifting power cannot be applied until the small cylinder has been brought into action, the relation of power to weight being so adjusted at the proper working pressure, that the slings are only held taut while the boat is rising or falling in the waves, provision being made for the escape of the water from beneath the ram as the weight of the boat forces it back against the pressure.

The cranes are revolved by means of a pair of rams 16 inches in diameter, placed vertically alongside the pillar of the crane. It has been necessary to provide considerably more power for this purpose than would be needed for a similar crane on shore, since it will be obvious that if boats are to be hoisted in a seaway, it is necessary to have sufficient holding power to overcome the additional twisting strains brought to bear when the ship is rolling. The direct thrusting power of the rams is 90 tons, and they operate a $2\frac{1}{2}$ inch chain cable which passes round, and is secured to, a steel sprocket drum at the foot of the crane, 6 feet, 6 inches in diameter, thence over a pulley at the head of each ram, the ends being secured to the framing which supports the ram cylinders. The cranes have a turning range of about 250 degrees, and the boats are so placed as to come fairly within the scope of one or other of them; but since the *Vulcan* is 58 feet wide, and the cranes 40 feet apart, it is obvious that all the boats cannot come within the scope of either crane. To provide for the contingency of one of the cranes becoming disabled, the torpedo boats— of which the ship carries six—are stowed in crutches fitted on trolleys, which may be traversed from one side of the ship to the other. It is anticipated that when the ship is in commission and the crew properly drilled, the whole of these boats may be lifted in or out in less than a quarter of an hour.

The boat equipment consists of six second-class torpedo-boats, a wooden vedette boat 53 feet in length, a 42 feet steam pinnace, and a steam cutter. The torpedo-boats are built entirely of steel, 60 feet in length, having a speed of over 16 knots an hour, the engines working up to about

230 horse-power, the boilers being of the ordinary loco-motive type, working under forced draught, with closed stokeholds. The vedette boat and steam pinnace are also fitted to work with closed stokeholds and forced draught.

The ship is electrically lighted throughout, and fitted with four electric search-lights, each of 25,000 candle-power. For these purposes three sets of Siemens' dynamos, driven direct by Willans' patent compound central valve engines are provided, each dynamo giving a current of 400 ampères at 80 volts E.M.F., when driven at about 420 revolutions per minute.

The propelling machinery and boilers were supplied by Messrs. Humphrys and Tennant. The main engines, of which there are two sets, driving twin screws, are of triple-expansion overhead cylinders, capable of developing 12,000 horse-power at 100 revolutions per minute. The cylinders are of 40 inches, 59 inches, and 88 inches diameter, and the stroke is 4 feet 3 inches. The air-pumps are driven directly off the low-pressure pistons, and the condensers are of gun-metal, giving a cooling surface of 13,500 square feet. The circulation of the cooling water through the condenser is maintained by independent centrifugal pumps, driven by Humphrys' single-cylinder overhead engines. These pumps are duplicated, to provide for the contingency of one becoming disabled, the old plan of fitting sea-injection cocks for use in case of emergency having been discontinued.

These pumps are also fitted to draw from the bilge, and guaranteed to take 1,000 tons per hour each from the bilge with 100 lb. pressure of steam. This they easily did at the trial, the total amount of water delivered by the four engines, as ascertained by experiment, being a little over 5,000 tons per hour. There are no feed pumps driven off the main engines, but separate feed engines, two main and two auxiliary, all of equal size and Admiralty pattern, are

fitted in the stokeholds for supplying the main boilers,
a smaller pattern being supplied for the auxiliary boiler.
In each engine-room there are also two fire and bilge
engines, one turning and one reversing engine, a distilling
pump, an auxiliary condenser, which takes the exhaust
steam from the whole of the auxiliary service, having its
own circulating engine and air-pump, and a Normandy's
double-distilling apparatus capable of providing 150 gallons
of fresh water per hour for the use of the crew.

Separate engine-rooms are provided for the hydraulic
engines, of which there are two complete sets, each set
equal to the task of supplying the pressure for the cranes
and bollards when hoisting in the boats. They are horizontal, tandem, compound type, two high-pressure cylinders
of $13\frac{1}{2}$ inches diameter, and two low-pressure cylinders,
27 inches diameter, with a stroke of 18 inches to each set,
the pumps, $5\frac{3}{4}$ inches diameter, being driven direct off the
pistons in the ordinary way. No hydraulic accumulator is
provided, but a hydraulic governor efficiently supplies its
place by controlling the supply of steam to the engines as
the water pressure varies. Murdock's steam governor is
also connected to the throttle valve in case of any mishap
to the pump, to prevent the engines running off at a breakdown speed. In each hydraulic engine-room there are also
one of Belliss's air-compressing engines and pumps, with
reservoir for supplying Whitehead torpedoes with air up to
a pressure of 1,700 lb. per square inch, ventilating and
exhaust fans driven by Brotherhood's three-cylinder
engines; and, on the starboard side only, one of the
dynamos—termed the war dynamo, because it is placed
under the protective deck—the other two being placed in
the workshop above the protective deck, where it is pre-
sumed they can be much better looked after, being under
the direct supervision of the officer in attendance there.

In the workshop there are five lathes of various sizes, from 15 feet bed and 9 inch centres, down to 3 feet 6 inches bed and 6 inch centres, two drilling machines, planing, slotting, shaping, and punching machines, a circular saw bench, a carpenter's bench and fitters' benches, and a Fletcher's air furnace, capable of melting down 2 cwt. of scrap steel in two hours. The pulley shafting is driven direct by a 6-inch belt of a small single-cylinder

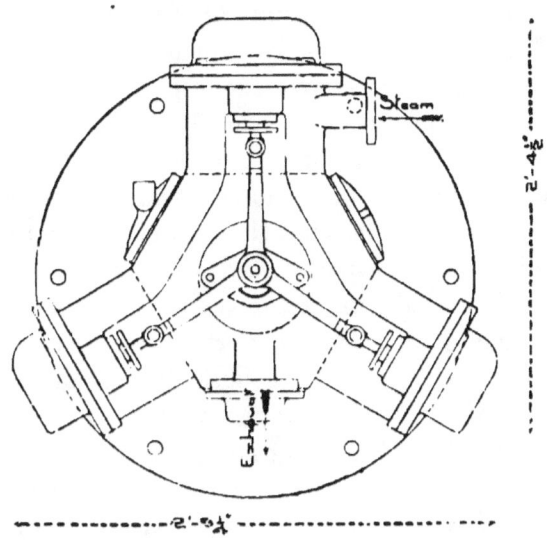

FIG. 8.—BROTHERHOOD'S THREE-CYLINDER ENGINE.

horizontal engine. In the blacksmith's shop on the upper deck is a powerful hydraulic forging press, a large forge, fitted with Root's blower and steam blast, also a coppersmith's forge and pipe-bending machine, together with a complete set of tools.

To supply steam there are four double-ended cylindrical boilers 17 feet long and 14 feet in diameter, with three furnaces each end, 3 feet 8½ inches diameter, 6 feet in length, leading to a common combustion chamber. There is also, in addition to these, a smaller boiler, single-ended, 12 feet 5 inches in diameter, and 9 feet 4 inches in length, with three furnaces, which is intended to be used generally for auxiliary purposes, but which is worked under the same conditions of forced draught as the main boilers. The stokeholds are closed, and fitted in the usual way with air locks for entrance, air-tight hatches, etc. The air for the fires is driven into the stokeholds—of course only when working with forced draught at full power—by eight 60-inch fans, driven by Brotherhood's three-cylinder engines, working at 600 revolutions per minute.

As originally designed, the total grate area was about 655 square feet, and the total heating surface about 19,000 square feet. Certain modifications, however, were suggested by experience with boilers in other ships, in order to prevent overheating of the tube-plates, and consequently leaky tubes. These, when carried out, reduced the grate area to about 543 square feet, and the heating surface to 16,740 square feet.

The earliest of our present first-class cruisers, officially described as of the *Edgar* type, are enlarged *Merseys* and diminished copies of the *Blake* and *Blenheim*. Their engines indicate 12,000 horse-power with forced draught and 10,000 with natural draught, which, says Brassey's "Naval Annual" for 1890, "it is expected will give them sea-going speeds of twenty knots and eighteen knots respectively; but if two knots be subtracted from each of these theoretical speeds, and the ships are able to accomplish even that much on actual service, we may consider ourselves well off." But prudent as it seemed at the time of writing to foretell such an approach to failure, the prophecy has turned out to be far too pessimistic.

The *Royal Arthur*, ordered to steam at her full natural draught speed for forty-eight hours, after she had been about eighteen months in commission as flagship of Rear-

Admiral Stephenson in the Pacific, averaged eighteen knots
for the whole period, and there is little doubt but that most
of her sisters could do as well under similar conditions.

When she is first commissioned nobody but the chief
engineer, and sometimes not he, knows everything there is
to be known about the complex machinery of a modern

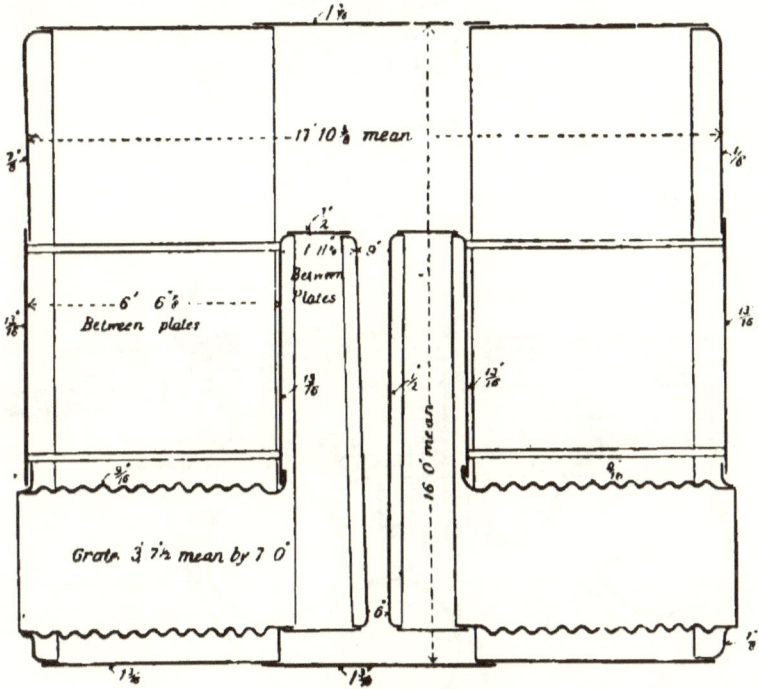

FIG. 9.—BOILER OF H.M.S. "EDGAR."

cruiser; what is called the human element is distinctly
weak, for nobody knows anybody else, but in a year or so
things are very much altered. Every man knows his place,
his duty, and how to do it. The consequence is that in ships of
a high power the results obtained on the trial trips are generally equalled, and sometimes, as in the case of the *Vulcan*,
actually surpassed—this ship having made for a forty-eight

hours' run in the Mediterranean about seventy horse-power, under natural draught, more than she did on her trials.

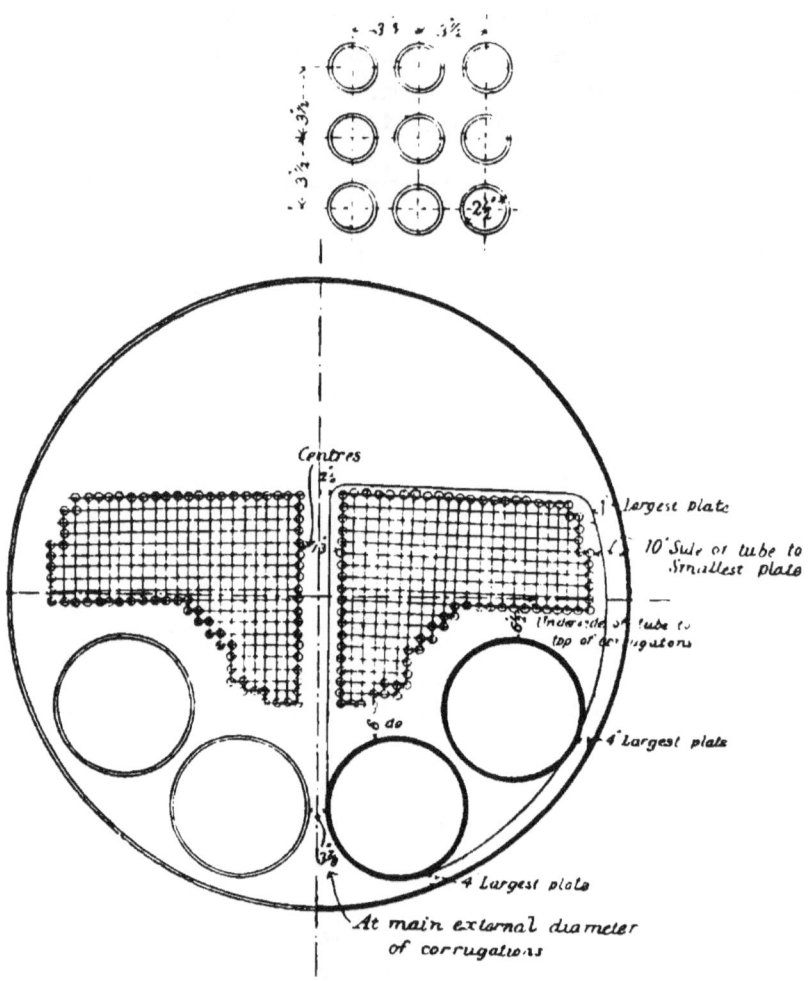

FIG. 10.--BOILER OF H.M.S. "EDGAR."

The *Royal Arthur*, like all other modern fighting ships, is fitted with twin screws, and a balanced rudder, capable of being worked either by steam or hand, her high speed

requiring this form of rudder to enable her to be kept
under proper control. Her engines were supplied by
Messrs. Maudslay, Sons, and Field. The estimated speed
was 18½ knots and 20½ knots for natural and forced
draught, but the real speed was half a knot less than this.
The amount of coal carried is 850 tons. The complement of

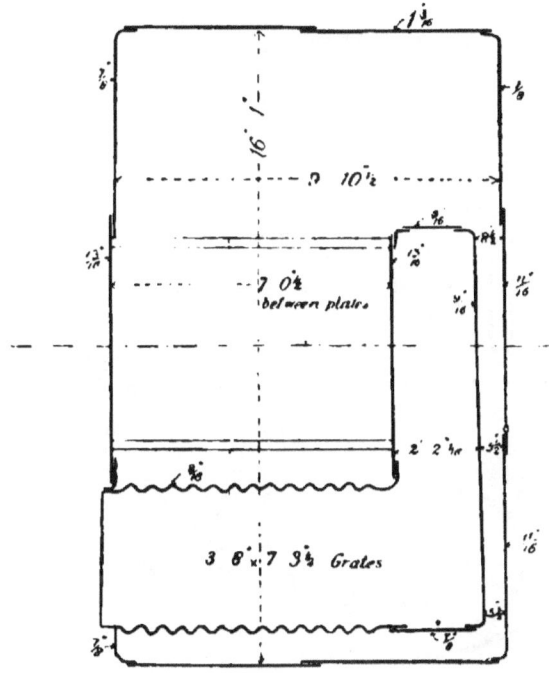

FIG. 11.—BOILER OF H.M.S. "CRESCENT."

officers and men is 520, of whom 123 belong to the engine-
room staff. The total cost of the ship was £402,414, and she
may be taken as a specimen of her class, which consists
of, besides her, the *Crescent, Edgar, Endymion, Gibraltar,
Grafton, Hawke, St. George,* and *Theseus.* All of these
vessels are, excepting the *Grafton* and *Theseus,* in commission as I write, and I venture to say that no country in the
world could produce a squadron to equal these nine ships.

The Admiralty specifications are so minutely drawn up nowadays, that there is not much room for the display of any great originality of design. In fact, the engines of the different makers only vary in details of arrangement that can hardly be called important. The relative capacities of

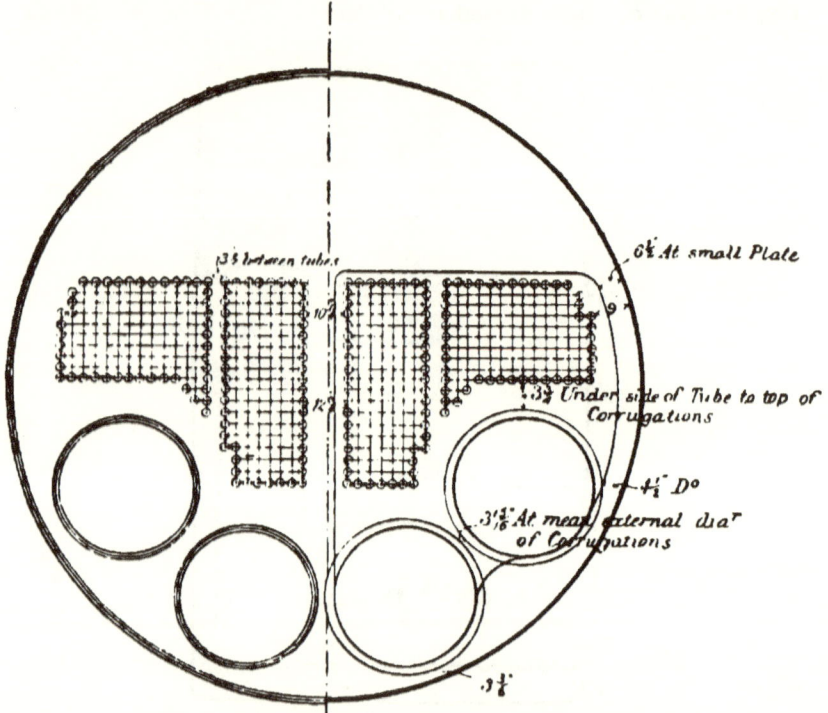

FIG. 12.—BOILER OF H.M.S. "CRESCENT."

the cylinders, for instance, are not quite the same in the *Royal Sovereign* as in the *Nile*. The engines of the *Royal Arthur*, by the same makers, are of the same type as those of the latter ship. It may be observed, however, to produce the 12,000 horse-power of the *Nile*, steam of a pressure of 135 lb., generated by the combustion of fuel on 603 square feet of grate surface was employed; while in the case of the *Royal Arthur*, to obtain the same power, Messrs. Maudslay use steam at 155 lb. pressure, while the grate surface is increased to 855 square feet; both undoubtedly changes for the better. The framing of the *Royal Arthur* is to a certain extent novel. Instead of the more usual plan of one strong standard at the back and two bright columns in front, the cylinders are each supported by four cast-steel columns, which allows of much easier access to the guides and other working parts of the machinery while under way. The weight of the *Royal Arthur's* engines, including the water in the boilers, is 1,180 tons, and this may be taken as about the weight allowed for all first-class cruisers of her class. In these latest engines there is no fancy valve gear, the old-fashioned link motion alone has been used.

The *Hawke*, a sister ship to the *Edgar*, and engined as that vessel is by the Fairfield Company, completed her trials in the most satisfactory manner. Each set of engines has three cylinders of 40 inches, 59 inches, and 88 inches in diameter, with a stroke of 4 feet 3 inches. Steam at 150 lb. pressure is supplied from four double-ended boilers of 16 feet in diameter and 18 feet in length, each end of the boilers having four furnaces and two combustion chambers. There is also an auxiliary boiler, 13 feet in diameter and 9 feet 3 inches in length. In all there are thirty-five furnaces and 20,000 square feet of heating surface.

The first set of trials was made on March 5th, the *Hawke* starting from Sheerness towards Dover, and making an eight hours' run, the speed being determined from the log. The Admiralty designated this as a natural draught trial, but perhaps it would be better to describe it as an assisted draught experiment, there being an air pressure equal to 0·3 inch of water in the stokehold. Under these conditions the engines worked during the eight hours' run at an

average rate of 98·46 revolutions per minute, and indicated
10,761 horse-power, which gave a mean speed of 19·5 knots.
A four hours' run was made over the same course three
days later, when the horse-power was 12,521, and the
mean speed about twenty knots. The question that naturally
arises is, whether it is worth while in vessels of this class
to spend so much money, to run such risks, and, not
the least thing, to endure such discomfort for the sake
of a contrivance that, at most, gives a knot an hour extra
speed, and that will probably never be used in time of
peace.

The use of triple-expansion engines in the Navy, though
not quite, perhaps, universally approved, has become
universal. No ship, whatever its size, is now fitted with
any other variety. The first in use in the service were
those of the *Rattlesnake*, which were finished in 1886,
by Messrs. Laird. The first triple-expansion engines made
by Messrs. Humphrys and Tennant were those for the
Victoria and *Sans Pareil*, the orders for which were received from the Admiralty in 1885. Messrs. Maudslay
completed some engines of this type in 1887 for H.M.S.
Nile, and at the same time for the small craft *Sandfly*,
Spider, *Grasshopper*, and three others. Messrs. Thornycroft completed their first set in August, 1887, and in
October, 1888, turned out, under Admiralty supervision,
some torpedo-boats for the Indian Government. Messrs.
Penn did not build any till 1890, when the Admiralty
ordered the *Sappho* and *Scylla*.

We now come to a consideration of the *Blake* and
Blenheim. Their engines are of a type never previously
adopted in this country, though it has in several instances
found favour with the Italian Government. They consist
of four distinct sets of triple-expansion, inverted-cylinder
engines, and occupy, with their adjuncts, nearly two-thirds

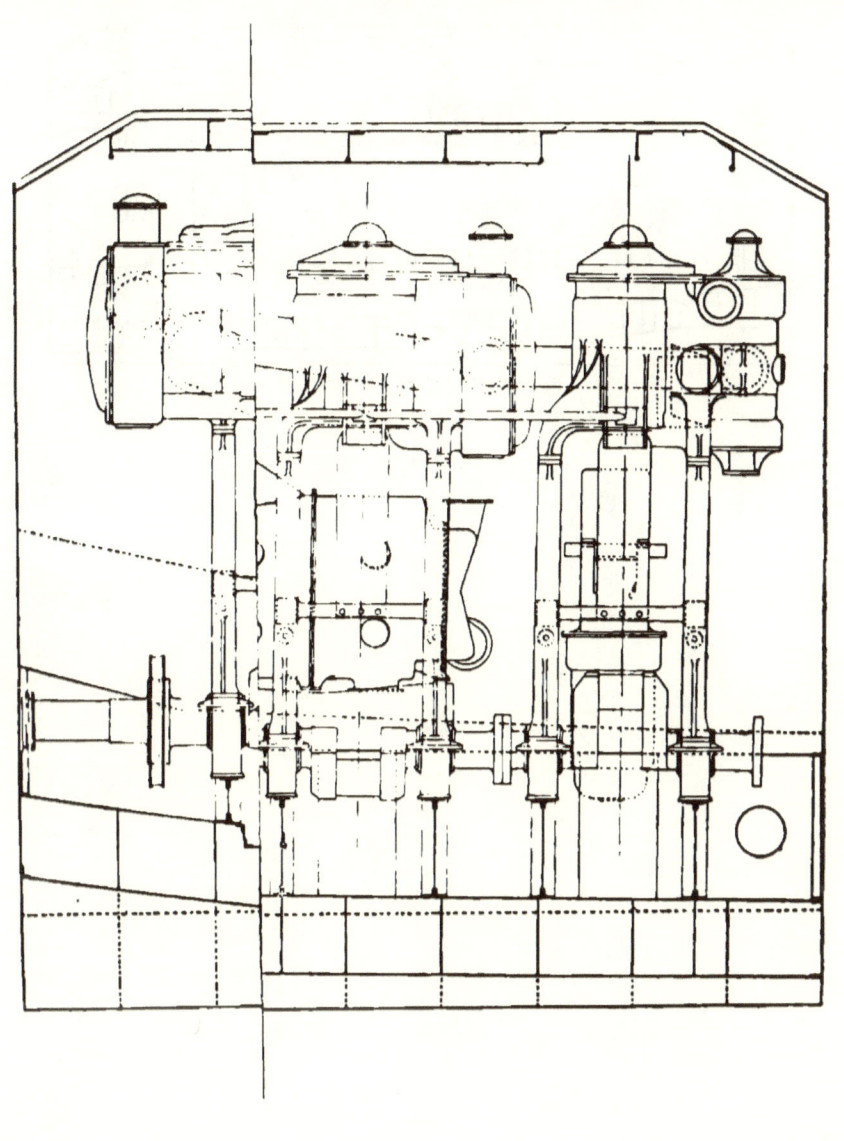

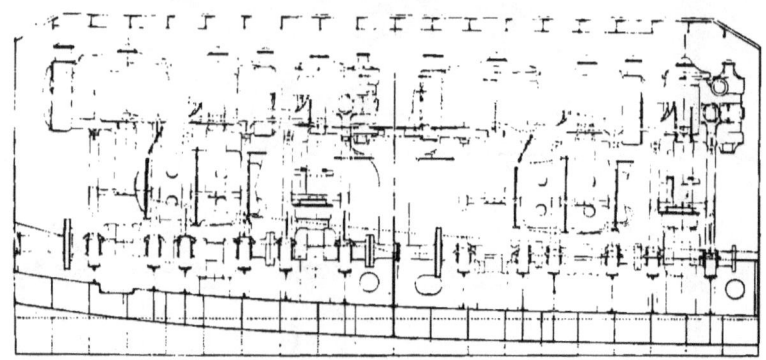

FIG. 13.—ENGINES OF THE "BLAKE," 20,000 HORSE-POWER.

of the length of a ship of 9,000 tons displacement. They are placed in four separate compartments, two sets being coupled together on the starboard and port sides respectively, for driving each propeller. There are a total of four high-pressure cylinders, 36 inches in diameter, four intermediate cylinders, 52 inches, and four low-pressure cylinders, 80 inches, with a stroke of 4 feet. Each set of engines has an air-pump 33 inches diameter and 2 feet stroke, and a surface condenser having 12,800 tubes, and an aggregate surface for cooling of 2,250 square feet, the length of the tubes between the tube-plates being 9 feet. There is also in each compartment one centrifugal circulating pump, 3 feet 9 inches in diameter, driven by a small independent engine, and capable of pumping from the bilge as well as the sea. The screw propellers are 18 feet 3 inches in diameter, with a mean pitch of 24 feet 6 inches. Steam is supplied by six double-ended boilers, having four furnaces at each end, and one auxiliary boiler. The total area of fire-grate surface is 863 square feet, and of heating surface, 26,936 square feet. Each engine-room is kept cool by four 4 feet 6 inch fans. Forced draught was intended to be produced by twelve 5 feet 6 inch fans, three in each stokehold.

The *Blenheim* is fitted with Normandy's improved double distillers, capable of furnishing 400 gallons of distilled water per hour. The electric lighting machinery consists of three dynamos of Siemens' manufacture, driven by a Willans' engine, each of which is capable of producing a current of 400 ampères. The after main engines can be easily disconnected and worked separately for slow or moderate speeds : and it is on this hitherto untried arrangement that naval sea-going engineers looked somewhat askance. The *Blake*, however, only returned in May, 1895, to England after a three years' commission on the North America and West Indies station, and, I believe, during this period none of the dreaded disadvantages were experienced. The trouble feared was that if the after engines were used much more than the forward ones, their bearings would wear down, and when, in case of it being necessary to get more power, the forward engines were coupled up, the shafts would be found to be "out of line." Nothing of the kind, however, occurred, or, at any rate, if there ever seemed any danger from this cause, the chief engineer probably recommended the use of one screw only, keeping the ship on a straight course by means of the helm.

On November 18th, 1891, the *Blake* went out for her official eight hours' trial with natural draught. The day was rather foggy, and towards the very end of the trial it was deemed advisable to be satisfied with the results of a seven hours' run, as these had been so satisfactory and the light was fading, while the engines were working with a smoothness and efficiency that showed no signs of flagging. The Admiralty orders were to run at about 13,000 horse-power, which was what had been stipulated for at natural draught, but with all four engines linked up and an abundance of steam, an average of 14,500 horse-power was easily obtained. At one time 15,000 was touched, but was not allowed to be maintained; but 16,000, or a little more, could readily have been indicated with the permitted half-inch of air pressure, if the engines had been allowed to use the steam as fast as it was generated. The Admiralty officials, however, perhaps acted wisely in not putting more power through the boilers than they could help, as the result was that not a sign of "weeping" or other complaint was shown by them. Engines never worked better or more smoothly, and the entire absence of vibration at all speeds was most remarkable. The speed of the ship was a little disappointing, but

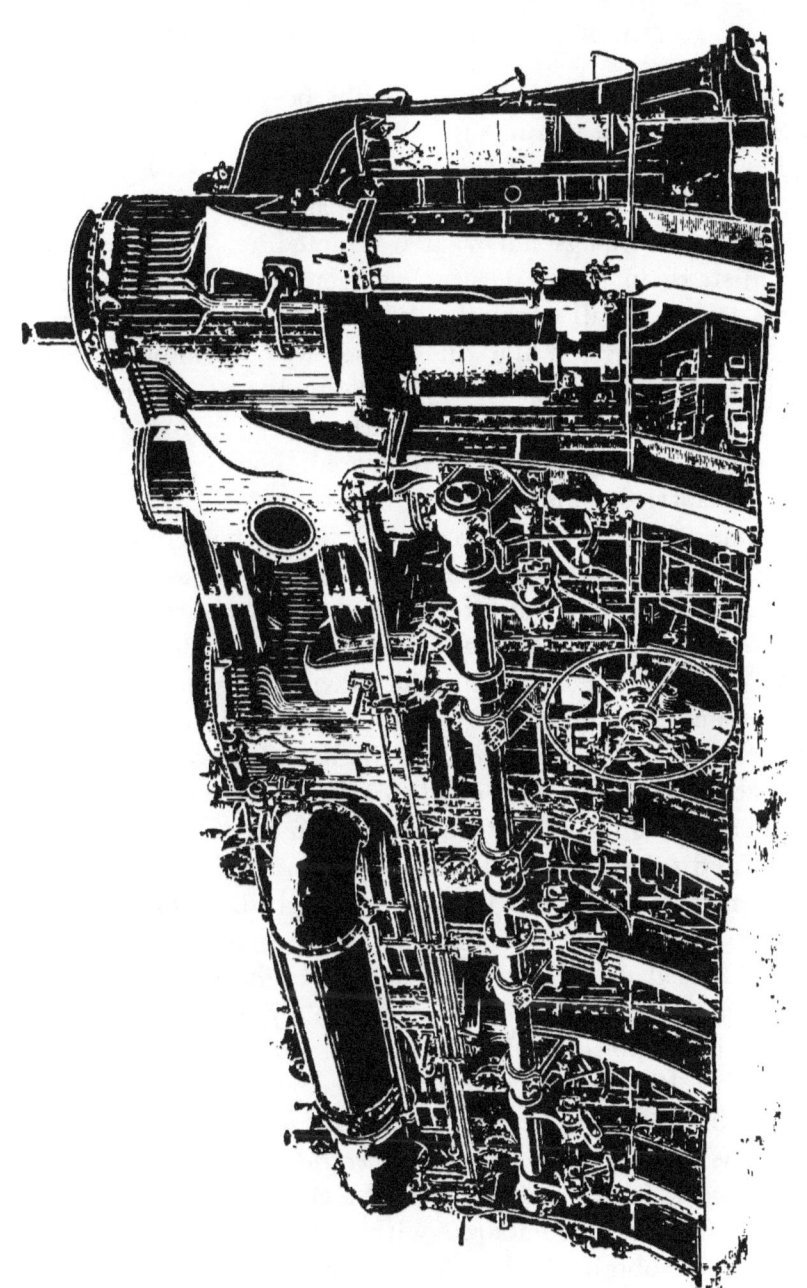

FIG. 14.—SIDE VIEW OF THE "TERRIBLE'S" ENGINES, 25,000 HORSE-POWER.

the loss of nearly half a knot should be put down to the trial having been run in such shoal water.

The *Blake's* sea speed for twenty-four hours with 14,500 horse-power, would probably be at least 19·7 knots. This is very good, though not what was aimed at; but now that the mistake in boiler design has been frankly recognized, the Admiralty will no doubt do much better than this in the near future. While this vessel was flagship of Sir John Hopkins at Bermuda, she had all her boiler-tubes "ferruled," and never gave any trouble to her engineers afterwards. It must be remembered, however, that she was never tried under forced draught.

Coming next to the *Blake* and *Blenheim*, both in chronological and progressive order, are the two largest cruisers in the world, which far exceed in size any vessels of their class that have gone before. These two ships, the *Powerful* and *Terrible*, one built by the Naval Construction and Armaments Company, at Barrow-in-Furness, the other by Messrs. J. and G. Thomson, of Clydebank, near Glasgow, are each 538 feet long over all, 71 feet wide, are designed to have a draught of 27 feet, and are to be of 14,200 tons each in displacement. The advance in engine power on the two former ships is hardly less marked. The engines of the *Blenheim*, which alone of the two ships was tried under forced draught, indicated 21,411 horse-power, the *Powerful* and *Terrible* are to be driven by engines exerting 25,000 horse-power. On the natural draught trials, however, the *Blake's* propelling machinery gave out 14,525 horse-power, much the same as the *Blenheim's*—a little less. As it is intended to run the *Powerful* and *Terrible*, says the "Times," with natural draught only, the powers just quoted should be compared with the 25,000 horse-power hoped to be obtained from the later vessels.

It may be stated here for the information of those who

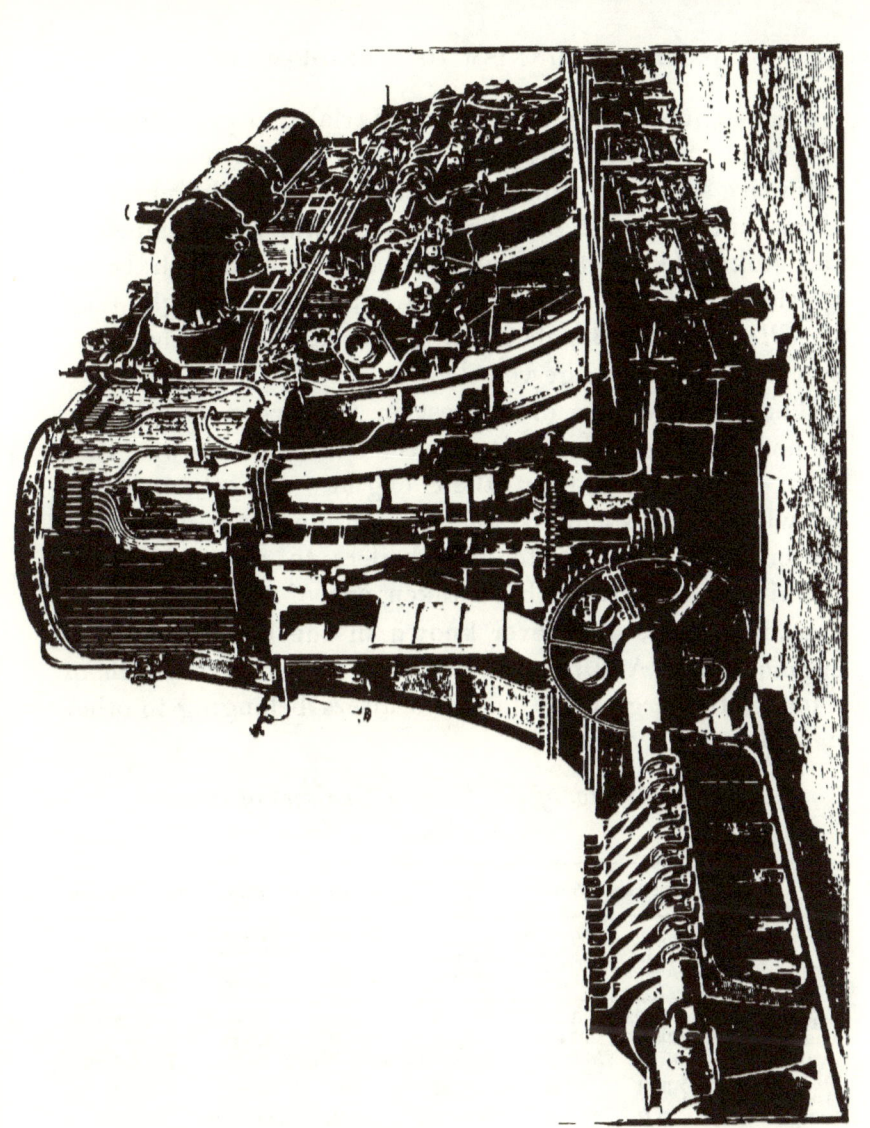

FIG. 15.—END VIEW OF THE "TERRIBLE'S" ENGINES.

are not acquainted with Admiralty trial-trip practice, that the term "natural draught" is not always used in its primitive sense of being the draught due to the chimney alone, but that a slight *plenum* is generally maintained in the stokehold, anything under about half an inch being considered natural draught. On her forced draught trial the *Blenheim* had 2 inches of air pressure, which is the *maximum* allowed for large vessels.

The chief feature of interest in the two new cruisers, is not, however, their size or the enormous power that is to be obtained from their engines, but the manner in which the steam is to be generated to supply that power. In fitting water-tube boilers to these ships the Admiralty authorities have taken one of the boldest and most important steps ever known in the history of naval engineering. And here it may be as well to give details of a few of the largest and fastest cruisers belonging to other nations :

Dimensions, etc. of the Largest Cruisers of Several Nations.[1]

	Russia.	France.	United States.	Germany.	Italy.	Great Britain.
	Rurik, Twin-screw.	Dupuy de Lôme, Triple-screw.	Columbia, Triple-screw.	Kaiserin Augusta, Triple-screw.	Giuseppe Garibaldi, Twin-screw.	Terrible, Twin-screw.
Displacement .	10,923	6,297	7,475	6,052	6,500	14,200
Length . .	396 ft.	374 ft.	412 ft.	393 ft.	325 ft.	500 ft.
Breadth . .	67 ft.	51 ft. 6 in.	58 ft. 2 in.	49 ft. 3 in.	59 ft.	71 ft. 6 in.
Ratio of length to breadth .	5·91	7·26	7·08	7·97	5·508	6·99
Draught . .	26 ft.	23 ft. 6 in.	22 ft. 6 in.	23 ft.	23 ft. 7 in.	27 ft.
Horse-power .	13,250	14,000	21,500	12,000	13,000	25,000
Speed . .	18·0	20·0	22·8	20·0	20·0	22·0 [2]
Coal capacity .	2,000	900	2,400	—	600	1,500 or 3,000

[1] The above table is taken from an exhaustive series of articles on the *Terrible*, published in "Engineering" of May 24th, 1895, and following numbers, from which I have largely borrowed.

[2] With natural draught only.

The stem, sternpost, rudder, and the brackets for carrying the screw shafts are all made of phosphor bronze, the blades of the twin-screw propellers being of manganese bronze. The total weight of bronze used is 120 tons, excluding the weight of the twin propellers, which are each 21 tons. The stem weighs 15 tons. It is of the usual ram form now universally adopted by the Admiralty. The twin-screws are each three-bladed, the diameter being 19 feet 6 inches. Both screws rotate inwards, which is the reverse of the ordinary practice, but recent experiments made by the Admiralty warrant the change.

The steering-gear is of the screw type, and is placed immediately under the protective deck, and aft over the rudder, which is of the balanced type and has an area of 250 square feet. The gear consists of a double-threaded right and left-handed screw on an 8-inch shaft, which carries a nut on the right-handed and another on the left-handed portion of the screw. The revolution of the shaft causes the nuts to approach to or recede from each other. The motion of the nuts is transmitted to the cast-steel crosshead on the rudder stock by means of heavy steel rods 10 inches in diameter and 10 feet long. The rudder stock is cast in one piece with the rudder frame, and is of manganese bronze, 24 inches in diameter, but with a 9-inch hole cored in it to reduce the weight. A brass stuffing-box has been placed at the point where the rudder stock passes through the sternpost, to maintain water-tightness. The weight of the rudder is taken up on a series of eight gun-metal rollers 6 inches in diameter, working on a roller path bolted to the sternpost. The steering-gear is actuated by two powerful steering-engines supplied by Messrs. Caldwell and Co., Limited, Glasgow, each having two vertical cylinders 13 inches diameter by 10 inches stroke. The engines are in duplicate to avoid the chance of a breakdown. They are placed in the engine-room, and the power is transmitted to the gear by hollow shafting 6 inches in diameter carrying the spur gear. The vessel can also be steered by four hand-wheels 6 feet 6 inches in diameter placed on the same shaft as the nuts, the gear being connected or disconnected to the steam engine or hand-wheels at will by a powerful screw clutch.

It may be added that the whole of the wheel gearing throughout the entire system has been machine cut, so as to reduce backlash and noise to a minimum. The motion of each of the steam-steering wheels corresponds with that of the ordinary hand-steering wheels, and they are carried on gun-metal pedestals, having indices to show the position in degrees of the rudder to starboard or port. In addition to the brass dials, those on the upper deck are fitted with glass segments and lanterns for illuminating the inside at night, and have the necessary figures and the information burned into these glass segments.

Of auxiliary engines it may be said that there are 85 in all. Here is a list:

Reversing engines, 2 sets; turning engines, 2 sets; main circulating pumps, 4 sets; auxiliary circulating pumps and air pumps, 2 sets; main feed pumps, 6 sets; auxiliary feed pumps, 8 sets; fire and bilge pumps, 4 sets; drain tank pump, 1 set; distiller pumps, 2 sets; air compressors for air jets in Belleville boilers, 8 sets; fan compressors for stokeholds, 12 sets; fan compressors for engine-rooms, 2 sets; fan compressors for ship ventilation, 4 sets; electric light engines, 3 sets; air compressors, 4 sets; steering-engines, 2 sets; boat-hoisting engines, 2 sets; coal-hoisting engines, 2 sets; ash-hoisting engines, 12 sets; engine for workshop, 1 set; capstans fore and aft, 2 sets.

These amount to a total of 85, or, including the main

engines, there are a total of 87 separate sets of steam engines altogether on board.

The main engines are of the four-cylinder triple-expansion type. Each of the two sets is designed to develop 12,500 indicated horse-power, giving a continued power of 25,000. Steam is supplied by 48 water-tube boilers of the Belleville type, to be described later. The safety valves on the boilers are loaded to a pressure of 260 lb. per square inch, this pressure being reduced to 210 lb. at the engines by means of a patent Belleville reducing valve, which is placed at the forward end of each engine-room. Each set of engines is placed in a separate engine-room, divided by a longitudinal water-tight bulkhead, which extends the whole length of the machinery space, and each engine-room is in all respects exactly similar to and entirely independent of the other.

The diameters of the high and intermediate pressure cylinders are 45 inches and 70 inches respectively, while the diameter of each of the low-pressure cylinders is 76 inches, all having a stroke of 48 inches. The high-pressure cylinders are placed forward, and are each fitted with piston valves of the inside type, having improved adjustable packing rings, while the intermediate and low-pressure cylinders are fitted with treble-ported flat slide-valves on their sides, having a special type of relief frame to relieve them of steam pressure, and the weight of all the valves is suitably balanced in order to reduce the strain on the valve-gear as far as possible. The cylinders, which are entirely independent castings, are bolted together to provide sufficient longitudinal stiffness, and to further increase their stability in case of ramming, strong struts are fitted between the high-pressure cylinder and the forward structure of the vessel, as well as transversely between the respective cylinders in each engine-room. The barrels of

all the cylinders are made of special close-grained cast iron,
and are steam-jacketed. The valve-gear is of the double
eccentric link motion type, and is reversed by means of a
double-cylinder engine attached to one of the cast steel
front columns at the level of the starting platform and be-
side the starting handles. Each of the reversing levers is
provided with screw gear, so that the valves of each
cylinder may be linked up independently.

The pistons, cylinder covers, and steam-chest doors are
of cast steel. The piston and connecting rods are of
Siemens-Martin steel, and metallic packing has been employed for all the stuffing-box glands of the piston-rods
and valve spindles of the main engines, as well as for all
the auxiliary engines throughout the vessel. The crank-
shafts are hollow, and each consists of four interchangeable
pieces, 20 inches in external diameter at the journals, and
10 inches in internal diameter. The crank arms are cut
away as much as possible for lightness, and for convenience
in fitting the centrifugal lubricators. The thrust shafts
and propeller shafting are also hollow, the shafting being
$18\frac{1}{2}$ inches diameter inboard, and 20 inches outside the ship.
As the vessel is copper-sheathed, the portions of the shafting abaft the stern tube stuffing-box have been cased with
gun-metal.

In conformity with Messrs. Thomson's practice for naval
machinery, as well as for the machinery of vessels intended
for express passenger service, the tube casing, as well as
the ends of the condensers, is built up entirely of naval
brass plates riveted together. The minimum weight
possible is thereby secured, and this condition is of the
greatest importance, as a combined cooling surface of
25,000 square feet is required in the *Terrible*. The
steam is condensed outside the tubes, which are $\frac{5}{8}$-in. in
external diameter by ·05 inch thick, the circulating water

passing through them. The water is supplied by four large 24-inch Gwynne's centrifugal pumps, each being driven by an independent engine. The pumps are large enough to supply sufficient condensing water for full power working. The pumps, also, with steam of 150 lb. pressure, are each capable of discharging per hour 1,500 tons of water from the bilge. The engines driving them may exhaust into the atmosphere, and work at a speed of 300 revolutions per minute.

The exhaust steam from the whole of the auxiliary machinery in the ship is led into the auxiliary exhaust pipes which are connected both with the atmosphere by the auxiliary exhaust pipe carried up the after funnel, and with the respective auxiliary condensers in either engine-room. Each of these condensers has its own air and auxiliary pump entirely independent of those for the main condensers, and driven by independent engines. The combined cooling surface of these two auxiliary condensers is 3,000 square feet, and their tube casings, like those of the main condensers, are built of naval brass plates, Messrs. J. and H. Gwynne supplying the pumping machinery in connection with them.

Besides the auxiliary engines already noticed, a double-cylinder reversible engine is conveniently placed above the starting platform on one of the after columns which support each of the low-pressure cylinders, for the purpose of turning the engines in harbour. This is effected by a set of compound worm gearing, the worm wheels having machine-cut gun-metal teeth, the main worms being of manganese bronze. These engines are capable of turning the main engines through one complete revolution in eight minutes with a steam pressure of 150 lb., and a hand-gear has also been arranged for the same purpose.

The electric machinery for generating the current for

internal lighting, search-lights, motors, etc., consists of three large sets of condensing engines and dynamos. The engines are of the open-fronted compound type, mounted on the same bed-plate, and coupled direct to dynamos which are of the direct current type, self-regulating, and each capable of maintaining on continous running 600 amperes with an electromotive force of 80 volts, at 300 revolutions per minute. Two of these sets are placed in a compartment adjacent to the main engine-room and under the protective deck, the third set being placed on the main-deck amidships. The electric light installation consists of about 800 50-candle-power and 16-candle-power lamps, laid out on the double-wired, water-tight distributing system. In addition to the lighting up of the interior spaces, including coal-bunkers and magazines, the decks will be illuminated by powerful lights suspended from the rigging. The compasses, telegraphs, masthead, side lamps, signal lanterns, semaphores, and military tops are all separately lighted, and under the immediate control of the officer on deck. Six search-lights of about 50,000 candle-power each are fitted up—two on the forward bridge, two on the after bridge, and one on the top of each mast. Each of these powerful lamps can project a beam of light right round the horizon. Electric motors are to be used throughout in lieu of the usual hydraulic appliances, and this applies not only to the training and elevation of the heavy guns, but also for the ammunition hoists, etc. Submerged torpedoes will also be fired by electricity from the torpedo director-house and conning towers. Voice tubes are fitted throughout, thus putting one compartment into communication with another, the necessary signalling appliances in connection therewith being entirely done by electrical apparatus.

An equally important feature with lighting in maintaining

all compartments of such structures habitable is an efficient supply of fresh air, and to effect the efficient ventilation of those portions of the ship underlying the protective deck and of the engine and boiler-rooms, 18 steam fans of large diameter are employed. These fans and engines have been made by Messrs. J. and G. Thomson, the contractors for the vessel, of an improved design, resulting from their long and varied experience in this class of auxiliary machinery. Two fans, 6 feet in diameter, are placed forward of the machinery space, and by means of two large trunks, air is led to the submerged torpedo-room, air-compressing space, and to the capstan engine-room, all these compartments being on the orlop deck. Where these trunks have occasion to pass through water-tight bulkheads, vertical and horizontal automatic valves are fitted over the opening, so that, in the event of a compartment being flooded, the adjacent compartments are kept dry, the valves automatically closing as the water rises. The quantity of fresh air required to supply these underwater compartments is enormous, involving ventilating trunks of very large section; and great skill has been displayed in the manner of carrying out this portion of the equipment so as to interfere as little as possible with the other fittings of the ship.

From the main supply trunks branches of greater or less dimensions, according to requirements, are led to every part of the ship. And not only is fresh air thus artificially supplied, but an equally efficient service of exhaust trunks is fitted throughout the vessel, by which means the foul air is carried aloft.

The air-compressing machinery for charging the torpedoes consists of four complete sets of air-compressing engines and pumps, and eight sets of air reservoir tubes with separators and charging columns. Two engines are placed in the forward part of the vessel and the other two in the after end. Each has three air pumps of large size, and all the parts of these engines as well as of all the other auxiliary engines throughout, are designed to work at the full boiler pressure of 260 lb. per square inch, which will be the pressure ordinarily employed. The air pressure employed is 1,700 lb. per square inch, the tubes for the separators, charging columns, and air reservoirs being made of the best open-hearth steel, and are free from grooves and surface imperfections of every kind, great care being taken to secure them of a perfect cylindrical form and of a uniform thickness throughout. Some indications may be given of the excellence of the workmanship employed in the manufacture of this class of machinery, so as to insure perfect tightness of the joints at each of these tube-ends, fifty of which form but one air reservoir, and also of the joints of the intermediate pipes connecting them to the air pumps, as well as of the various valves and fittings of the pumps themselves. The whole of the installation was tested to the working pressure of 1,700 lb. per square inch, and allowed to stand under this pressure for twenty-four hours, when it was ascertained that the loss of pressure was under six per cent. To attain this result only the very best materials can be employed, and the greatest care has to be exercised in selecting the copper, as well as in obtaining the most suitable alloys of this metal.

In a later number of "Engineering," that for June 28th, 1895, is a description of the *Terrible's* Belleville boilers, which is by far the best and clearest I have ever read. I prefer to give it here rather than in my own chapter on boilers, so as to preserve the continuity of the account of that ship's machinery, which ship, with her sister, the *Powerful*, forms the most splendid example of naval architecture and naval engineering that the world has ever seen. The Belleville boilers, as fitted to both these

vessels, *cannot* be failures, but will undoubtedly inaugurate
a fresh epoch in the propelling power of the Royal Navy.
But more of this hereafter.

" Each boiler consists of a series of sets of tubes, placed
side by side over the furnace, and inclosed in non-conducting

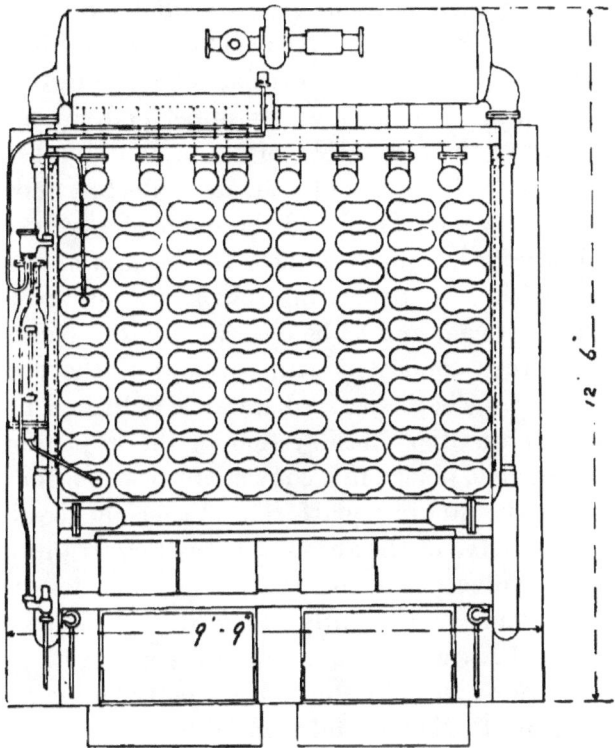

FIG. 16.—BELLEVILLE BOILER AS APPLIED TO THE "TERRIBLE."

casings. Each set of tubes, called an element, is constructed
in the form of a flattened spiral, and consists of a number of
straight tubes, connected at the ends by means of a spiral,
termed a junction-box. The junction-boxes of each element
are built vertically over each other, and tubes enter and
leave these on the same level. The boxes at the back end

of the boiler are close-ended, but those towards the stoking platform have holes in them to permit of the inspection of the inside of the tubes, these holes being closed by specially constructed doors, kept tight by the boiler pressure. The tubes are all slightly inclined to the horizontal, and the lowest box of each element is connected by means of a special form of conical joint, secured by bolts, to a horizontal cross-tube of square section, forming a feed collector. Each element is also connected at its upper end, by a similar bolted joint, to the lower side of a horizontal cross-drum, which performs the duties of a steam collector, and on the upper side of which is placed the main stop-valve. Two external circulating pipes connect the bottom of the steam collector with two depositing chambers or mud-boxes, placed at each end, and to be described later, whose upper ends are in turn connected with the end of the horizontal feed collector. The boiler feed-water is delivered by either the main or auxiliary feed system to the adjustable feed-regulating valve, placed in a convenient position for adjust-ment from the stoking platform. From thence it passes through the valve of the automatic feed regulator up to the feed check valve placed on the steam collector, midway between its ends and slightly below its horizontal centre. These special features we shall describe later.

"Circulation takes place by each element receiving a supply of water from the horizontal feed collector into its lowest tube; this water is partly evaporated here and passes, part as steam and part as water, through the back junction-box into the tube above it, where a further portion of the water is evaporated. Each tube, therefore, has to convey all the steam made in those tubes of the same element which are below it as well as that formed within itself. A mixture of steam and water is thus continuously discharged from each element into the collector. The water so circulated mixes

with the fresh feed-water, and both pass along the bottom
of the collector, and by means of the external circulating
pipes placed at either end, into their respective mud-boxes,
and thence into the feed collector, again to be circulated
through the elements.

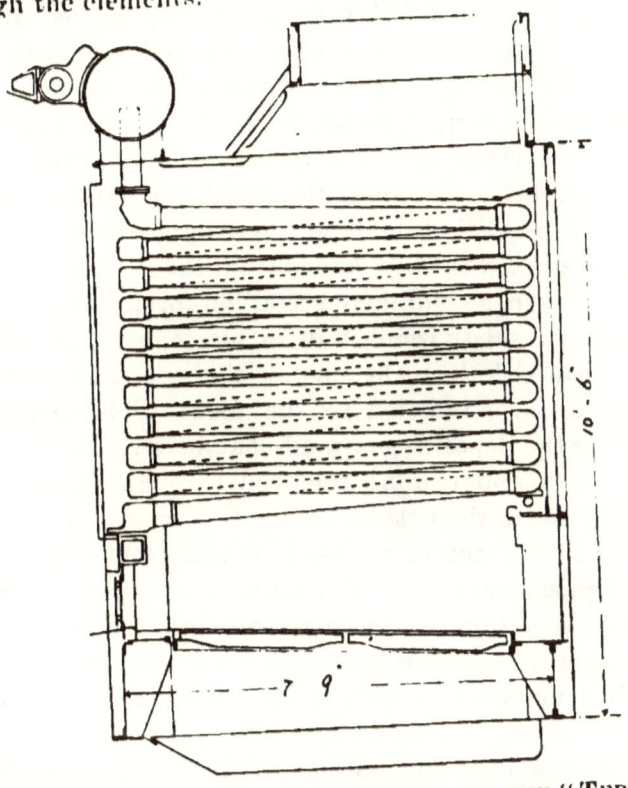

FIG. 17.—BELLEVILLE BOILER AS APPLIED TO THE "TERRIBLE."

" The function of the mud-boxes is important. Deposits
on the heating surface of marine boilers, arising from the
presence of small quantities of sea water and grease in the
boiler feed, have always been a source of trouble, and frequently of accident. It is with the view to obviating the
deposits on these surfaces that the depositing chambers or

mud-boxes have been arranged. Two tanks containing
lime-water are provided. In the lime tank an inlet pipe is
attached to the top, and the outlet is regulated by a cock
situated on the side of the tank, near the bottom. Lime is
put into the tank by a manhole, and the portion of the feed-
water diverted through the tank becomes impregnated to
the desired degree by means of the regulating valves provided. The diluted feed as it passes along the bottom of
the steam collector, together with the water that issues
from the various elements, is raised to the temperature of
evaporation before reaching the external circulating pipes.
Here it is found that the lime salts contained in the feed-
water, together with those added from the tanks to the feed,
separate out in a solid non-crystalline form, but in a state
of very high subdivision ; and in being precipitated they
carry down with them the small globules of oil which may
have obtained admission to the feed. This precipitate
gathers in the depositing or mud-chambers in the form of a
greasy mud, and can be removed through the blow-off
valves fitted at the bottom, while the purified feed-water
flows off the top into the cross feed collectors. There is a
vertical pipe screwed into the top of each mud-box, and it
conveys the return water, together with the boiler feed-
water from the steam collector, and a horizontal branch on
the side communicates with the feed collector. A vertical
web, extending from the top of the mud-box intervenes
between these inlet and outlet orifices, and is carried to a
sufficient depth to prevent the direct passage of water from
one to the other. The downcoming water, together with
the suspended greasy mud, descends along the side of the
mud-box, and as its movement is relatively slow, the precipitated mud and lime salts continue to descend by virtue
of their greater density, and are deposited at the bottom of
the vessel, while the purified water flows off at the top into

the feed collector by the exit branch. The blow-off valve for removing this deposit is on the bottom of the mud-box, and there is a valve fitted on the side for draining the boilers into the reserve fresh-water tanks, in accordance with the usual Admiralty requirements. A couple of hand-holes with doors, similar to those of the junction-boxes, are also provided.

"The Belleville automatic feed regulator, illustrated in detail by fig. 18, consists of a cast-steel vessel in direct communication with the boiler by two connections, one pipe entering its lower end and connecting it with the feed collector, the other pipe being attached to the top of the apparatus and connecting it with the seventh junction-box of the generating element nearest to it. The lower part of the vessel contains a float, guided at its lower end by a rod, which enters a hole in the bridge-piece carried by the bottom cover. The float is suspended by another rod from a lever which rests on knife-edges and which carries a roller at its other extremity. This roller lifts a rod, which is connected to an external lever, from one of whose ex-tremities is suspended a counter-weight consisting of a spring, bearing against a lug on the top cover, and of lead discs, of which some are placed on the upper end of the rod of the counter-weight, in order that their number may be more readily varied. The weight of the float is thus placed *in equilibrio*, partly on account of its displacement from the water of the vessel, and partly by the action of the counter-weights. In this condition the regulating feed valve uncovers its opening to a certain extent, and the inlet feed-water, entering through the outer check valve, flows through the regulating valve, and up to the feed check valve on the side of the steam collector. If the water level sinks, the float sinks also, to preserve its equilibrium, and the internal lever lifts the rod attached to the external lever,

H

which presses down the regulating feed valve, and so en-
larges the passage for the feed-water. If the water level
rises, the float rises also, in order to preserve its equilibrium,
and the roller on the end of the internal lever descends.
The counter-weight causes the rod which presses on this
roller to follow its motion, so that the external lever in sink-
ing on the side of the counter-weight, rises on the other
side, lifting the regulating feed valve, which diminishes the
section of the passage for feed-water. Thus the float acts
continuously for maintaining the water level at the same
height in the apparatus.

"This level will be higher or lower according as the
counter-weight is loaded with a greater or less number of
lead discs. Thus the level is raised by adding some discs,
and is lowered by removing some. It should be remarked
that the pressure exerted by the steam on the lower side of
the feed regulating valve always tends to close it, while, on
the other hand, the pressure of the steam in the apparatus,
which acts upon the rod in connection with the external
lever, tends, on the contrary, to open the feed valve. The
diameters of the feed regulating valve and of this rod,
together with the proportions of their respective levers, are
so regulated that these two pressures are *in equilibrio*, and
that therefore they have no influence upon the action of the
automatic apparatus.

"One of the most important features in the working of the
Belleville boilers is the regulation of the feed for a determined degree of dryness in the steam. When the boiler is
at rest, the water level is at the same height in the feed
apparatus and in the boiler; but when steam is being raised,
the resistance which the steam mixed with the water experiences in circulating through the tubes produces a reaction,
which causes the water level to rise in the feed apparatus
in proportion as the evaporation is more active. On the

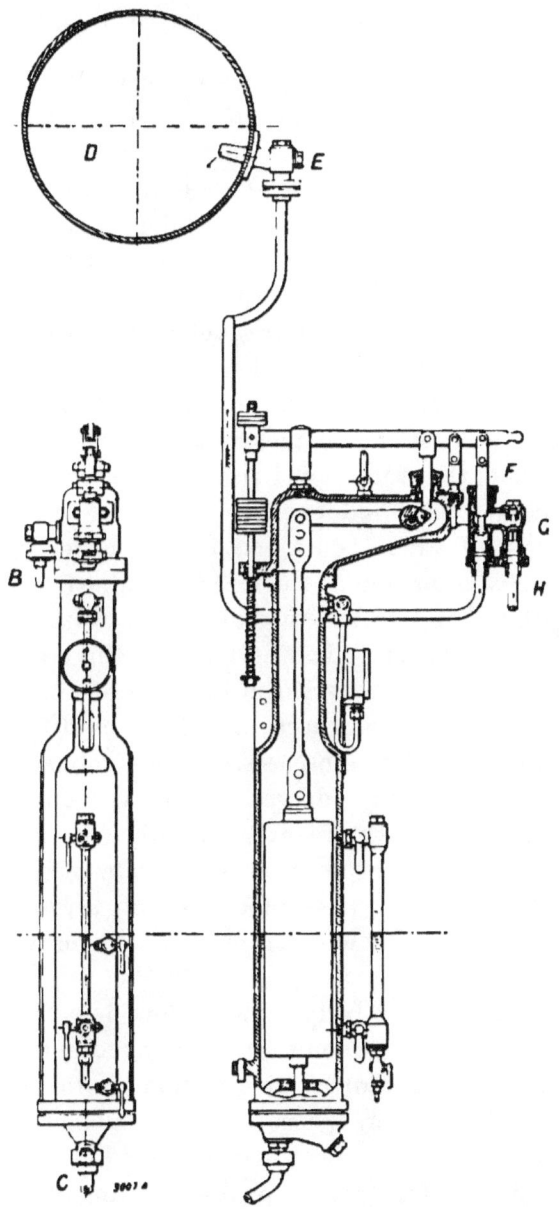

FIG. 18.—BELLEVILLE AUTOMATIC FEED REGULATOR.

other hand, as the quantity of water carried by the steam
tends to increase with the rate of evaporation, it is necessary in order that the steam should arrive in the steam
collector always at the same degree of dryness, that the
quantity of water contained in the boiler should vary in an
inverse ratio to the activity of the fire. This result is obtained by the automatic feed apparatus illustrated by fig.
18. The height of the water level in the feed regulator
being regulated once for all, the supply is cut off automatically when this level is attained. From this it results
that if the combustion becomes more active the evaporation
increases, and the water level rises in the regulator. The
balance arrangement reduces the passage of the feed, and
the quantity of water contained in the boiler diminishes
progressively, according as the rate of combustion increases.
On the other hand, if the rate of combustion diminishes,
the evaporation becomes less active, and the level sinks in
the apparatus which causes the opening of the feed regulating valves to be increased, and the quantity of water
contained in the boiler increases progressively according as
the rate of combustion decreases. In the one as in the
other case the quantity of water contained in the boiler is
always in an inverse proportion to the rate of combustion,
and the degree of dryness of the steam always remains
practically the same whatever may be the activity of the
fires.

"There are in all forty-eight boilers for the *Terrible*,
located in eight boiler-rooms, and arranged symmetrically
on each side of the central longitudinal water-tight bulkhead. The four after spaces on each side of the vessel
contain eight boilers, respectively arranged in three groups,
the forward and after groups, each consisting of two boilers
placed de by side, and the centre group of two pairs of
boilers placed back to back, and fired from athwartships

stokeholds. The remaining sixteen boilers are placed in
four forward boiler-rooms, situated likewise in pairs on
each side of the central bulkhead, and fired from longitudinal stokeholds. This difference in arrangement is necessitated by the fineness of form of the vessel at this part.
The funnels are four in number, of oval section, one to
each tranverse division. They are of different cross dimensions, to suit the number of boilers leading to each, but the
longitudinal dimensions have been kept the same in all
four, in order to accord with the general symmetry of the
ship. The height of each funnel from the grate is 80 feet.
To supply the air required for suitable deflection of the
furnace flames, and for admixture with the gases for insuring complete combustion, eight air-compressing engines
are supplied and fitted in the boiler-rooms, there being one
double-cylinder compressor for each of the four large compartments, and a single-cylinder compressor for each of the
four smaller forward spaces. The air is injected into the
furnace from a nozzle-box, placed on the front of the boiler
immediately above the furnace-doors, and extending the
whole width of the fire-grate. This air is discharged over
the fire through small nozzles, which divide it into thin
streams. The total grate surface is 2,200 square feet, and
the total heating surface 67,800 square feet, which should
give an ample margin of boiler power even when compared
with merchant service proportions.

"In the case of the *Terrible's* boilers, the junction-boxes
are malleable cast-iron, and the tubes are mild steel, lap-
welded, $4\frac{1}{2}$ inches outside diameter, and varying in thickness
from $\frac{3}{8}$ inch for those of the lower, to $\frac{3}{16}$ inch for the upper-
most rows. The tubes are screwed into the back boxes, the
pitch of the screw on the tube being very slightly different
from that of the box, so as to form a metallic joint between
them. A jam-nut is added for greater security. A similar

device is employed for the front ends, with this exception, that, instead of both tubes entering the box, one is connected by means of a screwed coupling-nut to a projecting nipple. This arrangement is adopted in order to facilitate the removal of the tubes which form the elements. The casings which inclose these elements are particularly deserving of notice from the careful manner in which they have been designed, so as to secure the requisite stability with a minimum of weight. The radiating surfaces of these casings, as well as of the steam collectors, have been covered with a layer of asbestos three inches thick, which is in turn protected by thin plates securely and neatly fastened.

" The feed arrangements for supplying the forty-eight boilers have been most carefully worked out, and every precaution has been taken to insure the system against any contingency. The arrangement comprises a main and auxiliary system of pumps and pipes, which are separate from and independent of each other. Four sets of evaporators and two distillery condensers have been provided in the aft auxiliary machinery space, together with the necessary pumps, etc., and these have been arranged so as to admit of triple and compound distillation, which greatly increases their efficiency over the ordinary method. The evaporators are capable of producing an aggregate of 26,880 gallons of fresh water per day from sea water, part of which is condensed in the condensers in the form of pure aërated fresh water for ship's drinking purposes, and the remainder is condensed in the auxiliary condensers situated in the engine-rooms. From thence it is conveyed to the main feed tanks, so as to make good any loss of water incurred by the machinery through escape of steam or other causes. The main feed system consists of six double-acting pumps of Messrs. G. and J. Weir's well-known special type, three in each engine-room. These draw by independent pipes

from the feed tanks, and each delivers by a separate pipe
to a compartment of eight boilers, whence the water is
distributed by branch pipes to the feed regulators attached
to the boilers. The eight pumps of the auxiliary feed
system, likewise of Messrs. Weir's manufacture, are placed
one in each boiler-room; those in the four after rooms are
the same size as the main feed-pumps, while all are
capable of supplying their own boiler-room at full power.
These auxiliary pumps are also connected to the main feed-
tanks by independent pipes, and in addition have separate
connection to the reserve fresh-water tanks and the sea,
and each discharges to the feed regulators in connection
with the boilers.

"The main steam supply is conveyed by six lines of steel
steam-pipes, three lines being arranged on each side of the
central bulkhead, and these being each entirely independent
of the other, as are also the connecting pipes from the
boilers to each of these lines. Any boiler may, therefore,
be cut out from the system without interfering with the
performance of the others in its compartment, as may also
any compartment from which any of these main steam-
pipes lead, without affecting the efficiency of the other
compartments. Any group of boilers may supply steam to
any of the engines.

"The reduction of the pressure of steam from 260 lb. to
210 lb. is secured by valves placed in the engine-room. It
is effected by means of wire-drawing. A cylindrical bell-
shaped 'gridiron' valve is employed, illustrated by figs.
marked 19 and 20. This valve has its ports cut in planes
at right angles to the axis, and extending about two-thirds
of the circumference. Similar ports are cut in the circular
valve-face, which is secured into the valve-chest in a
manner similar to the liner of a piston-valve into the
cylinder casting. The inlet steam is led round the back of

the valve-face, and thence flowing through the narrow circumferential openings between it and the valve, enters the centre of the hollow valve and escapes without further ob-

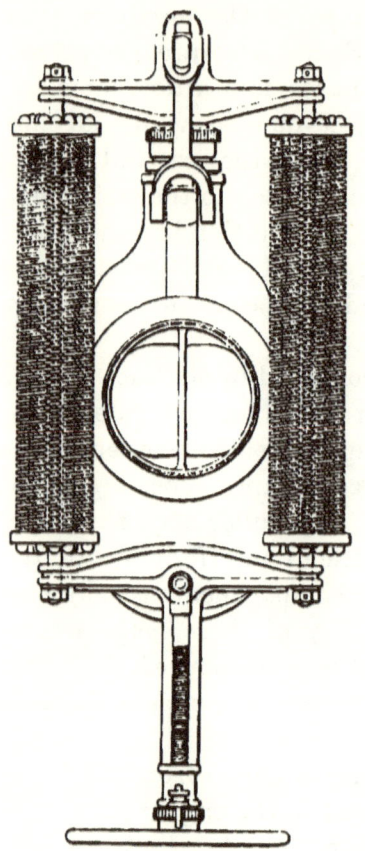

struction by the mouth of the bell to the outlet branch. The valve-chest is carried up over the dome of this valve, and through a special form of stuffing-box at the top projects a spindle, which is in connection with this dome. This spindle is jointed at its upper or exterior end to a lever, whose fulcrum is at its other extremity. At its centre is poised on steel knife-edges a crossbeam, from each of whose ends hangs a frame of springs. The lower ends of these frames are likewise attached to a similar crossbeam, and an adjusting hand-screw, yoked through a stiff projection from the bottom cover of the valve-chest, is attached to the centre of this beam.

FIG. 19.
BELLEVILLE REDUCING VALVE
FOR "TERRIBLE."

"As the space between the dome of the valve and the exterior valve-chest is, practically, not under steam pressure, it follows that the upward pressure of the steam, which has passed through the valve openings on the interior of the dome of the valve, is resisted by the extension of the springs. By adjusting this extension, either by adding more springs to the frame, or by removing some, as well as by means of the hand-screw for finer variations, the openings of the circumferential

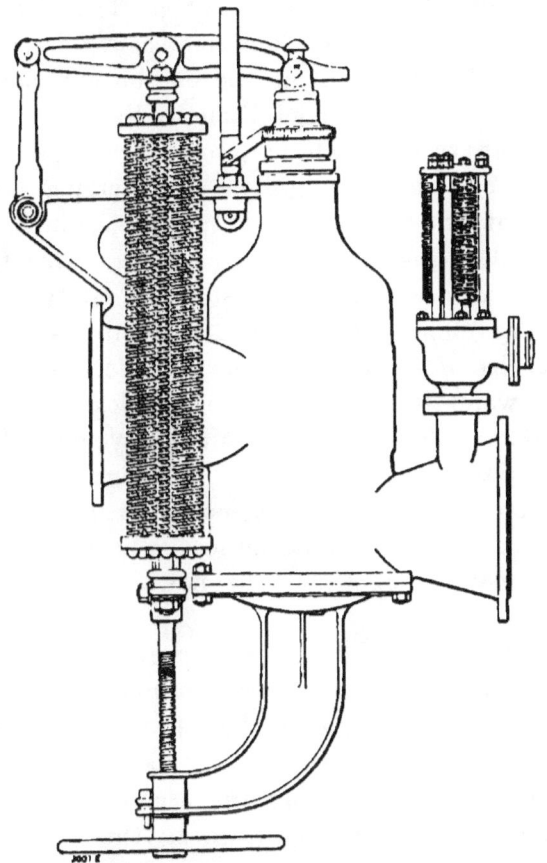

Fig. 20.—Belleville Reducing Valve for "Terrible."

ports may be regulated to any required degree, and in consequence a corresponding reduction of pressure may be effected. The details of these valves have been most carefully elaborated, and are the results of many years' experience on the part of Messrs. Delaunay, Belleville and Co.

A small safety-valve loaded so as to blow off at about the
' reduced pressure ' is placed on the outer branch.

" Before concluding, it may be remarked that two large
pumping engines of Messrs. J. and G. Thomson's duplex
pattern are also fitted in each engine-room to serve as fire-
engines and for pumping out the engine and boiler-room
and screw-alley bilges, in addition to the other compartments of the vessel. These pumps are capable of discharging a total of 90,000 gallons of water per hour, with
reduced steam pressure of 150 lb. per square inch, at about
eighty double strokes per minute. The drains from the
main and auxiliary steam-pipes, stop and safety valves, and
all auxiliary engines throughout the ship, are led by a
special service of piping to a special collecting-tank, from
which the water is pumped by the duplex drain pump to
the feed-tanks. This special drainage system, which was
initiated by the Admiralty some years ago, is a most important factor in reducing the loss of fresh water for the
boilers, the significance of which loss is naturally becoming
more and more apparent, as the power of the engines is
increased."

The *Terrible's* plant includes four evaporators, two distilling condensers, and two steam pumps. There are two
distinct or duplicate sets, and each may work independently of the other. Each set may be worked compound
or not compound, by using the secondary steam from
one evaporator as primary steam to the other. When
working not compound the four evaporators generate from
sea water 120 tons of gained fresh water per twenty-four
hours, and when working either compound or non-com-
pound, part of this gained fresh water is condensed in the
distilling plant into twenty-five tons of pure aërated drinking
water, the remainder being passed through the auxiliary
condensers to make up the boiler feed.

It would be interesting to compare these two new cruisers, the *Powerful* and *Terrible*, with the United States cruisers, *Columbia* and *Minneapolis*, the triple-screw vessels which attained such remarkable speed on their trials; but this may be better done when we have seen what our own ships can do.

The "Scientific American" believes, speaking of the commerce-destroyer *Columbia*, that she is the highest engined of any ship afloat for her size, but she is not the fastest. Her displacement is 7,350 tons, with an indicated horse-power of 22,000, and her speed 22·8 knots on a short trial trip, strained and driven to the utmost with the hottest fires imaginable, burning picked coal in quantities greatly in excess of any other ship, and every bearing flooded with oil. Even under these conditions her rate fell occasionally to 21 knots, and the indications are that she could not possibly maintain that speed from New York to Southampton. It is doubtful if on such a voyage she could keep up 19 knots. The power of the *Columbia* is far greater than that of the *Campania* and *Lucania*, and her displacement far less, yet they have maintained an average speed for 3,000 miles of 21·3 knots. The New York "Tribune," and other papers, similarly comment on the *Columbia's* trials.

In July, 1895, after the festivities at Kiel, the *Columbia* was ordered by the American authorities to make the best of her way from the Needles to Sandy Hook, and she averaged 18·4 knots for the whole distance. This was respectable, but no more, considering that she made on her full speed trial 22·8 knots. The time she took on the voyage was eleven minutes under a week, and her longest day's run was 473 knots. The Americans deserve the highest credit for having been sporting enough to set us the example of a voyage that has been often talked for a man-of-war,

but never previously performed.   The cost of the *Columbia*
was about £545,000.   About the same time the *Campania*,
a Cunard steamer, accomplished the voyage from New
York to Queenstown in five days twelve hours. This gives
a rate of 21·24 knots per hour, though it was necessary to
reduce speed for twelve hours on the eastward banks of
Newfoundland, an account of fog.

CHAPTER VI.

CRUISERS: SECOND AND THIRD-CLASS.

THE importance of this class of vessel for general sea work has long been recognized. But it was not till ten years ago that attempts were seriously made to improve the type in the first and most necessary quality of speed. The result was the building of a set of cruisers, of which the *Scout* was the pioneer, which are generally known to-day as the *Archer* class. Thirty-eight firms were invited to tender for the construction of six of these vessels in 1885, and the work was given to Messrs. J. and G. Thomson, of Clyde-bank, Glasgow. These ships, the *Archer*, *Brisk*, *Cossack*, *Mohawk*, *Porpoise*, and *Tartar*, were far from being perfect, but every one of them is in commission at the present day, and when in the course of nature they are absolutely worn out, there will be a serious lack of ships suitable for com-manders' commands, unless the Admiralty takes to build-ing some fresh ones. Two extra ships were added to the original six, built at Devonport, with an additional 1,000 horse-power each, named the *Serpent* and *Racoon*. Of these, the former was unhappily lost, with the greater part of her crew, through running ashore off the north-west coast of Spain, when proceeding on her first period of foreign ser-vice. The remaining ships mark an era in the history of the machinery of the Royal Navy. Probably no class of vessel has the machinery and boilers confined in such a cramped and inaccessible space as the whole of the above ships; but, notwithstanding this, and the inconveniences which are bound to arise from want of room in the engine-rooms and stokeholds, these vessels are, some of them, now doing their third commission abroad, and they have proved themselves fairly efficient, while their machinery and boilers have given no more trouble than has been easily overcome by their own engine-room staff, or the resources of the small foreign dockyards which exist on the stations where these ships are employed.

Their engines are of the double-compound, horizontal, direct-acting type, driving twin screws, and they are fitted with surface-condensers and separate double-acting air-pumps, which are fixed alongside the high-pressure cylinders, and worked by eccentrics fitted on the crank shafts of the main engines. When the engines are worked at from 140 to 150 revolutions per minute, the indicated horse-power is about 3,500, and the speed a little more than 17·5 knots per hour. The high-pressure cylinders are fitted with one slide-valve each, of the piston pattern, and the low-pressure cylinders have two slide-valves, also of the same type, which are worked by the ordinary eccentric and link gearing. Each set of the main engines has steam starting and reversing gear, in addition to ordinary hand-gear. The crank shafts and propelling shafting are of hollow steel, with the high-pressure and low-pressure cranks placed at an angle of 90 degrees from each other. The crank pins and brasses are fitted with centrifugal lubricating gear, in addition to the ordinary methods of lubrication. The "slippers," or cross-head guides, are forged in one piece with the piston-rods, and the guides work on a solid bed, which forms a portion of the bottom framing of the engines. The cylinders are fitted with steam jackets; there are two main circulating pumps for the condensers, of the usual centrifugal type,

FIG. 21.—ENGINES OF THE " ARCHER " CLASS.

one pump being sufficient for each engine when the
machinery is being worked at moderate speed.

The engine-rooms are divided by a transverse water-
tight bulkhead, having a water-tight door for communication between the two engine-rooms. The engines themselves are placed horizontally, each engine, with its condenser, occupying almost the entire breadth of the ship, the
propeller shafting of the forward, or port, engines—that is,
those which drive the port propeller—passing through the
after, or starboard, engine-room, between the condenser
and the backs of the two cylinders. This arrangement,
which is the only one possible in ships of this power and
class, having horizontal engines, renders the space for
moving about, or overhauling the machinery, extremely
limited. There are two stokeholds, with a water-tight
transverse bulkhead separating them, communication being
obtained by a water-tight door. Each stokehold has two
boilers, all of the same size and pattern. There is one
funnel common to all four boilers. The safety-valves are
loaded to 135 lb. per square inch. In each boiler-room
there are two forced-draught fan engines, one main and
one auxiliary feed-pump, and in addition there are in the
forward stokehold two sets of distillers, which have one
fresh-water pump for delivering the distilled water to the
fore-holds, or wherever it may be wanted. The other
auxiliary engines are, one capstan engine, one steering
engine, two sets of air-compressing machinery, two
dynamos, and two ash-hoist engines.

The vessels of the above class are the last of the protective deck type of cruisers which were fitted with horizontal
engines. As it is of supreme importance to place the
engines and boilers of a cruiser under protection, it becomes
somewhat difficult in a small vessel of 1,600 or 1,700 tons
to fit engines of 3,000 or 4,000 indicated horse-power in

the limited space available below the protective deck, and
so recourse was had to horizontal engines in the ships we
have been discussing.

In all the succeeding cruisers the horizontal type of
engine has been abandoned, even at the cost of fitting
sloping armoured coamings round the tops of the cylinders
above the protective deck. The advantages of increased
accessibility, more space in the engine-room, and better
ventilation in the later types, are sufficiently manifest.

The next type of second-class cruisers was ordered
under the provisions of the Naval Defence Act, and the
Naiad may be taken as a fair sample of the lot. She
was built and engined by the Naval Construction and
Armaments Company at Barrow-in-Furness. It goes without saying that her engines are vertical and triple-expansion. Each cylinder is separately carried on a tripod,
formed of a cast-steel back column, which also acts as
a guide, and two turned-steel columns in front. These
latter are braced and tied by diagonal stays, and the
cylinder tops are further stayed by two fore-and-aft steel
stays. Any tendency to vibration, even at high speeds,
is thus counteracted. The cylinders are 32½, 49, and
74 inches in diameter, and are jacketed and drained in the
ordinary way. There are no receivers proper, but the
eduction pipes from each cylinder act as such. All the
pistons are of cast steel, and are of the dished form.
Piston valves are fitted to the high-pressure and intermediate cylinders, and ordinary slide-valves to the low
pressure cylinders. In the south the more usual practice
is to employ piston valves only for the high-pressure
cylinders. All the valves are balanced. There are no tail-
rods. The valves are worked by ordinary link motion, and
the reversing is done by means of simple gear of the all-
round type of special design, whereby all jarring motion is

I

taken from the reversing levers. The main condensers, electric light, air compression, and steering machinery are abaft the engines, and the arrangement of the machinery is such that there is ample room, and access to it is easy.

There are five boilers, placed in two separate stokeholds; of these boilers two are single-ended and three are double-ended. There are twenty-four furnaces, each with a separate combustion chamber. The total heating surface is 15,880 square feet, and the total grate area is 580 square feet; this gives about 16 horse-power for each square foot of grate—a very fair allowance. Under each furnace is a water ash-pan. In each boiler-room are two feed pumps, and in each stokehold are two fans which supply air to the furnaces. Each of the two sets of boilers can supply steam to each of the two sets of engines; thus, when cruising, one set of boilers can be shut off for cleaning or repairs. To render this possible of course a good deal of extra steam piping has had to be fitted. All the steam-pipes are of copper, and those of large size have been served—*i.e.*, carefully wrapped round—with copper wire. On this subject the Engineer-in-Chief of the Navy said, in a recent paper: " On account of the occasionally uncertain behaviour of the copper composing our copper steam-pipes, it has been found advisable in pipes over 8 inches to wind them with $\frac{3}{16}$-inch copper wire, stretched while winding to a uniform tension of 3,600 lb. per square inch, the ends of the wire being secured to the flanges. Only straight lengths of copper pipe are used, elbows and ends entering stuffing-boxes being made of gun metal or cast steel, and in certain cases large steam-pipes have been made of forged steel."

For forced draught purposes there are in each of the *Naiad's* stokeholds two fans, driven by Brotherhood's engines, equal to maintaining a pressure equivalent to

3 inches of water—a pressure that will never be employed. The total weight of the machinery, including the water in boilers and condensers, is about 650 tons, giving about 165 lb. per indicated horse-power. This looks very light if the ship were always going to steam at full speed like an Atlantic liner, but as she will under ordinary cruising conditions rarely develop more than 1,500 horse-power, which gives a weight of machinery equal to 1,000 lb. per unit of horse-power, the engines must be considered, for these latter days, of fairly sufficient solidity.

The *Naiad*, like all her sisters, carries 400 tons of coal, supposed to give her a radius of action of 4,000 knots, at 10-knot speed. The coal-bunkers are arranged so as to afford the greatest possible protection to the machinery, which implies a cellular arrangement, requiring much manual labour to get the coal from the boxes to the fires. This is a detail that has not received anything like the attention it deserves. In too many ships of recent design the gentlemen whose business it was to get out plans for a cruiser, one of whose qualities was to be large coal-carrying capacity, have so managed matters that a great portion of this coal is stowed away in inaccessible "pockets," whence it can only be extracted by requisitioning the services of seamen as well as stokers—which should always be avoided unless absolutely necessary.

The Liverpool "Journal of Commerce," to which I am indebted for many of the above particulars, says that the electric installation is very complete, and is entirely depended on for artificial light, and goes on to remark, "There are, in addition to the usual fixed and portable lamps, three search-lights, which is usual in all warships, just where they can be manipulated with the greatest risk to the operator, and where they would form a convenient and eligible target to the enemy."

The *Naiad* ran her natural draught eight hours' trial at Spithead on October 1st, 1891. She indicated 7,521 horse-power, with a speed of 18·6 knots. As she had been in the water for twelve months before without docking, this result was eminently satisfactory. From her trials, more-over, a very useful "wrinkle" was gained. For a long time great trouble had been experienced with the steel gudgeon-pins of fast-moving engines; they simply pul-verised the brass of the bearings in which they worked. The *Naiad* had two of her pins made of iron, case-hardened, as an experiment, and the result was so satisfactory that the steel pins of the *Pallas*, a third-class cruiser, which had given an infinity of trouble, were removed, and iron ones substituted. After a hard run these were found to be in splendid condition, and the ship left for China at last, having been long delayed on account of her gudgeons.

Some months before the trials of the *Naiad*, the *Latona*, a sister ship built and engined by the same firm, was despatched to Malta and back on an experimental cruise. The results were respectable, but not splendid. On the outward voyage the passage to Gibraltar was accomplished at an average speed of 15 knots, while 17 knots was main-tained for twenty-four hours between Gibraltar and Malta. The return voyage was made under easier conditions of steaming at 12 knots speed. Under forced draught the *Latona* realized, on the measured mile at Stokes Bay, just over 20 knots, with 9,438 horse-power, and the boilers did not leak. This trip of the *Latona's* was considered by the Admiralty sufficiently typical and important for a special report of the proceedings to be issued to the public. Had the Admiralty known then as much as they do now, it is probable that very little fuss would have been made about such a mediocre performance. Had the *Latona* been put into commission it is more than likely that she would in a

year or so's time have averaged 17 instead of 15 knots from
England to Gibraltar, thus showing how much depends
on officers and stokers getting used to their machinery.

There are two other second-class cruisers, the machinery
of which may well get a word of description, the *Andromache* and the *Apollo*.   Their engines differ but slightly
from those of similar ships by other makers, but they have
original points.   They were designed and manufactured by
Earle's Shipbuilding and Engineering Company, Hull.
Steel is extensively used in their construction, the main
framing, back columns, cylinder and valve-chest covers, and
piston-rod crossheads being cast, and the piston and connecting rods, working barrels of the cylinders, shafting,
bracing-rods, etc., are of wrought steel.   On their front
side the cylinders are carried on round columns, turned up
bright and well tied together to prevent vibration, and
at the back by two columns to each, of special shape,
arranged so as to carry the cast-iron guides and to give the
greatest available base, thus ensuring stiffness to the structure.   The whole of the columns are well braced together
fore and aft, as well as athwartships.   The cylinders are all
independent of one another, but connected by copper steam-
pipes and stayed together with steel rods.   The condensers
are cylindrical, of cast naval brass, placed at the after end of
the engines, and connected to the low-pressure engines
by copper exhaust pipes.   The air pumps are bolted to the
engine framing and the foundations, and are worked
by levers off the low-pressure piston-rod crosshead.

The following are the leading dimensions of the engines :
High-pressure cylinders, $33\frac{1}{2}$ inches ; intermediate-pressure
cylinders, 49 inches ; low-pressure cylinders, 74 inches ;
stroke, 39 inches ; air pump, diameter, 30 inches ; air
pump, stroke, 13 inches ; connecting-rod centres, 6 feet
6 inches ; piston rods, diameter, $7\frac{1}{4}$ inches : crank-shafts,

diameter, external, 12¾ inches; crank shafts, diameter, internal, 6¾ inches; cooling surface, two condensers, 10,000 square feet. Water is circulated through the main condensers by a centrifugal pump to each, having 42-inch discs.

It is pretty certain that these second-class cruisers, of which at the moment of writing we have thirteen in commission and at least twenty-one in reserve, ready for sea, are among the handiest and most useful vessels we possess. The *Rainbow*, built and engined by Palmer's Company, Jarrow-on-Tyne, on her eight hours' natural draught trial, with 7,780 horse-power, attained a speed of 19·45 knots; with forced draught for four hours, her 9,681 horse-power gave her a speed of 20·20 knots. The *Intrepid*, at full power, with 9,471 horse-power, managed to do 19·80 knots. The *Brilliant*, with natural draught, developing 7,512 horse-power, ran for eight hours at a mean rate of 19·20 knots. In fact, the greater number of this class of ship, with natural draught, which alone is likely to be used on service, are good for 19 knots, and with forced draught can manage 20 knots.

Now it is a question well worthy of discussion and consideration by the general public, who have to bear the whole of the expense of the additional fittings for forced draught, whether a knot an hour for a very few hours is worth the money and the risk involved by the use of this system. It is quite certain that it would only be for a very few hours, for no tubes will stand forced draught for more, whereas with natural draught most of the modern engines will go at nearly full power as long as the coal holds out. Then, too, the extra horse-power to get the extra knot, and consequently the extra consumption of coal,—is something enormous. In the *Rainbow*, for instance, it took 1,901 horse-power to increase the speed by three-quarters of a knot. Surely this is a big price to pay for a very little

FIG. 22.—ENGINES OF THE "ANDROMACHE."

good. Apparently, the Admiralty think so too, for in the trials of the new battleships they have forbidden the use of anything but natural draught, giving a horse-power of 9,000 instead of 13,000. Of course there will always be people who will be in favour of providing the ship with means whereby, in case of extremity, she can obtain an extra knot of speed, but the extreme cases are likely to be so few and far between that they need not be reckoned, knowing as we do that the use of forced draught will inevitably cripple the boilers of any large vessel.

No other nation has anything like such a grand fleet of 19-knot cruisers, sufficiently heavily armed, and growing more powerful as each new individual is added to it, always an improvement on its immediate predecessors. As was said only the other day, in ships we are probably quite equal, with those we are building, to the combined fleets of our two most powerful enemies, but if it came to war we should be hard pushed to find crews to man our ships, more particularly in the engine-room departments.

Probably all of our successful second-class cruisers, such as the *Sirius*, *Andromache*, and others referred to above, are the lineal descendants of five, called the "M" or *Medea* class, all of which were launched in 1888, and though two of them, the *Magicienne* and the *Marathon*, are still in commission, they were undoubted failures as far as their machinery went. The "Broad Arrow" of that date said : "The second-class cruiser *Medusa*, 2,800 tons and 9,000 horse-power, went out for her forced draught trial in the Solent on Wednesday. The five vessels of this class which were designed by Mr. W. H. White as 19·75 and 20-knot cruisers, have now all been tried, with the result that they average about 19 knots on the measured mile with forced draught. The *Magicienne* and *Marathon* get very little more speed with forced than with natural draught. The ships are

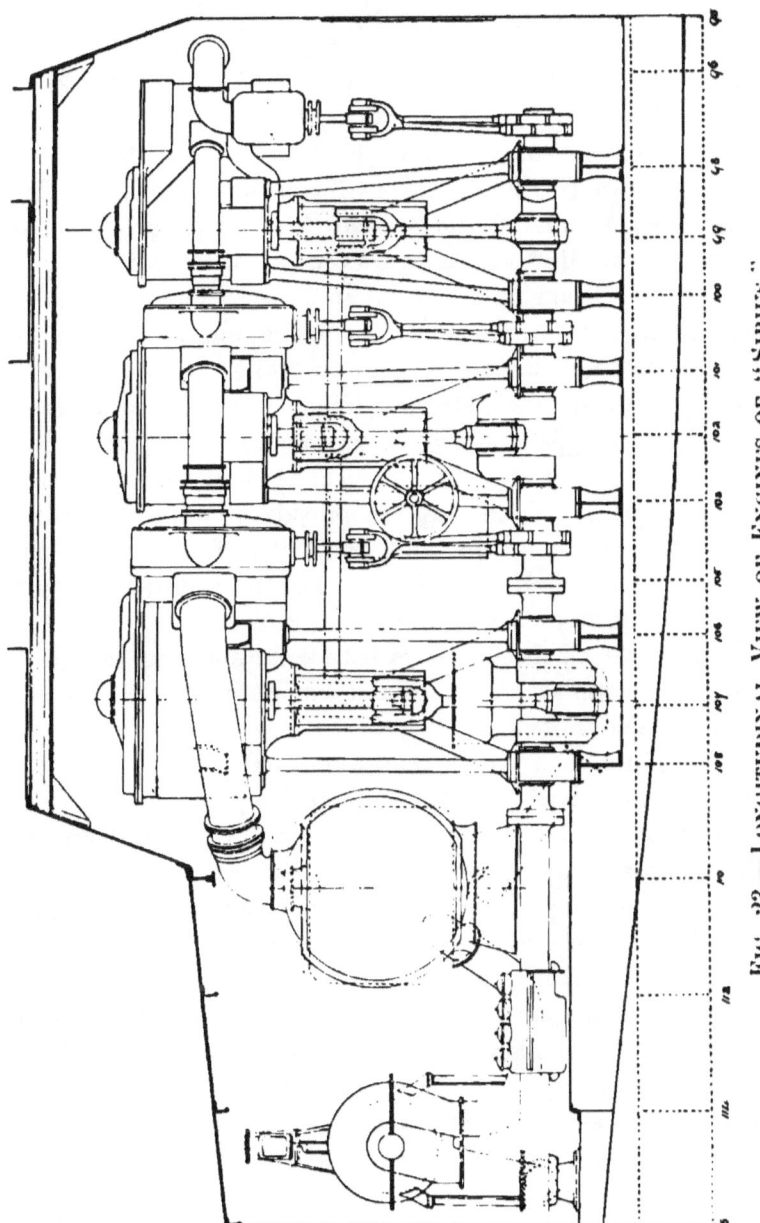

FIG. 23.—LONGITUDINAL VIEW OF ENGINES OF "SIRIUS."

too cramped, as most naval men foretold when their keels
were laid, and the improved *Medeas* are to be 300 feet by
43 feet instead of 265 feet by 41 feet, which are the
dimensions of the five vessels of the *Medea* class." The
general dimensions of the second-class cruisers that have
succeeded the *Medea* class are as stated here, but a few of
them have a beam of 43 feet 8 inches. "The latter ships
have boilers too small for their large engines, and the
stokers have not sufficient room to stoke; consequently it
is difficult to maintain steam. Their freeboard is too low,
and they are particularly low-waisted, while the gun
sponsons are very low, and the electric light sponsons seem
to be designed with the express purpose of throwing water
up on the after bridge and poop; the fore part of the
Medusa's electric light sponsons has been filled in with
wood to counteract this defect to a certain extent. . . .
The result of all these defects is that the ships are very wet,
and their ocean speed would not be more than 16 knots,"
and very seldom that.

Mr. White, in a paper read about this time before the
Institute of Naval Architects, dealt fully and successfully
with many of the criticisms that had been passed on the
Medea class, but—he never built any more. Lord Brassey
said that, having heard Mr. White, than whom he considered the country had had no abler or more faithful
public servant, he remained of opinion that in the ships
under consideration too much had been attempted within
the limits of tonnage. To secure the steaming qualities
and the fighting power required in the *Medea* class, the
constructors should have been allowed to go to a displacement not inferior to the 3,730 tons of the *Iris* and *Mercury*.
With an addition of 50 feet to the length, the same speed
would probably have been attained in smooth water. In a
seaway the falling off would have been much less.

It is when driving at a head sea that the inferiority of the short ship is most conspicuous. It would be a great advantage incidental to an increase of length that a considerably increased space would be gained for engines and boilers and for the convenient stowage of coal. The engine-rooms of the *Medea* class are crammed with machinery to a degree which must be detrimental to efficiency. When working at high speed the physical

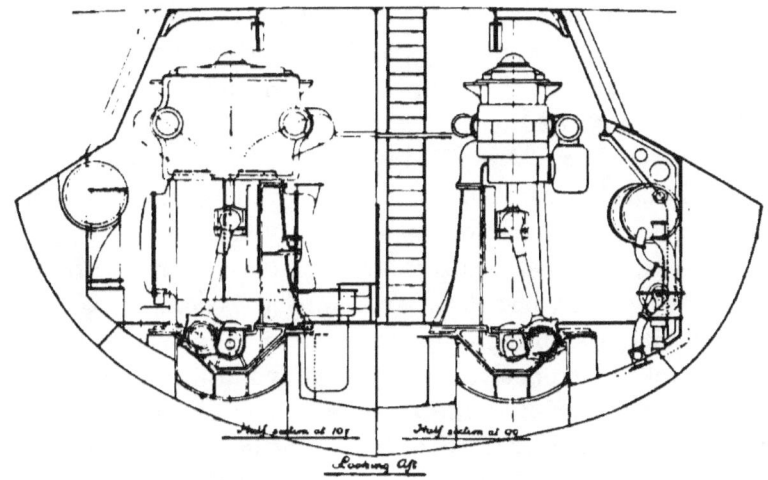

FIG. 24.—SECTIONS OF "SIRIUS."

sufferings of the engine-room complement are such that they could not be endured in a continuous run. The trouble experienced in taking coal from the bunkers to the furnaces in the *Medea* class has brought the engineers into conflict with the constructors, the latter insisting on the necessity of having an almost unpierced protected deck, covering engines, boilers, bunkers, and magazines, and a series of water-tight bulkheads minutely subdividing the ship into water-tight compartments. The engineers contend that in practice it is impossible either to feed the fires with sufficient rapidity to enable the ship to maintain her proper speed, or even to work her with due regard to safety, when all the water-tight doors are closed.

Lord Brassey was undoubtedly a true prophet when he said the *Medeas* were much too small, and foretold the great alteration for good that would ensue from an addition of 50 feet to their length, 450 tons to their displacement, and 1,500 to their natural draught horse-power, while several of the latest second-class cruisers now building are of 5,600 tons, 350 feet long, and 8,000 horse-power natural draught, reaching these dimensions through the *Fox* class, of 4,360 tons, 320 feet long, and 7,000 horse-power. The only excuse for calling ships of 5,600 tons' displacement second-class cruisers is that what we are now building for the first-class are so considerably larger.

The second-class cruisers are no doubt very swift and powerful vessels, but there are many occasions for service, particularly on foreign stations, when they would be too large and too expensive, and, without counting a number of obsolete craft, such as the *Pylades*, which are only fit to be broken up, it has been thought wise of late years to increase our fleet of third-class cruisers to about thirty, of which we have some twenty in commission, the places of most of the others being occupied by useless old tubs. It always has been so, and, I suppose, it always will be, that while we have beautiful new fast ships rusting away in the basins of our dockyards, we yet for commission after commission abroad keep ships running, such as the *Caroline*, *Rapid*, *Satellite*, and others that could not possibly fight or run away.

But, to return for a moment to the *Archer* class, Lord Brassey says, in his "Annual" for 1890, that these vessels were strongly recommended to Lord Northbrook by the late Sir Cooper Key and his naval colleagues. It was

desired to secure a speed and coal endurance far exceeding
what had previously been attained in vessels of similar
dimensions, combined with an armament of sufficient power
to deal with any raiders on commerce likely to be met with
on distant foreign stations. The *Archers* were intended,
when acting independently, to give protection to commerce.
They were to be the scouts or look-out vessels of a fleet.
In battle, as sea-going torpedo vessels, it was believed that
they might be effective auxiliaries to the heavy ships.   It
cannot be said that the result has been a failure.

Recently the *Brisk* steamed the 1,200 miles from St.
Paul's to St. Helena in four days and one hour.   During
the trip she did her four hours' full-speed trial, covering a
distance of sixty miles in a rather heavy sea and with a full
stock of coal, water, and provisions on board.   At a
cruising speed of 10 knots the coal endurance of the *Archer*
class is 7,000 knots.   In proportion to their tonnage they
are powerfully armed.   It has recently been stated that in
going to the Cape from St. Helena the speed of the *Brisk*
when meeting a strong wind and sea was reduced to five
knots, as the vessel was being buried under water forward,
the forecastle bending down three or four inches under the
weight of superincumbent water.   On another occasion the
Brisk was steaming before a strong wind, and was taking
in so much water on the poop that she had to be turned
round, and steamed against the wind and sea for thirty
hours until the weather moderated.   In any case, no more
Archers have been built.

The next third-class cruisers were five built for the protection of floating trade in Australasian waters.   These
were larger considerably than the *Archers*, being of 2,575
tons against 1,170 tons, and 7,500 horse-power against
3,500.   They were intended to have a maximum measured
mile speed of 19 knots, but they never approached it in

Australia. The propelling machinery consisted of twin-screw triple-expansion vertical engines. The diameter of the high-pressure cylinders is 30½ inches, of the intermediate 45 inches, and of the low-pressure 68 inches, the length of stroke being 33 inches. The engines run at a very high speed, and are very compactly arranged with the view of economizing the room, which is limited, owing to the protective deck. Steam of 150 lb. to the square inch is supplied from four double-ended boilers, each 11 feet 6 inches in diameter and 17 feet long, having in all sixteen furnaces, with a grate surface of 375 square feet, and a heating surface of 9,400 square feet. These ships were a decided step in advance, but they were spoiled by the fatal fault of trying to get too much power out of too little space, which inevitably led to a pestilent lightness of machinery.

The *Pearl*, *Philomel*, *Phœbe*, and *Pallas*, were almost identical with the *Mildura* and her Australian sisters, except that provision was made for 500 more horse-power at natural draught, which was the beginning of a much greater equalization between natural and forced draught. The *Pallas*, which was floated out of dock at Portsmouth on June 30th, 1890, the first of the ships building in the dockyards under the Naval Defence Act, had 4,500 horse-power under natural draught, and 7,500 under forced draught. The *Diana*, *Dido*, and *Doris*, now building, are to have 8,000 horse-power natural draught, and 9,600 forced draught. This is, of course, because it is gradually coming to be believed that forced draught will never be used on active service. The total cost of each of these ships was about £148,000.

About 1890, two third-class cruisers, the *Barham* and *Bellona*, were introduced into the Navy, which were the *ne plus ultra* of the attempt to get enormous power and

speed out of insufficient material. These vessels were 280
feet long, 35 feet beam, tonnage 1,830, fitted with two
torpedo tubes, and, on each broadside six 4·7-inch guns and
a number of machine guns. They were fitted with twin-
screw triple-expansion vertical engines, the cylinders standing on wrought-steel columns, diagonally braced and tied.
The crank-shaft of hollow steel by Beardmore of Glasgow,
the bed plate of cast steel, the slide valves for the high-
pressure cylinders of the piston type, for the intermediate
and low-pressure of the ordinary flat double-ported variety,
the slide valves being in addition fitted with a balance
cylinder to take the weight of the slide gear. The engines
were fitted with steam starting or reversing gear, of the all
round or continuous working description, in addition to the
usual hand-starting and reversing gear. The intermediate
and low-pressure cylinders were fitted with steam jackets.
The propellers were three-bladed and made of manganese
bronze. The engines were originally designed to develop
6,000 horse-power, which was estimated to drive the ships
at 19·75 knots per hour. The condensers are of the ordinary surface condensing type, with sea water circulating
inside the tubes, and are so arranged that they can be used
either as main condensers, or, when the main engines are
not being used, as auxiliary condensers for the steam exhausting from such auxiliary engines as may be working ;
large gridiron valves being fitted in the eduction pipes
between the low-pressure cylinders and the condensers, for
the purpose of shutting off communication between the condensers and cylinders when the former were being used for
auxiliary purposes. The air pumps are worked by rocking
levers attached to the crosshead of the intermediate cylinders,
these rocking levers being supported by long sleeve bearings
on the weigh shafts of the starting gear, which runs fore
and aft the whole length of the engines. In addition to the

main engines, which are contained in two separate engine-rooms, divided by a longitudinal water-tight bulkhead, there are about seventeen auxiliary engines, all comprised in the main engine-rooms, leaving only the feed pumps and capstan engine outside.

There are two separate boiler-rooms, each containing a set of three boilers and one main and one auxiliary feed engine. The boilers were expected when designed to produce sufficient steam for 6,000 horse-power in the engines with 3 inches of water pressure in the stokeholds, but, owing to difficulties with leaky tubes in both ships, as in most if not all of the vessels fitted with a similar type of boiler, it was decided to reduce the maximum horse-power to its present amount of 4,700, at which neither ship is ever run, as that involves forced draught. Both vessels are now fairly efficient cruisers; the *Barham* is attached to the Mediterranean Squadron, and the *Bellona* replaced the *Curlew* with the Channel Fleet, both as dispatch vessels. From being utterly untrustworthy ships with a possible speed of 19 knots, they may now be depended on for ordinary service at about 16 knots, a speed not to be despised even now. The boiler-rooms are arranged one forward of, and one abaft the engine-rooms, which gives the ships rather a peculiar appearance, as the two funnels are necessarily nearer the bow and stern than is usual, the forward funnel being between the fore and main-mast, and the after funnel between the main and mizen-mast. The *Barham* and *Bellona* were the only two ships of the type built, at a time when the irrational craze for light machinery and boilers had reached its height. Messrs. Hawthorne, Leslie and Co. built and engined the *Bellona*, and the same firm put the engines into the *Barham*, which was built at Portsmouth Dockyard. The *Barham* was launched in 1889, the *Bellona* in the following year.

Both ships were first commissioned for service during the naval manœuvres of 1891. The correspondent of the "Globe," who was afloat with the "Western" Fleet, says, that on Tuesday, July 28th, the *Forth* was the first to discover the approach of the enemy's scouts, *Narcissus* and *Barham*, which had steamed up from Ushant at full speed. Their approach was, of course, at once signalled to the other ships of the British fleet, and the *Forth* speedily got into action with the *Narcissus*, and afterwards with the *Barham*. By-and-by the *Bellona* was ordered to join the *Barham* in giving chase, but she had the disadvantage of being a long way out of position at the start. The *Barham* was steaming at least 17·5 knots, and the other ships from 15·5 knots downwards. Probably the *Bellona* was doing as well as the *Barham*, but as she had five miles to pick up, it would have been a question between the two ships of efficiency in stoking and coal endurance, had the chase been persisted in.

Late news from the Mediterranean, where the *Barham* has now been in commission for over two years, conveys the information that she does a great deal of running about with mails and the like, and generally does her work very creditably. At first she could not steam a bit, for the ferrules would choke after two or three hours, but now experience has been gained as to clearing the ferrules the ship does 18 knots easily for four hours, and 15·2 knots, or even 16·5 with a clean bottom, for thirty hours. This is no doubt respectable going, but is not what was expected from the *Barham*, which was designed for 19 knots. Anyhow, forty modern *Barhams*, to replace that number of "duffers," would be a great acquisition to the fleet.

Before leaving the subject of third-class cruisers, I may be permitted to call attention to a ship which, in time of need, would undoubtedly come under that description, though her name is not to be found in the "Navy List."

K

At the end of last year Mr. M'Calmont's twin-screw steam yacht *Giralda* was completed. Never was such a yacht of the power and capacity of the *Giralda* dreamed of before, and only to a man of boundless wealth would her creation have been possible. Her chief characteristic is that she combines all the features of a first-class pleasure yacht with the speed of the fastest ocean-going steamers within the compass of 1,500 tons, which is, however, only about 200 tons less than the cruisers of the *Archer* class, and she has a coal-carrying capacity enabling her to make a voyage of over 3,500 miles at a speed of 15 knots, or of nearly 6,000 miles at a speed of 12 knots. Upon the measured mile on the Clyde she obtained a speed of 20·9 knots, and she practically steamed at the same rate for a lengthened run in the Solent.

The ship was designed and constructed by the Fairfield Company, of Govan, and with their experience of Atlantic liners and first-class cruisers they have satisfactorily proved that high speed and abundant accommodation can be secured in vessels of small tonnage. The "Times" says, and it is from that paper that most of my information about the *Giralda* is gleaned, that it has been hitherto held that the capacity of an ocean-going steamer was necessary to provide engine-power for a speed of over 20 knots, if in addition to the boilers and coal bunkers there should be provided the ordinary complement of state rooms. It has never before been realized that in anything but a torpedo-catcher, where the personal accommodation is reduced to a few holes and corners, and where practically the entire hull has been given up to boilers and coal-bunkers, a vessel of comparatively small tonnage could carry a pleasure party at the rate of 24 land miles per hour with the *maximum* of comfort and without the slightest vibration.

The trials of the *Giralda* have provided some interesting

data on the question of vibration. At a speed of 17 knots the vibration is excessive, but above and below that speed the vibration disappears. This curious fact illustrates, with something like precision, the accepted theory that when the revolutions or vibrations of the engines synchronise with the natural vibrations of the vessel, the agitation throughout the hull must necessarily be exceptional; but as soon as the speed passes this synchronising point the vibrations of the screw and of the vessel neutralize each other, and repose is the result.

The *Giralda* is 275 feet long, 35 feet beam, and 19 feet in depth. Mr. M'Calmont holds a master's certificate, and navigates the boat himself. The engines are of special interest in view of the speed attained. They develop 8,000 horse-power from five boilers of the ordinary cylindrical type, three of which are double-ended and two single-ended. Fans furnish additional draught when a high speed is required, but there is no forced draught in the true sense of the term. The engines have each four cylinders, a high-pressure of 25 inches in diameter, an intermediate of 40 inches, and two low-pressure cylinders of 48 inches each. The four cranks are set at the four quarters of the circle, and by this arrangement an unusually smooth motion is secured. The smallness in diameter of the low-pressure cylinders causes them to occupy a comparatively small space, and brings the screw-shafts and the two triple-bladed propellers well within the body of the hull. At full speed the revolutions of the engines reach 220 per minute, and the boilers are worked at 175 lb. on the square inch.

The parallel between an ocean-going steamer and the *Giralda* is maintained by the provision of water-tight compartments cutting off the engines from the boilers, and dividing one set of boilers from another. Some of the water-tight compartments are wholly separate, and the others are provided with doors that can be closed from the main deck. The coal-bunkers completely surround the boiler-rooms, and the side bunkers are carried inwards over the top of the boilers to the height of the upper deck. Two Gardner guns and four Hotchkiss guns, with two electric search-lights of Admiralty pattern, assist the conception of an amateur cruiser ; and her crew of sixty Naval Reserve men, procured from the Orient service, encourage the idea that, although a private yacht, the *Giralda* may be regarded as at any time available as an Admiralty despatch boat.

CHAPTER VII.

As ships grew to be larger and larger, and their propelling engines became more powerful, so, as a matter of course, did the number of the small engines used for various purposes on board increase. I can well remember the time when a small "donkey" for supplying extra feed water to the boilers, or by pumping in cold water after coming to an anchor to prevent or mitigate the nuisance of steam blowing off, was the only bit of auxiliary machinery in the ship. But things have altered remarkably since then. In the *Vulcan*, for instance, there are no fewer than 98 separate engines with 194 cylinders, and 30 torpedoes with 90 cylinders, making a total of 128 engines with 284 cylinders. It may be as well to set down here the duties of these numerous engines, observing that I doubt if a first-class battleship or cruiser carries quite so many engines as the *Vulcan*. Here is the list :

Main engines, 2 ; reversing, 2 ; circulating, main, 4 ; circulating, auxiliary, 2 ; turning, 2 ; fresh water, 2 ; fire-engines, 4 ; distilling, 2 ; hydraulic, 2 ; ventilating fans, 4 ; dynamos, 3 ; dynamo, portable, 1 ; dynamo, auxiliary feed, 1 ; air compressing, 4 ; steering, 1 ; main feed, 4 ; auxiliary feed, 1 ; evaporator pumps, 2 ; workshop, 1 ; capstan, 1 ; ash hoists, 4 ; forced draught. 8. Torpedo boats :—main engines, 6 ; circulating engines, 6 ; fan engines, 6; auxiliary feed, 6. Other steam-boats:—main engines, 4; auxiliary feed, 3; fan engines, 2; circulating engines, 1; hydraulic bollards, 4; crane hoists, 3: Total, 98.

Now all these engines are in so many cases so absolutely necessary that to lump them all together as "auxiliary" seems almost a misnomer. In the following pages it will be endeavoured to mention these auxiliary engines in the order of their necessity, or, I might better write, indispensability.

To take the case of the common jet condensers, with which the engines of the earlier steamships were universally fitted, we find that no special machines for circulating the cooling water in the condensers were required. The sea-water which was used was admitted into the same chamber as the exhaust steam by a pipe which led directly from the sea to the interior of the condenser, and the portion of the pipe which was inside the condenser was perforated so as to allow the sea-water to flow through the perforations in a series of small streams or jets, hence the term "jet" condenser. The amount of water which came through these jets was regulated by a valve, which could be worked from the engine-room platform. There was no circulation of sea-water required in these old-time condensers. The sea-water and condensed steam became mixed together, and were pumped overboard by the air-pump, with the exception of a small portion which was required for feeding the boilers, and was abstracted by the main feed pump and delivered into the boilers.

With the introduction of the surface condenser, in which the exhaust steam, after it has become condensed into fresh water, is kept separate from the cooling sea-water, it became necessary to fit a special pump for forcing or circulating the sea-water through, or as was sometimes the case, round the cooling tubes of the condenser, and the amount of cooling water which is circulated through the tubes in a given time regulates, in a great measure, the efficiency of the condenser. Thus, the pump used for circulating cold water through the condensers became known as the " circulating pump."

The type now universally fitted for this purpose is the centrifugal pump, the impeller, or turbine, of which is driven by a small steam-engine, to the crank-shaft of which the impeller is attached. As the impeller is caused to revolve at a very high rate of speed, it consequently gives a very rapid circulating motion to the water it is acting on, and so sets a considerable amount in motion through the condenser.

This property of the centrifugal pump is also made use of to clear the ship of large quantities of intrusive water which may have found its way inboard through a leak or some other accident. Suitable suction and discharge pipes being fitted to the pump, in addition to those required for the condensing water, many hundreds of tons per hour may be, and often have been, dealt with by the centrifugal pumps.

All modern engines are now fitted with surface condensers, and so the centrifugal circulating pump has become an indispensable adjunct to the main engines, and cannot, perhaps, be correctly termed an "auxiliary."

For the same reason, in the modern engine the main feed pumps, which are used for maintaining a proper supply of water to the boilers, without which they would inevitably explode or be seriously injured, can hardly be classed as distinct auxiliary engines, seeing that they are as necessary a part of the equipment of a modern ship as the main engines are.

It has been stated above, that in a surface-condensing engine the exhaust steam from the engines is cooled and condensed with sea-water from which it is kept separate.

This condensed exhaust steam is practically fresh or distilled water, and is therefore most useful as feed water for the boilers. It is delivered from the condensers by the air pump into a separate tank, called the feed tank, and is pumped thence into the boilers by the main feed pumps, which are now fitted separately, as independent engines from the main engines.

There are several types of feed pumps in the Royal Navy, all being either "lift" or "force" pumps, but a detailed description would be too technical and tedious for the general reader.

In the older types of marine engines, in which it was customary to attach the main feed pumps to some convenient part of the main engines, it was also found necessary to fit an additional feed pump, mentioned above as the "donkey," for supplying water to the boilers in the case of accident to the main feeds, or when the engines were not working and the fires were "banked," or being used for distilling purposes. Before the introduction of surface condensers, the boilers were fed with the mixture of salt water and condensed steam from the condensers during such time as the main engines and feed pumps were working, but under other conditions the "donkey" obtained its supply of feed water directly from the sea.

In modern boilers salt water is never used, if it can possibly be avoided, and special distilling appliances, to be hereafter described, are fitted for obtaining an ample supply of fresh water for all ordinary emergencies.

It is the custom now in vessels fitted with modern machinery to supply them, in addition, with large freshwater tanks for the use of the boilers. These tanks carry the reserve feed water for the boilers. The duties of the main and auxiliary feed pumps are now made nearly interchangeable; that is, they are so arranged that each pump

will pump water into the boilers from any part desired,
either from the main condensers, the main feed tanks,
or the reserve feed tanks.   The exceptions being that each
pump has a separate and independent delivery into the
boilers, and that the auxiliary feed pump can draw water
from the sea in the event of all other sources of supply
failing.   By the system of interchangeability just described
it is almost impossible that a warship's machinery could be
disabled altogether by the failure of all her feed pumps at
one time ; and their pumping capacity is also so designed,
that one half the number of either the main or auxiliary
feed pumps is sufficient to supply all the boilers with water
in the event of the remainder of the feed pumps becoming
inoperative.

The auxiliary feed pumps may be reckoned as the most
important of the auxiliary engines, as it would be quite impossible to keep the boilers in use with fires alight unless
they were supplied with a sufficient quantity of water.

Next, perhaps, in importance to the feed pumps is
the distilling apparatus of the modern ship.   This is fitted
for providing a supply of pure water for drinking and
culinary purposes for the crew, and also for augmenting the
supply of feed water for the boiler, for it must be remembered that the escape of ever so little waste steam from the
safety valves means a proportionate diminution in the fresh
water available to feed the boilers and be again converted
into steam.   In theory, there should be no waste ; in practice, there always is.   In the earlier ships the distillers
were only required to furnish enough water for domestic
use, and the steam for them was taken direct from one of
the boilers, which had—or had not—been previously prepared for distilling purposes by the use of proper appliances
for getting rid of all traces of grease or oil in the boiler
water.   This steam was passed into a small distiller, where

it was condensed into fresh water. The distiller consisted
of a box of tubes opening into a chamber at either end,
steam from the boiler being admitted into one chamber and
passing through the tubes to the chamber at the opposite
end. The tubes were surrounded by cool sea-water, which
was kept entirely separate from the steam which was being
condensed inside the tubes. Of course, in case of a leak
the intended fresh water was more or less tainted with
salt.

As the steam traversed the tubes it lost its heat by
coming into contact with the cool surface of the tubes, and
so reached the bottom chamber in the form of fresh water.
From this chamber the water was either drained or forced
into tanks, whence it was conveyed by pumps, worked
either by hand or steam, into the fresh-water tanks situated
in the ship's hold, and there kept in readiness for use by the
crew.

In order to facilitate the process of distillation it became
necessary to accelerate the natural flow of the cooling sea-
water around the tubes of the distillers, by utilizing a
steam pump which had been fitted for some other purpose,
such as the bilge pump, or the fire-engine, as a circulating
pump for the distillers. This pump, in addition to its
ordinary functions, fulfilled the same purpose with regard
to the distillers as the main circulating or centrifugal
pumps already described did with the main condensers.

An improvement was very early made in the distillation
of sea-water for drinking and culinary purposes on board
ship by fitting a filter, usually of charcoal, for the more
effectual removal of any traces of oil or grease from
the steam from the boilers, and by providing also a special
circulating pump for the distilling apparatus, and cooling and aërating the distilled water, so as to make it
ready for immediate use when distilled.

The next step in the process was what was called the "double distillation" of sea-water, by which the steam from the boiler which was being used for distilling purposes was not itself converted into fresh drinking water, but was used for the purpose of heating and evaporating sea-water contained in a special chamber of the distilling apparatus, known as the "evaporating" chamber. The vapour or steam from the evaporating chamber is passed through a series of tubes or coils contained in another chamber, and there cooled and condensed into absolutely pure fresh water, which can be used for drinking, cooking, or any other purpose.

The steam used in the first instance from the boiler for heating and evaporating the water contained in the evaporating chamber becomes itself condensed, and is pumped back into the boiler as feed water by a special pump. The heating steam from the boiler is termed "primary" steam, and the steam generated by its heat in the evaporating chamber is called "secondary" steam.

Of late years, owing to the altered conditions under which marine boilers are worked, and also to the altered types of boilers now being fitted to warships, it has become almost imperative to feed them with nothing but perfectly pure fresh water. To meet this increased demand for fresh water, the system of double distillation just described has become more developed, and a separate and special vessel of large dimensions is now fitted, termed an "evaporator," which can be used in conjunction with the ordinary distilling apparatus for obtaining larger supplies of fresh water, to be used either for drinking purposes, or for accumulating a reserve feed supply for the boilers; or the evaporator can be used in direct conjunction with the main or auxiliary condensers of the ship, by passing the steam direct from the evaporated sea-water into either, and so converting it into extra or " make-up " feed water.

The evaporator is a cylindrical vessel or boiler containing a certain amount of sea-water to be evaporated. A series of tubes or coils is placed in the interior of the evaporator, and so arranged that steam can be passed through the coils, which steam in its passage evaporates the salt water by which the coils are surrounded, the steam formed from this salt water being used as already described above. The evaporator coils are so fitted that they can readily be removed and replaced. This admits of the large deposits of salt and other solid matter, with which they become incrusted during the process of evaporation, being easily and frequently removed. It is the custom in most ships to fit two evaporators at least, so that one can always be kept ready for use while the other is being cleaned or repaired. Suitable feed pumps are fitted for supplying the evaporators with sea-water, and, as before mentioned, proper arrangements are made for the circulation of sea-water around the tubes of the distiller, and for the disposal of the distilled water and make-up feed water from the evaporators. The system of double distillation and evaporation now fitted in all modern fighting ships provides an ample supply of fresh water for all purposes, whether for the crew or for the boilers.

The remaining auxiliary engines usually fitted in warships, although of great importance to the efficiency of the vessel, are not of so essential a character as are those with which I have just dealt. They may nearly all be described as labour-saving machines, for it is possible, in the case of most of the engines I am about to refer to, to perform their work by human muscle instead of steam.

I will deal first with those which are used principally in connection with the main propelling engines. The most

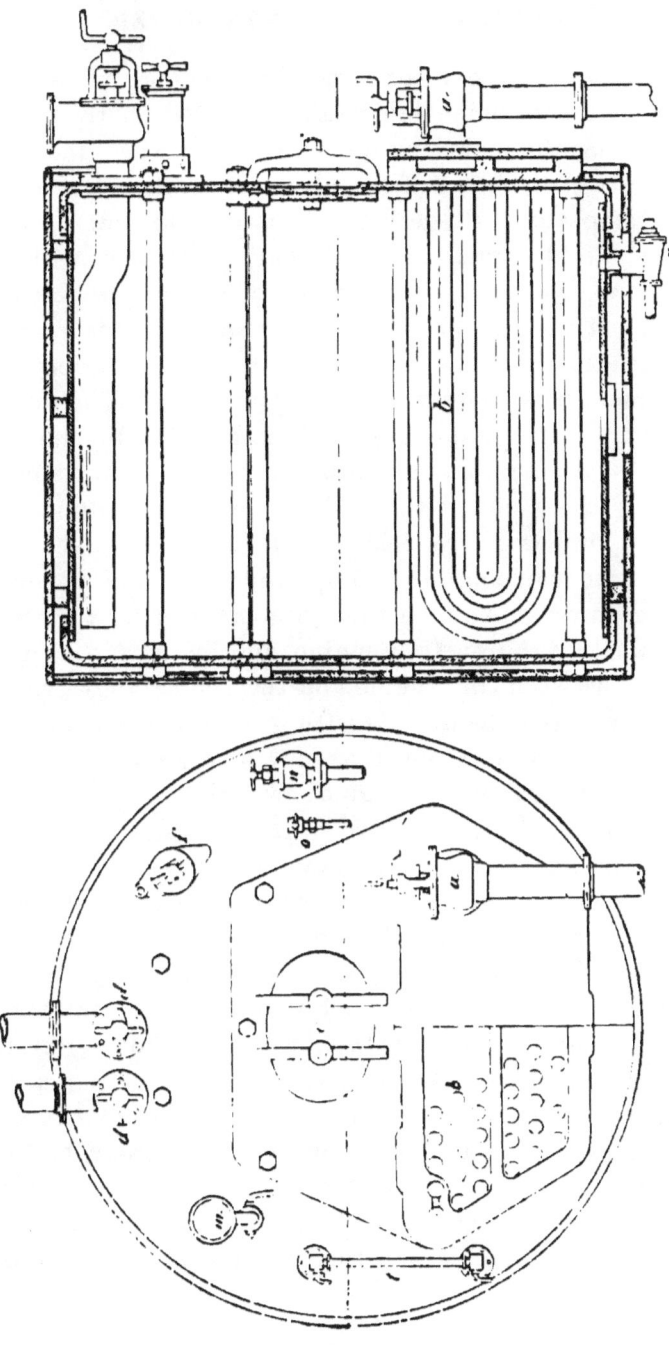

important of these is perhaps the starting, or reversing engine. As its name indicates, it is used for the purpose of assisting the main engines to start, or when under way to reverse their motion from ahead to astern, or *vice versâ*, or to stop them altogether. It is a small but powerful engine, fitted sometimes with one, sometimes with two cylinders, or else with steam and hydraulic cylinders combined. It can be worked at a high speed, and is generally attached to the front framing of the main engines, in a convenient position on the starting platform. The working part of the reversing engine is connected by means of suitable gearing to the weigh-shaft of the main engines, whereby the whole of the slide valves which admit steam to the cylinders are worked. Thus, the slide valves which actuate the main engines by regulating the admission of the motive power, steam, to the cylinders, can be themselves controlled by the starting engine, and, by means of proper gearing between this engine and the main slide valves, the main engines can be worked with great rapidity from ahead to astern, eased, or stopped as may be desired.

Starting or reversing engines are only fitted to the main engines when these latter are large, and when the ordinary hand-starting and reversing gear, which is always fitted in addition to the steam or hydraulic gear, is of necessity cumbrous and heavy, and where the task of moving it so as to readily start, reverse, or stop the main engines is too great to be performed so quickly as may be desirable. In small engines steam gear would be superfluous, for they can be handled with as much ease as the starting engines themselves. The object then of the steam starting and reversing engine is to save both time and labour, and as it is of the utmost importance that the main engines of a ship should admit of being worked with the least possible delay, it will be seen that the starting and reversing engine is an important auxiliary to the main engine. In all cases where it is fitted, it is so arranged that the hand and steam or hydraulic gear can be used in conjunction or independently.

Another useful auxiliary to the main propelling engines is the turning engine, which is used to move or turn the main engines when the ship is at anchor, or the engines are not being used. It is of great importance in such cases that the main engines should be periodically caused to revolve from one position to another. In the old days to move them by hand "a piston's depth" was considered sufficient, as it was on ordinary occasions, but I have seen, when repairs were being executed, a large number of stokers employed most of the day in using a worm and spindle to move the engines from one position to another by manual labour. To save time and muscle, it is now the custom with all large engines to fit a small steam engine for turning the main engines when they may be required to be moved for any necessary refit, or to keep their moving parts in proper order when not at work. The turning engine is so arranged that it will move the same worm and spindle as the hand-gear does, so that if steam is not up in any of the boilers—a most unlikely thing to happen, however—or the turning engine itself is disabled or being refitted, the main engines can be slowly moved by the hand-turning gear.

Yet another class of auxiliary engine which finds a place in the engine-rooms of our warships is the fire and bilge engine. It is used for pumping water from the sea to any part of the ship by means of a suitable arrangement of pipes and hoses, so that in the event of fire occurring at one or at several places in the ship at the same time, there shall always be a plentiful supply of water ready to hand for extinguishing purposes. The fire and bilge pump is also used for pumping the bilges clear of water, discharging the water overboard. It usually has a suction leading from each large compartment in the ship, and can also be employed for getting rid of the ordinary drainage from the engine and boiler compartments.

Another and most useful purpose to which the fire and bilge engine is put is to provide an ample supply of sea-water for washing the ship's decks, and this is obtained by the same arrangement of pipes and hoses that are intended for use in case of fire.

In the earlier steamships, before the introduction of surface condensers with their accompanying circulating or centrifugal pumps, the fire and bilge engine was a most important auxiliary to the ship's machinery. It was the sole steam pump capable of ejecting or discharging large bodies of water overboard in the event of leaks, or the like; but as it was found that the centrifugal pumps were capable of dealing with still larger quantities of water, it became no longer necessary to make the fire and bilge pump of such large dimensions and capacity.

The centrifugal pump having usurped one of the principal functions of the feed and bilge pump, the latter was reduced to smaller limits and power, and is now made generally of the same pattern as the main and auxiliary sea-pumps of the ship, with a view to interchangeability of parts and readier repair in the event of a breakdown occurring in either pump.

The pumps are generally fitted with two steam cylinders, and are direct double-acting, capable of discharging a considerable quantity of water. It is sometimes arranged in the larger battleships to have an engine or two, specially reserved for use in the case of fire, of the same type as the ordinary fire and bilge pumps, supplied for the combined purpose.

Formerly the cylinder drains from all engines were led

directly into the bilges, but it is now considered an advantage, when fresh water—which, of course, the condensed steam of the cylinders becomes—is so valuable, to fit a special tank for the purpose of collecting the drainage water from the various engines. A small engine or pump is also fitted in most modern ships for clearing the tanks, situated in the bilges, of the fresh water that has collected in them.

The ash-hoist engines are fitted on board ship for the purpose of hoisting the ashes, dirt, and furnace refuse from the boiler-rooms or stokeholds to the upper deck, where it is thrown overboard. These engines are placed at or near the upper deck of the vessel, in close proximity to the trunks through which the buckets containing the dirt and refuse are hoisted from the stokehold. The engine itself actuates a drum to which a long chain, having a hook at the lower end of it, is attached, and to which the buckets are hooked when it is desired to send them to the upper air and get rid of their contents. As the engine causes the drum to revolve, the chain to which the buckets are suspended becomes wound up, and the buckets of ashes are drawn from the stokehold platform to the upper deck. When they get there, they are unhooked by men stationed for the purpose—always bluejackets, not stokers—and are either carried by them to ash shoots in the vessel's side, and emptied overboard, or are hooked to a roller running along an overhead rail which leads from the ash trunk to the ash shoot, to be emptied as just mentioned; after which the empty buckets are returned to the stokehold to be filled, hoisted, and returned again as often as may be necessary.

The ash-hoist engine saves a considerable amount of labour and time, which is of much importance when the ship is steaming fast, and the consequent production of

L

ashes, clinker, etc., is great. For it is at such times very necessary to keep the stokehold platforms clear of refuse, so as to leave enough room for the coal which is wanted for the furnaces; and, unless the ashes can be removed with sufficient rapidity, it is not always possible to keep the fires in such a clear and good condition that steam can be maintained at the high and constant pressure required for the engines.

Engines called coal hoists, for hoisting coal on board from wharves or colliers alongside, are now generally fitted in the larger vessels of war, in case they should not be supplied to the merchant ships, where, however, they are generally to be found. These are also labour and time-saving appliances.

It may be of the utmost importance in war time that a fighting ship should be coaled with the greatest possible celerity, and it might also happen that it would be in the highest degree injudicious to expose the crews to long continuous spells of hard work, such as would be the case if they were kept constantly on the alert night and day, when the vessels were keeping the sea, and, in addition to this continuous work, when they went into harbour, to get stores and refit, to saddle them with still extra labour. Instead of this, at such a time opportunity would be taken to give the crews a short spell of much needed rest. Most of our large vessels carry as their fuel supply from one to two thousands tons of coal, or even more, and the amount of fatigue that would be imposed on the crew had this quantity to be hoisted inboard by manual labour would be enormous. To save all this labour, and the long and perhaps valuable time it would take to accomplish the operation of coaling by such means, it is the practice to supply steam-engines, which hoist the bags of coal from the lighters and lower them on the deck of the ship herself, by an arrangement somewhat similar to that described in the case of the ash-hoist engines.

Boat-hoist engines are also very similar to the ash and coal hoists, and are used for hoisting in and out of the

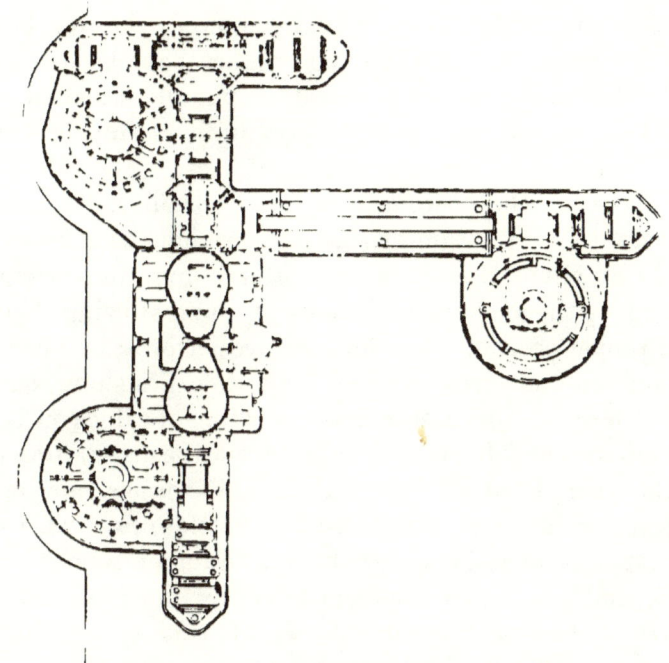

FIG. 26.—" VICTORIOUS' " ANCHOR GEAR.

vessel the heavy torpedo, steam, and other large boats which are carried on board battleships as a part of their warlike complement.

In the French Navy their larger ships are fitted with heavy davits to which the boats are suspended when hoisted, and to which the steam hoisting gear is attached ; but in the British Navy large derricks, " stepped " close to the foot of the military masts, are used. The boat-hoisting engines actuate the gear attached to the derrick, for hoisting and lowering the boats, as may be necessary, the derrick itself being capable of being swung into any required position, either overhanging the water at the ship's side into which the boats may be lowered or from which they may be hoisted, or immediately above the cradles or crutches into which the boats are stowed when on board. In a few cases the boat-hoisting engines have been worked by hydraulic power, but steam is usually adopted. It would seem better to keep the hydraulic engine, such as I describe later on, for its own special uses.

It has been the custom, now for a considerable number of years, to use a steam-engine for working the capstan, by means of which the operations of mooring, unmooring, or getting up the anchors, and " catting " and stowing them in their proper position when hoisted, are performed. The illustrations on the foregoing and opposite pages show some of the modern improvements in the working of cables on board men-of-war, and have been taken from the actual drawings of the gear fitted on board H.M.S. *Victorious*, one of the largest and latest of the first-class battleships. This type of gear was introduced by the late Samuel Baxter about 1884, and has since been considerably modified and improved. Among the advantages of this system is the readiness with which all working parts may be removed, cleaned, and overhauled, and the independent means of raising the anchor, should either of the three means be disabled by bad weather or carried away by shot.

The plan recommends itself in a great measure by its adaptability in meeting present requirements that all machinery shall be below the armoured deck, and also that as worm-gearing is of so much importance in this class of gear, all the main spindles are in a vertical position, and enable the driving worms to work horizontally in oil baths. The frictional plates, which have always been more or less a source of trouble, on account of the difficulty of getting at them, can now be readily removed without dismounting any portion of the gear. The cylindrical bearings, through which the vertical spindles are passed, are securely bolted to the deck, and upon these bearings the cable-holders revolve, thus freeing the spindles from all shocks, and forming an absolute safeguard against breakdowns. Formerly the capstan was worked entirely by manual labour;

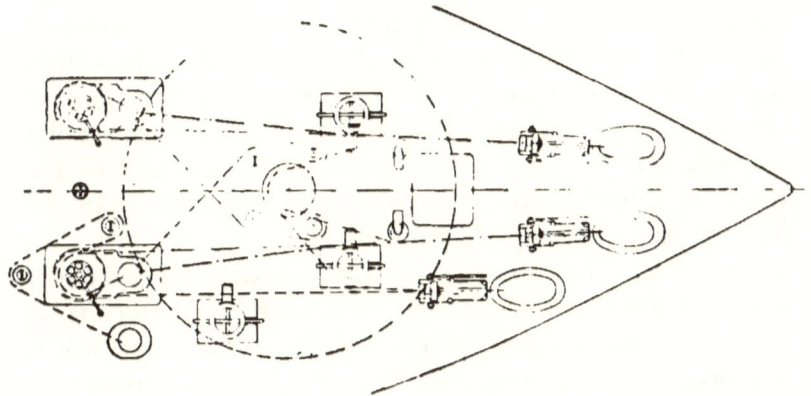

Fig. 27.—" Victorious."

huge wooden handspikes, or capstan bars, as they were called, were used as the levers by which the men caused the capstan to wind up the anchor-cable and anchor from the bottom of the sea, or to warp the ship from one position to another when shifting berth. Who has not read of the fiddler's jocund tune as, seated on the top of the capstan, he discoursed hornpipes, reels, and other such lively music to the merry tramp of the sailors' feet as they ran around, each pressing his capstan-bar, and thus lifted the anchor? But fiddler and fiddle are no longer the

picturesque accompaniments of a vessel's getting under
way.

The operation of hoisting the ponderous anchors and
chains which are necessary for the monster battleships of
the present day is a task far too laborious for their crews,
and so that steam, without which no battleship could exist
in the present day, is again called into requisition for
hoisting the anchor, as well as for most other necessary
work in a modern ship of war.

The capstan engine is situate in the forward part of the
ship, if possible well under protection and close to its work,
where it can easily be controlled from the forecastle, and
performs all its duties with no more music than the grinding of the chain through the hawse-holes, or the clank of
the pawls upon the rack of the capstan as it revolves rapidly
and effectually, doing treble the work in one-third of the
time taken in the older days, when ironclads were unknown
and steam was hardly thought of.

The first thing to be done upon getting a ship under
way, or after releasing her from her anchorage, is to
guide and control her on her course, and here again it is
necessary in the large and swift battleships and cruisers to
provide more powerful and effective appliances than can be
obtained by manual labour alone for moving the rudder
and directing the path of the ship. It is with this object
that the steam steering engine is fitted.

This engine is sometimes placed in the main engine-
room, but more often works in a special compartment of its
own, near the rudder or tiller, as may be found most convenient; and as it is such a vital portion of the ship's
auxiliary machinery it is always arranged to place it under
protection, well below the water-line, and out of the reach
of the enemy's shot or shell.

A very few years ago, a fleet seldom went to sea without

one or more ships making the signal, " Am not under control," which, in nine cases out of ten, meant that something had gone wrong with the steam steering gear.

In Lord Brassey's " Naval Annual " for 1892 I read, " The man who shall invent a system of steam steering that should be as trustworthy as, say, the propelling engines of an average man-of-war, will deserve well of his country. At present no such system exists."

In " The Times " of February 22nd of the same year, in an account of a run of the *Sybille* from the Tyne to Devonport, I am told," The steam steering gear worked badly, and ultimately broke down when off the Start." In various papers of the following day it was stated that " The Peninsular and Oriental steamer *Carthage* experienced very bad weather on her voyage from Gibraltar, and in the Channel on Monday night her steam steering gear broke down, and a collision was narrowly averted.

" When we consider that in the *Sans Pareil* there are no fewer than fifty-eight auxiliary steam-engines on board, and that of these there are some whose failure would mean the disabling for an uncertain period of the ship herself, it cannot be wrong to urge that the utmost care should be exercised by the inspecting officers to see, according to their lights, that these small engines are as scientifically constructed, and as accurately fitted in place, as are the large ones. There is no direction in which ingenuity could be more profitably applied than in devising small engines for use on board ship that shall, practically, never break down ; and the first step towards success is to recognize that the cause of nine out of ten breakdowns is flimsiness."

It is more than three years since the above words were written, but in that time a marvellous improvement has taken place. Nobody hears now of steam steering gear giving way, and during the recent naval war between Japan and China I do not call to mind a single instance where either it or the main machinery was damaged in action.

Although the steering engine itself is properly cared for in the way of protection, it is not possible to afford the same protection to the whole of the apparatus, called the "controlling" gear, by which the engine actuating the rudder is worked or controlled. This controlling gear connects the steering engine with the steering stations situated in various parts of the vessel, as, for instance, on the bridges, the upper deck, the conning towers, and even in the steering compartments and engine-rooms themselves.

It is usually the custom for ordinary work in peace time to steer the ship from the bridges, whence a good look-out can always be kept, and where the helmsman is within easy access and under the eye of the navigating officer, or officer of the watch on deck; but in war time it is possible to steer the ship by a helmsman stationed below, in close proximity to the steering engine itself, to whom the necessary directions can be transmitted either by electric or mechanical telegraphs, by voice tubes, or by a messenger. This arrangement would of course be adopted in the event of the mechanical connections between the bridges, upper decks, or conning towers—which are all in exposed situations—and the steering engine being disabled or shot away. The controlling gear, then, is simply the gear by which the steering engine can be worked from any steering station.

At each steering station a small hand-wheel with spokes is fitted on a pedestal, and to this hand-wheel the steering engine valve, technically known as the controlling valve, is attached by a series of rods and bevel wheel gearing; the rods of course reaching from the upper bridges and other stations right away down to the depths of the ships where the steering engines may be situated. The motion of the hand steering wheel on deck, or wherever it may be worked from, is conveyed to the engine by means of the rods and the controlling valve, and the whole apparatus is so arranged that the rudder which is being moved by the engine follows the motions of the hand steering wheel exactly.

The controlling valve is a special feature of the steam steering engine. It not only admits steam to the engine, so that the rudder is moved to port or starboard as may be desired, but it is so fitted that while the rudder is attaining the wished-for position the steering engine itself, which causes the rudder to move, is also actuating and closing the controlling valve, so that as soon as the helmsman on the upper deck, or bridge, or wherever he may be, ceases to operate the hand steering wheel and the helm has been placed where he wants it to be, the controlling valve shuts off steam and the steering engine stops, remaining stopped until the helm is required to be moved again, when the controlling gear and steering engine are once again brought into operation.

The motion of the steering engine is transmitted to the tiller and rudder by a system of powerful bevelled wheel gearing and shafting, extending right along the lower parts of the ship from the engine to the rudder, and this shafting is caused to revolve either in one direction or the opposite by the engine being started either to port or starboard. The arrangement whereby the rotary motion of the shaft is converted into a port or starboard motion in the rudder itself is an ingenious adaptation, in most cases, of a right and left-handed screw, cut on the end of the rotating shaft, near the tiller.

To the best of my belief the first instance of the employment of a right and left-handed screw was in the screw-ship *Lancefield*, built and engined by Robert Napier and Sons, of Glasgow, in 1861, and the accompanying sketch is a copy of one made by me at Lisbon for the late Admiral Sir Richard Colpoys Dacres at the end of that year. This right and left-handed screw mentioned above works a right and left-handed nut, that is, one nut at each end of the screw; to each nut are attached rods, which are also

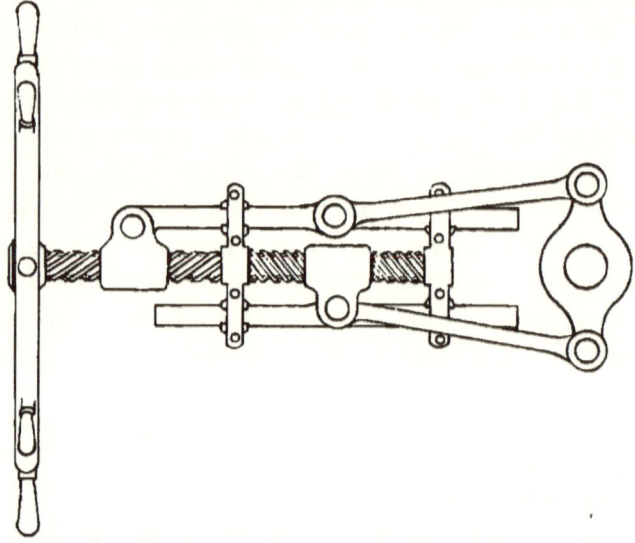

FIG. 28.—STEERING GEAR OF THE "LANCEFIELD."

attached to the tiller or yoke on the rudder head, and as these nuts approach or recede from each other, according as the rotating screw revolves in one direction or the other, the necessary motion to port or starboard is communicated to the rudder.

As with most other auxiliary machinery which is fitted to save labour or time, it is usual to supply the ordinary hand steering wheels, in addition to steam steering gear, so that, should the latter be disabled, the ship can still be guided or steered. Hydraulic gear for steering has been fitted in one or two vessels of the Navy, but it is now out of date.

The steam gear of Messrs. Forester, of Glasgow, was for some years, say, in the period of nearly thirty years ago, the system usually adopted in her Majesty's service, but of late years, among many makers, perhaps Messrs. Harfield and Co., and Messrs. Davis and Co., have been most generally employed.

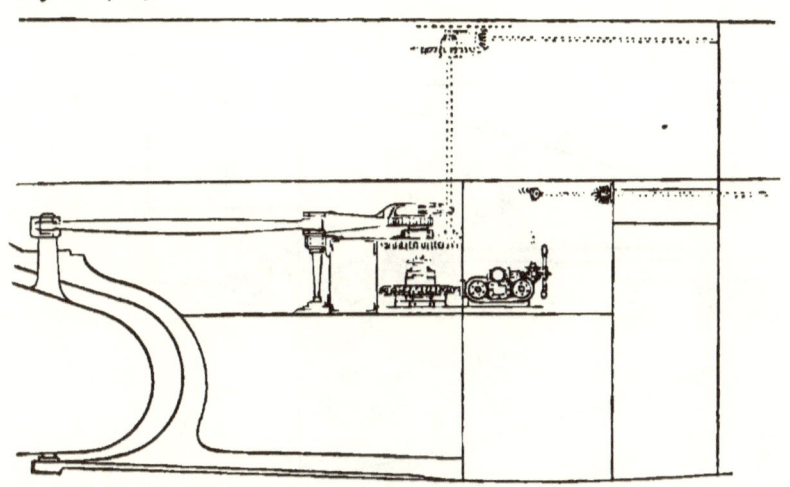

Fig. 29.—Elevation of Harfield's Steering Gear.

On June 1st. 1894, Admiral Sir John Fisher, Controller of the Navy, wrote to Harfield's firm : " With reference to the further trials of your patent steam steering gear, fitted in H.M.S. *Spartan*, I have to inform you that the working of similar gear in H.M.S. *Hermione* was entirely satisfactory at all speeds.

" *Ship going Full speed.*

Shifting from steam to hand gear occupied   12 seconds.
Shifting from hand to steam gear   „   40   „

" *With Steam gear.*

From amidships to hard a-starboard   occupied   7 seconds.
From hard a-starboard to hard a-port   „   16   „
From hard a-port to amidships   „   6   „

" One man only working the wheel, movement easy and smooth.

" *Using Hand gear.*

" With six men ship was steered easily, and helm put hard over in 55 seconds."

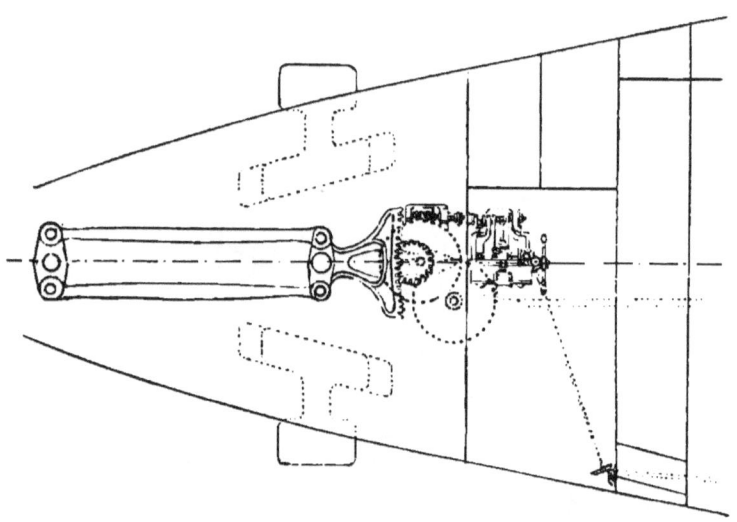

FIG. 30.—PLAN OF HARFIELD'S STEERING GEAR.

The " Globe," May 22nd, 1894, says : " Some interesting results were obtained from the new steam and hand steering gear supplied by Messrs. Harfield and Co. to the *Hermione*, second-class cruiser, 4,360 tons, which worked with the same satisfactory results as in all previous vessels. The gear, which is on the compensating principle, has the advantage of acting with increased power in proportion as the load increases. At the trial it was tested both by steam and hand. . . . In this vessel two men would have been amply sufficient to steer well and swiftly, as was proved in the *Spartan*, fitted with the same gear, but the officer in charge would not consent to less than six, which is half the usual number. There has never been any hitch with the 'Harfield' gear supplied, and it has the further advantage of being cheap."

This gear is practically noiseless, and in the wardroom,

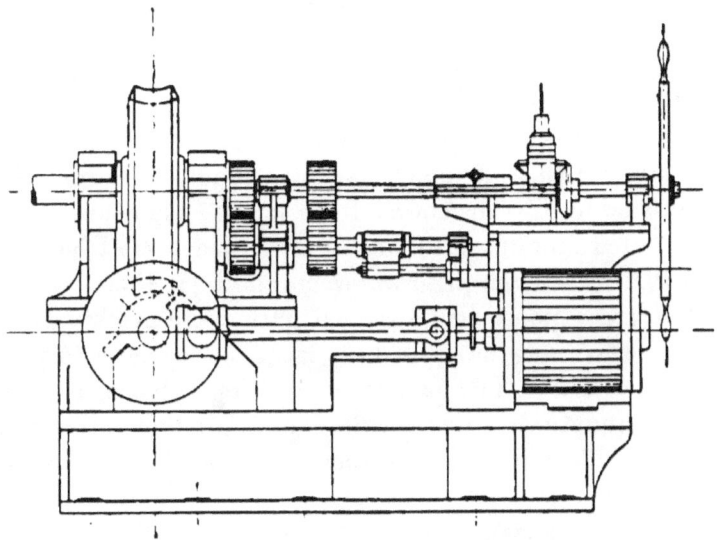

FIG. 31.—ELEVATION OF DAVIS AND CO.'S STEERING GEAR.

over the steering engine, it could not be detected whether it was at work or not.

Coming next to Davis and Co., Limited, there is no doubt but that they do an immense amount of work, not only for war purposes, but also for the mercantile marine. The largest ship they have hitherto fitted is the Russian armoured cruiser *Rurik*, with a speed of eighteen knots, and a twenty-two inch rudder head. They say, "Our steering machinery is perfectly noiseless, is constructed with machine-cut teeth, and now possesses the advantage of fifty per cent. saving over others." Messrs. Davis have fitted their gear in four first-class battleships, eight first-class cruisers, and a large number of smaller vessels in the British Navy.

A patent controlling valve has recently been perfected and patented by this firm, the principal object of which is to economize steam. This valve is actuated by the helm indicator, and wire-draws the steam when the helm is in the mid-position, opening gradually as the helm goes over, and thus increasing the power as the load becomes greater. By this means also all shocks of admission of steam are done away with, and the engine runs much more smoothly, which enables a truer course to be kept. There are several other noted manufacturers of steering gear, but I have not been fortunate enough to know much about them.

The great point to be gained with these machines is to keep the wearing surfaces very large, so as to reduce the wear and tear. The patent controlling valve also effects great economy in the working, and produces the same effect as increasing the number of revolutions per degree as the helm gets over.

On the importance of good steering gear it is not here requisite to dwell. For some years its giving way was a constant source of dread to the admirals of squadrons and the captains under them. No very serious accident ever happened from this cause, but the escapes sometimes seemed almost miraculous.

Until a comparatively recent period in the history of the marine engine the supply of air to the furnaces of the boilers was obtained entirely by the ordinary flow of air from the atmosphere, the quantity of air thus entering the furnaces being due to the draught in the funnels, the strength of the draught being regulated by the height of their tops above the furnace grates. The stokeholds were entirely open to the atmosphere, and the passage of air to the stokeholds was assisted by ventilating tubes descending from the upper deck. The tops of these tubes, usually about a foot in diameter, were opened out into a bell-

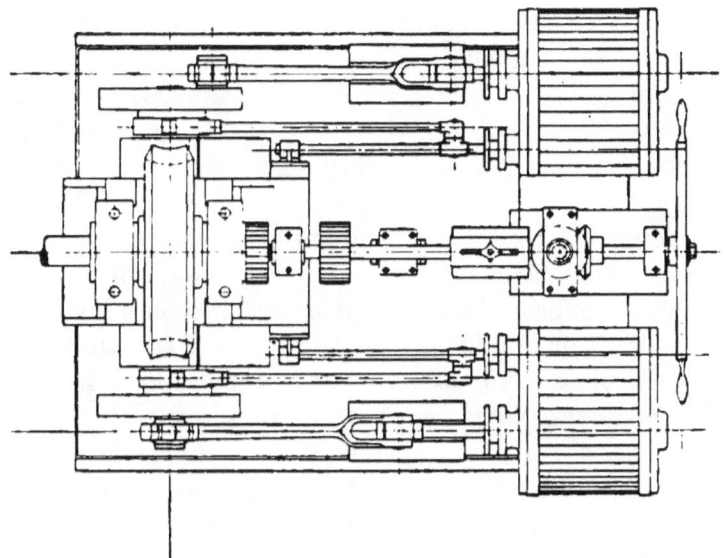

Fig. 32.—Plan of Davis and Co.'s Steering Gear.

shaped curve, capable of catching the wind, and of being "trimmed," or turned with its mouth open to the wind.

With the increases in speed, and consequently power and steam generation, which have been demanded in our modern fighting ships, it has been found that the ordinary atmospheric, or "natural" draught, as it is generally called, is not sufficient, unless the boilers are made very large, and of greater heating capacity than it is conveniently possible to give them, to generate steam with sufficient rapidity, and in the necessary quantity for the more powerful engines now fitted.

To get this supply of steam, as the heating surface cannot be enlarged without unduly increasing the size and weight of the boilers, recourse has been had to " forced " draught, and the fires have occasionally been made to burn more rapidly and to generate more steam in a given time, so that intensity and rapidity of combustion are employed to procure the same effect as larger heating surfaces; that is, in much the same manner as a housewife uses a pair of bellows when she wants an increased fire to make the kettle boil more quickly. There are two or three systems of forced draught to which I shall possibly refer again in my chapter on boilers.

In some vessels of the mercantile marine warm air is supplied to the furnaces under a certain amount of pressure, the air being brought by suitable arrangements inside the smoke-boxes or uptake of the boiler itself, the stokeholds being left open to the atmosphere in the ordinary way.

In the Royal Navy the plan almost universally adopted is the closed stokehold system. Here the stokeholds or boiler-rooms are entirely shut off, by means of suitable doors, from the atmosphere, and cold air is pumped down to them by means of large centrifugal fans, revolving at a high velocity, and situated at the base of the air supply trunks. By these fans the air is delivered into the stokeholds, where it soon attains pressure by being slightly compressed. This compressed air is admitted to the furnace bars at a much higher velocity than air which has only the ordinary atmospheric pressure; that is, a greater quantity of air is supplied by means of forced draught than can be obtained by natural means, and so the combustion of the fuel in the furnace, with consequent generation of steam in the boilers, becomes more rapid.

I doubt very much whether during the last three years forced draught has been used many times in any ship in the Navy. The fans have often been kept going in hot climates, but the stokeholds have been left open.

Forced draught is said to be advantageous in that it enables a warship to be totally independent of the ordinary atmospheric supply of air, and, no doubt, it would be extremely useful for such occasions as chasing or escaping from an enemy, when it would perhaps be impossible to maintain a high speed for any length of time without its use.

It also provides an efficient system of ventilation for the stokehold, and renders the task of the firemen below at the flaming, heated furnaces much easier than it would be without its aid, especially when steaming in tropical climates.

Closely related to the forced draught fans for the furnaces are the ventilating fans for the vessel herself. These fans are always of the centrifugal type, and resemble those already described for the main circulating engines. They are fitted in various parts of the vessel, and serve to render all the different compartments habitable by either exhausting the foul air, or supplying fresh air, or doing both.

In the old wooden line-of-battle ships, with their tiers of decks and row upon row of large open square ports, the ventilation of the habited and fighting parts of the ship arranged itself, in a natural manner with few exceptions, without any difficulty or any special trouble to the naval architect. The open gun-ports and the many hatchways from the upper deck downwards provided an ample supply of air and light for ordinary occasions. It was only in very bad weather that it became necessary to close the ports or to batten down the hatches, and at such times the atmosphere between decks was apt to become stuffy. But even

M

in such cases the work or duty of the officers and crew invariably took them on deck. All the various operations connected with the navigation and sailing of the ship took place in the free air of heaven, and a four hours' watch on deck completely neutralized the ill effects of a watch below in vitiated or close atmosphere.

In the modern battleship all is changed! The lofty, towering masts with their pyramids of canvas are swept away, nothing much now remains to be done in the open. In action the captain and navigator will control the ship from the conning tower by means of voice tubes and telegraphs leading to every station. A few machine guns here and there in the military tops and on the bulwarks, a few signalmen on the upper deck to answer and transmit messages from and to other vessels, a few men for the search-light projectiles, and an officer or two to look after these matters, form about the present staff required above decks; but the monster guns of the ship, the machinery which works the guns and turrets, the mighty engines by which the ship is propelled, the torpedoes and their launching tubes, the pumps for extinguishing fire, or clearing the compartments of water, all these, with their necessary crews, are stationed below, out of sight, and many of them far below the water-line, and entirely shut off by water-tight doors from any communication with the open air or the light of day.

It thus becomes necessary to supply to the men in an artificial manner the air which they can obtain by no other method. Thus the ventilating fans, which obtain their air supply by means of proper trunks open to the atmosphere, can also deliver their air to all such confined spaces in the vessel as may require it, or it can be arranged that the foul, vitiated air in a compartment can be exhausted by some fans while fresh air is supplied either naturally, in downcast trunks from the upper deck, or by delivery from the ventilating fans, as may be found convenient.

With such arrangements for ventilation the modern
battleship becomes quite as habitable and comfortable as
her predecessor of half a century ago.

With this consideration of ventilating the interior of a
battleship of the present day comes intimately the method
of providing artificial light as well. Candles or lanterns
can of course be used, and are even now supplied for
employment in case of emergency when other systems may
fail; but candles and lanterns will not burn without air,
and the products of their combustion go far to destroy the
benefits derived from the system of artificial ventilation
just described.

The method of artificially lighting our fighting ships, or,
indeed, those of any other people, is by making use of the
electric current, which acting through the highly resisting
substance, carbon, is made to produce the powerful illumination known as the electric light. By the passage of a
strong current of electricity, which is generated by suitable
machinery, through a film of carbon, the latter is made to
glow with an intense white heat, emitting sufficient light
to efficiently illumine a large area. The carbon filament
which produces this light, or, rather, by whose resistance to the passage of the current the development of heat
and consequent light is due, is itself inclosed in vacuum
in a perfectly air-tight glass globe, forming a lamp. Thus
it needs no air for its production, and therefore consumes no air; there are no products of combustion evolved,
and so the air between decks, or wherever the light may be,
is neither consumed nor fouled. Added to this, there is no
great amount of heat given off by each incandescent light;
and the wires from the electric machine, and the lamps
which emit the light, can be led anywhere and fixed any-

where, and so it happens that electric lighting lends itself more readily than any other plan yet devised to the illumination of our men-of-war. Small wonder, then, that such an excellent system is now universally adopted.

The electric current is obtained by using a dynamo, driven by a very fast engine, and as it is not attempted here to give more than a general description of any kind of machinery used in the Navy, it will be assumed that the reader has a sufficient acquaintance with magnetism and electricity to know that an electric current is produced whenever one magnet is moved in the vicinity of other magnets. This principle is made use of in the dynamo, the armature (or one magnet) of which is caused to revolve very rapidly in the neighbourhood of the field magnets (the other magnets) by a steam-engine working at a very high speed, whereby a powerful electric current is produced.

Various types of dynamos and engines have been fitted and are still in use in the Navy, and they are now, in nearly, if not all cases, sufficiently powerful to generate an electric current to burn a "search light," as well as to illuminate the interior of the ship.

In the search-light the carbons, by the resistance of which the light is produced, are considerably larger than in the incandescent, or "glow," lamp; they are burnt in the open air, and the intense light produced, in some cases 30,000 candle-power, or over, is concentrated by means of a mirror into one huge beam, and by suitably working the projector, as it is called, which holds the mirror, and also the lamps containing the carbons, the beam of light can be thrown a long distance in any required direction.

For this purpose the electric search-light projectors are usually placed either upon pedestals upon the upper deck or bridges, or else on projecting "sponsons" on the broad-side of the ship, so as to occupy such a commanding posi-

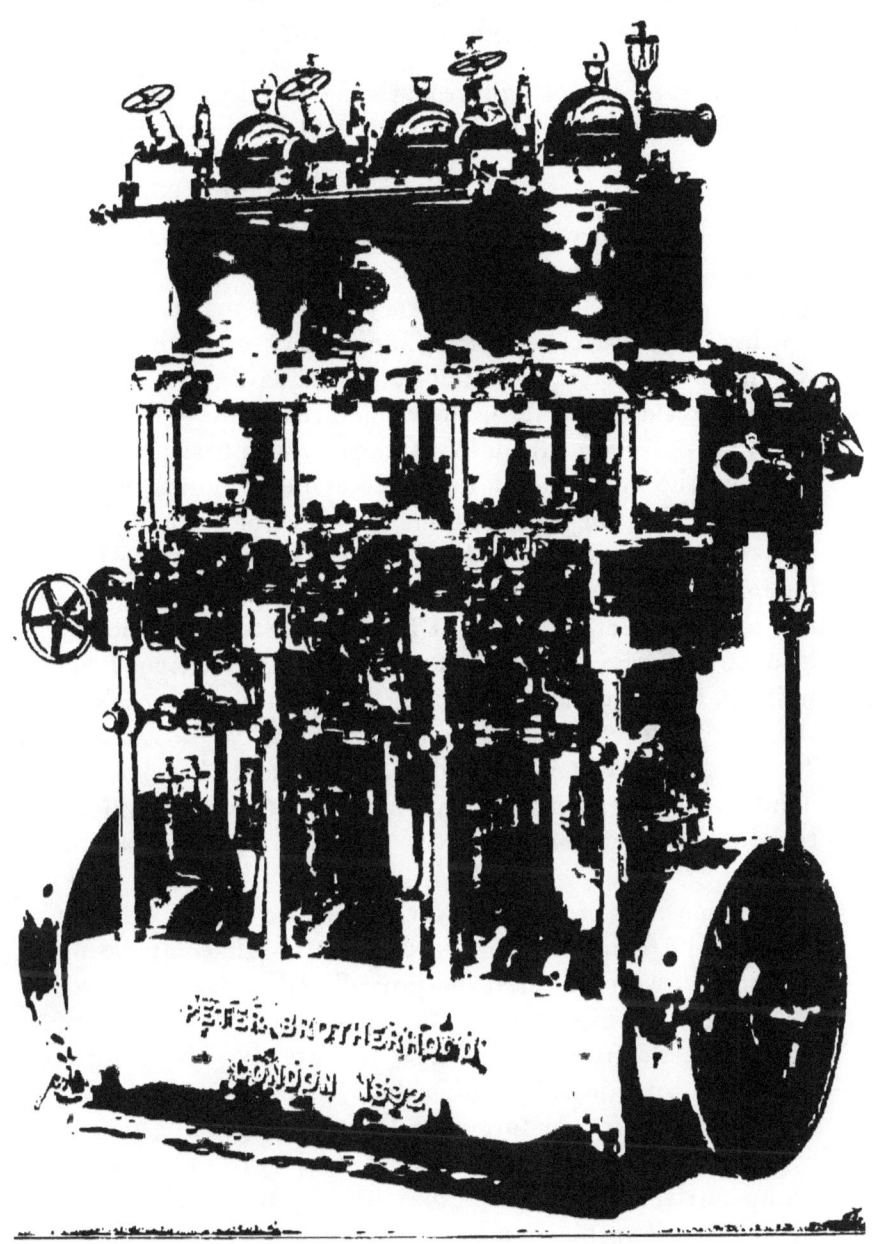

FIG. 33.—BROTHERHOOD'S AIR COMPRESSOR.

tion that the beam of light from the projector can be thrown over a large area, sweep it in fact, surrounding or near to the ship.

The electric light machinery, then, in addition to supplying a means of comfortably and luxuriously illuminating the interior of a war vessel, is also extremely useful for defensive purposes, providing a very efficient means of preventing, or at least discovering, any attack upon the vessel which may be attempted under cover of darkness.

Many of these engines are manufactured by Peter Brotherhood, of Belvedere Road, Westminster, who first made his name by the invention of the three-cylinder engine, which has been used in scores of men-of-war for such diverse purposes as propelling Whitehead torpedoes, driving fans for forced draught and ventilating purposes, air compressing, and the electric light, but for these last two objects the firm now employs a different pattern. At the time I am writing, they are supplying four compressors for each of the following vessels :—*Powerful*, *Terrible*, *Jupiter*, *Mars*, *Prince George*, *Victorious*, and *Hannibal*, and they have in hand electric light machinery for *Prince George* and *Mars*, three sets for each ship, and two sets each for *Barham* and *Bellona*.

Another class of machinery which is also fitted as part of the warlike equipment of a ship is the air-compressing machinery, which is used for providing the motive power for, generally, ejecting the torpedoes on their errand of death and destruction, and also for working the engines inside the torpedoes, by which they travel at a high speed against the enemy, or target, as the case may be.

The air compressors consist of one, two, or more air pumps, driven by steam-engines having one, two, or more cylinders. The air pumps are so arranged that during their action air is drawn from the surrounding atmosphere through suitable valves into the pumps, which valves open inwards only, towards the compressing chambers of the air pumps. The air thus drawn in becomes compressed through several stages by the action of the air pumps on the air contained in their barrels, and eventually emerges, or is discharged, into a reservoir at a pressure of many pounds per square inch.

From this reservoir the compressed air can be supplied by proper pipes and valves to various parts of the ship, for the purposes of charging the torpedoes themselves with the requisite amount of motive power for their propelling engines, and also for supplying the reservoirs of the air tubes for the expulsion of the torpedoes.

I mentioned above that compressed air was " generally " the means employed for starting torpedoes on their way, but the explosion of a small charge of gunpowder has also frequently been used ; but I do not think it found much favour with practical officers, as the use of powder impulse for expelling torpedoes fouls the insides of the torpedo tubes.

The air pumps of the compressing engine are driven direct from their steam-engine, the plungers of the air pumps and the pistons of the steam cylinders being generally coupled together, tandem fashion, on one rod. The engines are designed in a very compact form, occupying but little space, and are driven at high speed, their pumping capacity being so arranged that they can supply compressed air of sufficient quantity and pressure to meet such demands as may be made upon their power during an action, when it may be required to fire off the whole of the torpedoes against an enemy.

In all vessels of moderate size it is customary to have at least two sets of air-compressing engines, and these, with their proper equipment of torpedoes, form a very important and valuable factor in the fighting efficiency of the ship. They are therefore placed as much under protection as possible, either, as is the case with the steering engines and dynamos, in their own special compartments, or else in the main engine-rooms of the ship herself, as may be found most convenient.

In all, or nearly all, the battleships of her Majesty's Navy, the large guns which form the main armament of the vessel are, or were till the other day, so heavy that it is impossible to work either them or their turrets by hand, or to provide fit machines for that purpose in the limited space available to the naval architect when designing the vessel.

There are some few people, but very few, who still object to the application of hydraulic power to the working of heavy guns, and who shout with an exceeding great joy whenever it is announced that a weapon of this description has been so fitted that only manual labour would, in case of necessity, be necessary to use it, but, in spite of all that can be urged to the contrary, there can be no doubt that hydraulic power offers a much safer, surer, and easier method; quicker in its action, and, taking all things into consideration, less liable to derangement, than any system of wheels and ratchets, levers and handles, with which it is absolutely necessary to provide our heavy guns and their gear if they are to be worked by manual labour.

The hydraulic machinery, then, of a modern battleship is fitted for the purpose of training, or elevating, or depressing the heavy guns, which weigh from 29 tons to 67 tons, and in two ships, the *Benbow* and *Sans Pareil*, 101 tons, according to the class of ship in which they are fitted. It also provides a means of revolving the turrets in which the heavy guns are sometimes placed; of opening and closing the breech mechanism of the guns; of hoisting the heavy shell, or other ammunition, from the magazines situated below in the very depths of the vessel; of working the rammers by which the charges of ammunition are pushed into the guns; and of sponging and washing out the bores of the guns after each charge has been fired, so as to clean and cool them in readiness for being loaded again.

The hydraulic pumps and engines by whose work all these different operations can be performed are so simple and easy of manipulation, in their applied stage, that the control of their power can be finally left to the ability of one man, selected from among many others in the ship who have been trained to the same duty.

The pumps themselves are situated well underneath the armoured deck of a battleship, so as to be secure from damage from an enemy's fire. They are water pumps of special design, worked by steam, and generally placed in a compartment specially arranged for them, and they obtain their supply of water, by the pressure of which the heavy guns are worked, from tanks situated also in the bottoms of the ship, and are capable of generating a pressure of several hundred pounds per square inch.

The water pipes which transmit this pressure to the guns, turrets, and other parts required, can be easily led to any part of the ship, and are protected throughout their whole length either by being placed under the armoured deck, or led up to the guns, turrets, etc., through an armoured trunk.

This arrangement provides an efficient system by which the monster ordnance of a battleship can be safely and easily worked, and it also enables the same pressure to be made use of for working small hydraulic engines for the ammunition hoists.

In the earlier types of ironclad the turrets were turned by steam-engines, and this method still exists in a few ships, but, if only for the sake of coolness, the hydraulic plan is infinitely preferable.

In some of the later battleships electric motors have been supplied for working the heavy guns, which system has, so far, had the happiest results; but its application is at present so limited that it has scarcely yet emerged from the experimental stage.

In the later and larger types of war vessels it is now customary to supply auxiliary condensers for the purpose of collecting the exhaust steam from such auxiliary engines as may be in use, condensing this steam, and returning it to the boiler in the shape of fresh feed water.

If the main engines are at work, there is no difficulty in saving the waste steam from the auxiliary machinery, as it can be led directly to the main condensers; but there are many of the auxiliary engines that are constantly or frequently required to be in use when the ship is in harbour—such as ventilating engines, dynamos, air compressors, distilling machinery, boat hoists, coal hoists, or the hydraulic machinery for working and drilling with the heavy guns. At such times it would often be inconvenient to use the main condensers for the auxiliary exhaust steam. It may be necessary to overhaul or repair these condensers while in harbour, so a small condenser is now fitted in all vessels above a certain size or horse-power, with its proper arrangement of circulating pumps and pumps for abstracting the water due to the condensation of the steam from the auxiliary engines, and returning it through the feed tanks to the boilers that may happen to be alight at the time.

It is not usual, however, to fit an air pump to an auxiliary condenser; but with such a large number of auxiliary engines as were enumerated at the beginning of this chapter, it is of the utmost advantage to save this exhaust steam and the resultant feed water, which would be lost if the exhaust steam were allowed to pass through the waste steam-pipe into the atmosphere. The auxiliary condenser can also be used most efficiently in conjunction with the evaporators for obtaining a supply of reserve or "make-up" feed water for the boilers.

To keep all the machinery I have endeavoured to describe in order, it is necessary to carry a large amount of repairing plant, tools, and machines, and a proper engineering workshop with all necessary appliances, including smith's forge, moulding gear for making castings, coppersmith's tools of all kinds; while a proper complement of lathes, shaping and planing machines, punching, shearing, and drilling machines, is now to be found in all large ships.

It is the function of the workshop engine to drive all the machinery above mentioned, and it is of the highest importance that a war vessel shall be able to maintain herself in a constant state of efficiency, as far as the ordinary wear and tear of her machinery and casualties are concerned.

It is the province and duty of the engineer staff of the ship to carry out such repairs as can be effected on board with the plant and means at their disposal, and it is at such times, when the repairs may be of an extensive nature, involving perhaps the use of many or all of the machines which are supplied for the engineer workshops, that the workshop engine becomes a valuable auxiliary to the repairing or recuperative powers of the vessel, and enables her to become in a great measure a self-sustaining and self-sustained engine of war.

When the number of auxiliary engines, and the various purposes for which they are fitted in a modern battleship, are taken into account, and when it is considered that the whole of these engines, in addition to the main propelling machinery, and various portions of the ship herself, are intrusted to the engineer staff for their proper care and for their maintenance in a state of constant efficiency, some small idea may be formed of the endless anxiety, the ceaseless vigilance, and the ability which must be displayed if the British Navy is always to maintain the motto of "Ready, aye ready!"

CHAPTER VIII

BOILERS.

In a book about mechanism in a man-of-war, boilers are almost the most important subject for discussion. Although I have necessarily had often to speak of them before this, I consider a chapter on their different varieties will not here be inappropriate, and I take this opportunity of expressing my gratitude to Passed Assistant Engineer Robert S. Griffin, United States Navy, for much valuable information obtained from his paper on Marine Boilers, printed in the last issue of "Notes on this Year's Naval Progress," from the Office of Naval Intelligence, Washington.

Mr. Griffin, of course, begins by saying that nearly all the great powers are either using or experimenting with some form of the water-tube boiler. The Belleville has been in use in the French navy for the past fifteen years, and the Russians subsequently used the same type for the *Minin* in their navy. In the United States navy the *Monterey*, with Ward "coil" boilers, is probably the first vessel of any navy, other than torpedo-boats, to be fitted with bent-pipe boilers, and thus far they have worked satisfactorily, and given little or no trouble.

The next most important adaptation of them in America is for Gunboat No. 7, now building. She is to have four water-tube boilers of 1,600 horse-power, besides two cylindrical boilers; the latter are for use in long-distance steaming at an economical rate of speed, and are of such construction that they can readily be scaled, provision being made in their design for feeding them with salt water in case of necessity, so as to keep up a supply of fresh water for the water-tube boilers. There are, besides, a liberal evaporating plant and fresh-water tanks, so that the water-tube boilers may be used in ordinary steaming if necessary or desirable. The type of boiler to be fitted in this vessel had not been determined upon when Mr. Griffin wrote, but he thought it would probably be the Yarrow.

In the new design of machinery for the *Chicago*, it is probable that more than half the power will be in water-tube boilers, sufficient power in cylindrical boilers being provided for 10 to 12 knots cruising speed.

In France nearly every new vessel building is being supplied with some type of water-tube boiler, the preference apparently being for the Belleville and the Lagrafel D'Allest, though many other types are being tried. In the larger vessels it is invariably a straight-tube boiler, while in torpedo-boats the bent tubes seem to be in the majority.

In Germany little has been done in this direction as yet, though Mr. Thornycroft stated at a meeting of the Institution of Naval Architects, that his firm had been given a contract to put boilers of his *Speedy* type in the *Siegfried*. Nearly all the German torpedo-boats are by Schichau, and are therefore fitted with the locomotive boiler. In fact, Herr Schichau is about the only torpedo-boat builder of any note who has not either designed a water-tube boiler of his own, or tried one of another's make.

Russia is also trying the Belleville in a ship of about

15,000 horse-power, after having tried it in one of 2,000, and has recently entered into contract with Messrs. Yarrow for a torpedo-boat destroyer, which has been fitted with boilers similar to the *Hornet's.*

Before passing to a description of some of the types of water-tube boilers, it will be well to show what has led up to the sudden abandonment of the cylindrical boiler in England for vessels of high power. Attempts have been made to get an indicated horse-power from less than 1·5 foot of heating surface, and the result has been, as might have been expected, that the power was not obtained, and the boilers practically ruined before being turned over to the government. Then the type which seems to have commended itself, on account of economy in space, was the common combustion chamber boiler. In consequence of the trouble with boilers, due to leaky tubes, and the repeated failure of vessels on trial, and especially of those with boilers of the last-named type, a commission composed of engineer officers of the Navy, and engineering representatives of the Board of Trade and Lloyd's, was appointed to inquire into the subject, and to recommend such alterations and modifications in design as might obviate the difficulties hitherto encountered, and to submit such suggestions as might result in the production of a design which would insure the attainment of the stipulated power without injury to the boilers. The result of their deliberations has been the practical abandonment of the common combustion chamber boiler, and an increase in heating surface per horse-power.

In looking over an American engineering book the first thing that strikes one is the large number of boilers described and illustrated, the very names of which are hardly known in Great Britain. Who, for instance, ever heard of the Ward's Royal Arch, the Mosher, the Roberts, the Almy, the Towne, the Seabury, the M'Bride and Fisher, or the Warrington boilers? But when we come to the Babcock and Wilcox boiler, we are on a little firmer

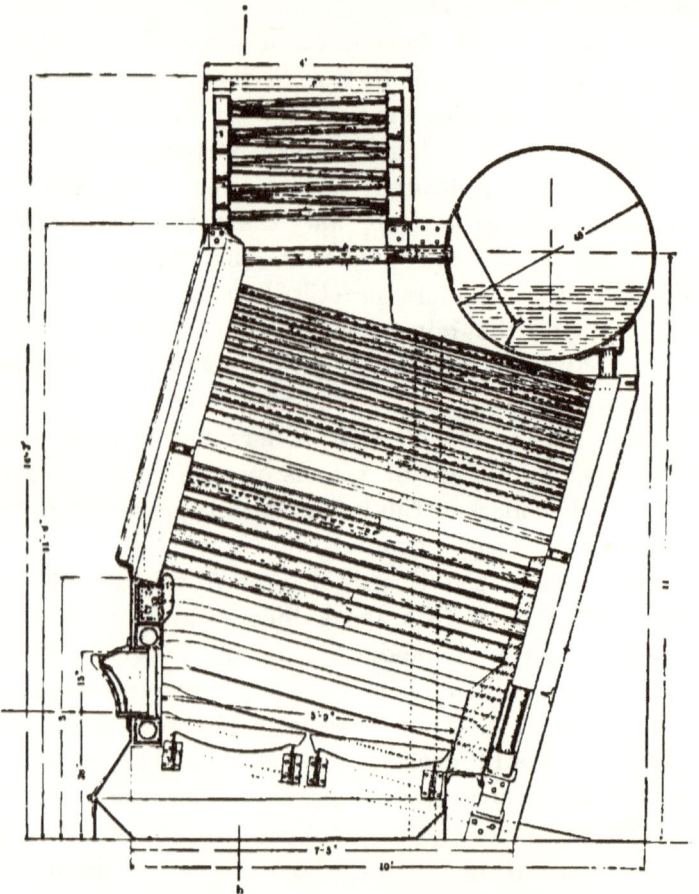

FIG. 34.—BABCOCK AND WILCOX BOILER.

ground. Mr. Milton, in his paper read before the Royal United Service Institution in June last, says that it has been fitted into the largest number of British merchant vessels. These boilers are modifications of the well-known land boiler made by the same firm. The products of combustion are brought immediately in contact with the heating surfaces, and the tubes are arranged to have a rise of about one in four, in order to cause a circulation. Above the boiler proper there is a feed-water heater, so arranged

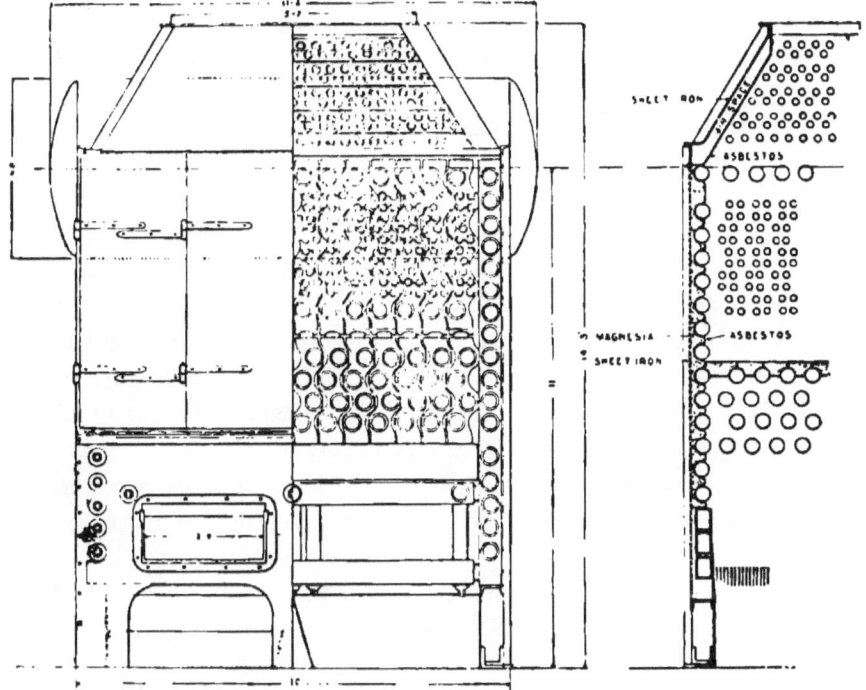

FIG. 35.—BABCOCK AND WILCOX BOILER.

that it may be shut off, and the feed introduced directly into the drum.

The Belleville boiler has been fully dealt with in the description of the machinery of the *Terrible* and *Powerful*. During the past four or five years the Messageries Maritimes have continued to fit them in their steamers which run from Marseilles to Australia, and are so well satisfied

with them, that they have recently ordered another set of
6,000 horse-power for their new steamer, *Chili*.   As a
result of experience it has been found necessary in recent
designs to increase the diameter as well as the thickness of
the lower rows of tubes, until now they are 4·92 inches
diameter and ·394 inch thick.   This was found necessary
on account of the bending of the tubes, the curvature in
some cases amounting to as much as one inch, and constantly increasing.

It was also demonstrated that the boilers could not be
successfully fed with salt water, except for short periods,
and so a special distilling boiler is now fitted in these
vessels to make up the loss of feed.   The saturation is
never allowed to exceed 2·5 or 3, and when the boilers are
not in use they are kept full of water.   After runs of three
or four weeks the tubes are cleaned inside, the deposit in the
upper ones being from 0·04 to 0·12 inch thick, and more in
the lower rows.   The zinc plates in the feed collectors and
in the purifying chamber are renewed at the same time.
The upper rows of tubes are found to suffer from erosion,
although there is little or no pitting of the lower tubes.
The life of the tubes is from four to six years.

The automatic feed regulator, which is the bugbear of all
practical engineers, is said to work well and to be thoroughly
satisfactory, regardless of the condition of the sea.

The Belleville boiler occupies more space fore and aft in
a ship than double-ended cylindrical boilers do, but less
athwartships.   They are generally placed back to back
along the centre-line with the stokeholds outboard.   They
are less economical than cylindrical boilers—the loss by
radiation is greater, and the heating surface is not as
effective—and weigh less than cylindrical boilers for
natural draught working; but for forced draught working,
more power can be obtained, thinks Mr. Griflin, from the

same weight of cylindrical boilers. They cannot be forced
to any extent, but inasmuch as they contain a much
greater proportion of grate surface to floor space than
cylindrical boilers do, it is not necessary to force them
much to obtain a reasonable amount of power per square
foot of floor space occupied.

If a tube gives out it can be replaced without disturbing
any of the elements, except the one containing the tube;
but the repair takes considerable time, as the boiler must
of course be cold before work can be done upon it. It is
necessary to carry a considerable weight of spare parts, the
last Messageries boat having spare sections for two whole
boilers, besides spare tubes with boxes, and about 25 per
cent. of all boiler fittings, including the moving parts of
the feed-pumps. As will be seen further on, the weight of
spare parts carried by some of the naval vessels forms a
considerable percentage of the weight of the boilers.

The following table gives such particulars of these
boilers in naval vessels as are attainable, mostly from the
"Journal of the American Society of Naval Engineers":

Name of Vessel.	No.	Steam Pressure.	I.H.P.	Grate Surface.	Heating Surface.	Weight of Boilers with Water.		
						Total.	Per sq. ft of Heating Surface.	Per I.H.P.
				sq. ft.	sq. ft.	tons.	lbs.	lbs.
Alger	24	—	7,890	753	22,265	342·6	34·46	97·3
Latouche-Tréville	12	242	7,300	694	19,525	303	34·80	93·1
Brennus . . .	32	242	13,810	1,100	35,030	529·6	33·87	85·9
Descartes . . .	16	242	8,384	700	21,503	282	29·4	75·3
Bouvet	32	242	13,810	1,136	32,761	400	27·3	64·9
Galilée	16	242	6,510	530	15,944	190	26·7	65·4
Powerful . . .	48	260	25,000	2,196	67,803	850	28·1	76·2
Sharpshooter . .	8	250	3,238	269	7,693	104	30·2	71·9

Seven other vessels are given in the original table, but
they are unimportant, comparatively, but besides them
the following French fighting ships are to be fitted with
Belleville boilers: *Tréhouart*, 7,500 horse-power; *Bruix*,

8,800 ; *Bugeaud*, 9,000 ; *Pothuau*, 10,000 ; *Pascal*, 8,500 ; and *Catinat*, 9,000. It is fitted in six vessels of the Russian navy, the largest installation being in the imperial yacht, *Standard*, of 15,000 indicated horse-power. Of late the tendency has been to increase the diameter of the tubes, the necessity for which has been demonstrated by experience in the merchant service. Nevertheless, where the

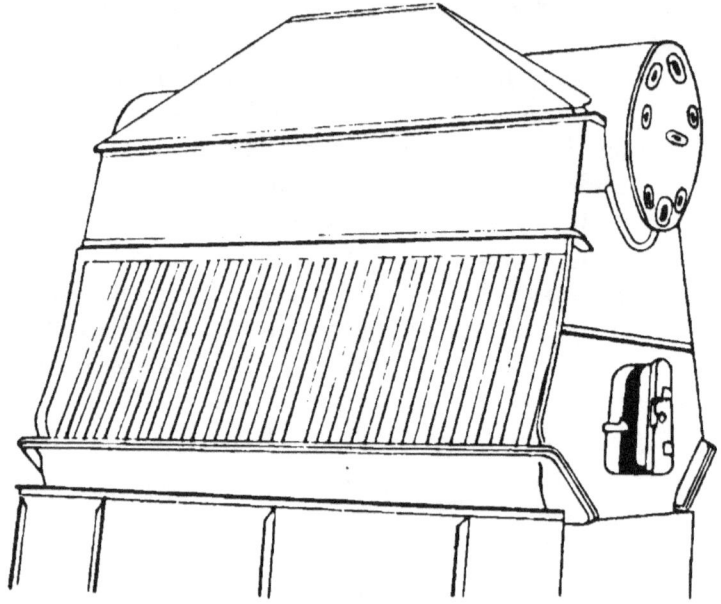

FIG. 36.—DIAGRAM OF YARROW BOILER.

aim is to keep down the weights, the smaller tubes are retained. Thus, the *Galilée* has 3·23 inch tubes, the *Bouvet*, the *Brennus*, and the *Sharpshooter*, 3·93 inch ones, and the *Descartes*, *Powerful*, and *Terrible*, 4·53 inch ones. The thickness of the two lower rows of tubes is almost invariably made 0·394 inch.

One of the most remarkable water-tube boilers in the world is the one invented by Mr. A. Yarrow, of Poplar,

and known by his name. It has long been famous for its
use in torpedo boats, but when it was applied to the *Hornet*,
it literally took the world by storm. The *Hornet* was, for
the time being, the fastest vessel in the world, and was
fitted with triple - expansion twin-screw engines with
cylinders of 18 inches, 26 inches, and $39\frac{1}{2}$ inches diameter,
and 18 inches stroke. Her eight boilers, weighing 43 tons,

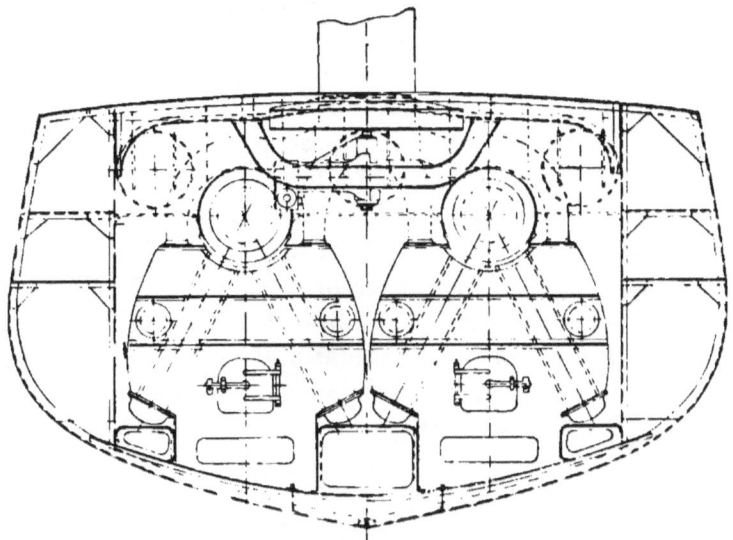

FIG. 37.—SECTION OF H.M.S. "HORNET," FITTED WITH
YARROW BOILER.

had each 21 square feet of grate, and 1,020 square feet of
heating surface, with 980 tubes, 1 inch external diameter.
The steam pressure was 180 lb. The boat was of 180 feet
length, 18 feet 6 inches beam, and 5 feet 3 inches draught.
Her displacement was 220 tons, or about the same as that
of the many gunboats built for the Crimean war, but her
horse-power was about 4,300, and she made a continuous
run of three hours' duration at a speed of 27·628 knots,
while a sister vessel, the *Havock*, also built by Yarrow and

fitted with locomotive boilers, made only 26·125 knots on
3,500 horse-power and 54 tons of boilers.

These boilers are built with straight copper tubes one inch
in diameter, and Mr. Yarrow states that a defective tube
was on one occasion cut out and replaced in forty minutes.[1]

The eight boilers of the *Hornet* contain 165 square feet
of grate and 8,216 of heating surface, the grates being
6 feet 6 inches, and the drums about 7 feet 6 inches long.
Before placing them in the vessel one of them was subjected
to an evaporative test of short duration, during which it
evaporated at the rate of 12,500 lb. per hour of water of
60 degrees into steam at 180 lb. pressure.

Meeting the common objection to his boiler that straight
tubes with fixed ends have no room for expansion, and
consequently must leak, Mr. Yarrow, at a recent meeting
of the Institution of Naval Architects, said: "Although
his firm had built a large number of water-tight boilers
during the last seven years with straight tubes, it might be
of interest to the meeting to know that they had never had
a single leakage between the tube and tube-plate. This fact
proved, they believed, that there was nothing objectionable
in the straight tube system, whilst it clearly offered many
advantages, both in construction and in service. Experience had shown that steel tubes, whether galvanized or
not, rapidly deteriorated, and if the tubes were galvanized
on the inside, a rough surface was produced, which in
some instances retarded the circulation of the water.

" There was also the possibility of portions of spelter
lodging in the tubes, and partially blocking up the passage,
or causing such an obstruction as would allow sediment to
collect. So far as his experience went, it led to the con-

---

[1] Since the above was written, orders have been given which
will probably have the effect of replacing all copper tubes in naval
boilers by steel ones.

clusion that copper tubes were more durable than steel,[1] but
in the use of copper it was essential that it should be very
pure, and that the tube, under all circumstances, should be
below the level of the water, and always filled, otherwise
the copper might become overheated.

"They had every reason to fear, from what they had
been told, that trouble would be experienced in working a
group of small rapidly-evaporating boilers in the *Hornet*,
but, as a matter of fact, they had experienced no difficulty
whatever, the feed being arranged in, as it were, two stages.
The feed-pumps on the engine take their suction from the
hot-well, and deliver into reservoirs at 50 lb. pressure, and
from this reservoir the donkeys take their suction, each
boiler being provided with an independent donkey. By
this means a very ample supply of water was always insured
on the suction side of the donkeys, and the pipes leading to
them could be of moderate dimensions, in consequence of
the 50 lb. pressure delivering the water readily to the suction
side of the pumps. To insure the reservoir always being
well filled, there was a small amount of auxiliary feed constantly passing into it, the surplus, beyond that which was
necessary for the supply of the boilers, being returned to
the tank through a relief valve loaded to 50 lb."

The sketch of the *Hornet's* boilers was kindly supplied me
by Mr. Yarrow. The first one of these boilers built was put
into a second-class torpedo-boat for the Argentine government. This boiler had a steam drum 6 feet long and 20
inches diameter, and had galvanized steel tubes. The boat
was 60 feet long and 9 feet 3 inches beam, and had a load
displacement of 15 tons. Her speed on trial, carrying a
load of 2 tons, was 18·113 knots, with 250 horse-power.
Since that time the Yarrow boiler has been very extensively used, both in our Navy and in those of foreign powers.

[1] Mr. Yarrow's opinion has probably changed since then.

Not less celebrated than the Yarrow boiler is the Thorny-croft, which has been brought very nearly to perfection in what is known as the *Daring* type, which is the latest variety. The Thornycroft boiler, from its flexibility, due to the use of curvilinear tubes, and from the large propor-tion of heating to grate surface, can stand a high degree of forcing, and is, besides, economical at ordinary rates of

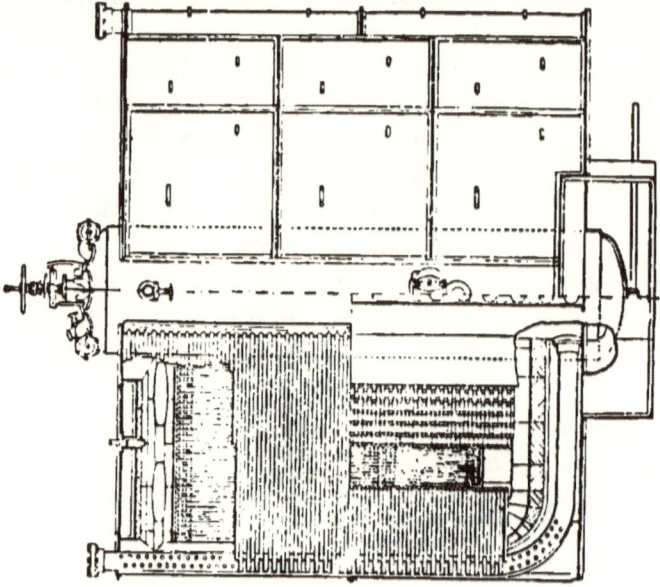

FIG. 38.—THORNYCROFT BOILER. "DARING" TYPE.

combustion. When the tubes are made heavy and the boiler properly cared for, there is no reason to believe that it is not a very durable one; and in this connection it may be mentioned that the boilers of this class in the United States first-class torpedo boat *Cushing* have been in her for five years, and during this time it has been necessary to replace but one tube in the two boilers. In 1891 the Danish Government, which had had some experience with the

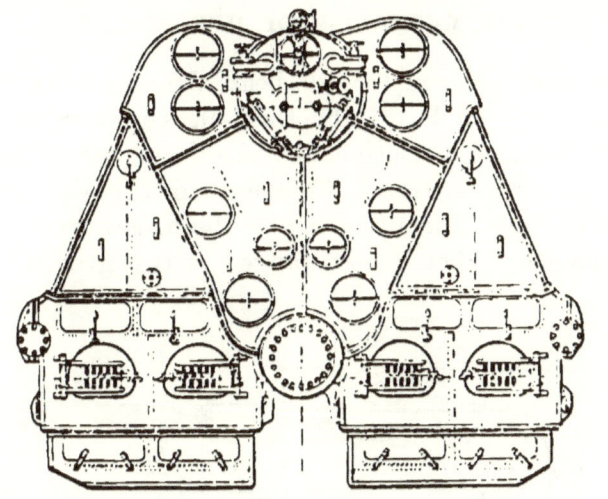

FIG. 39.—THORNYCROFT BOILER. "DARING" TYPE.

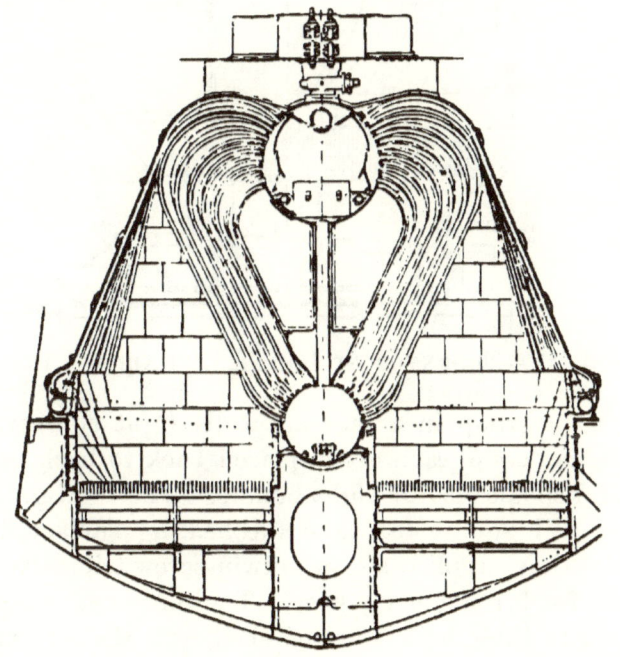

FIG. 40.—THORNYCROFT BOILER. "DARING" TYPE.

Thornycroft boiler in torpedo boats, determined to fit them
"in battery" on board the third-class cruiser *Geiser*, of
about 1,300 tons displacement.   An order was accordingly
given to the Thornycroft Company for a design of eight
boilers of 3,000 horse-power, and the boilers were built at
Copenhagen.   They were arranged in two groups of four

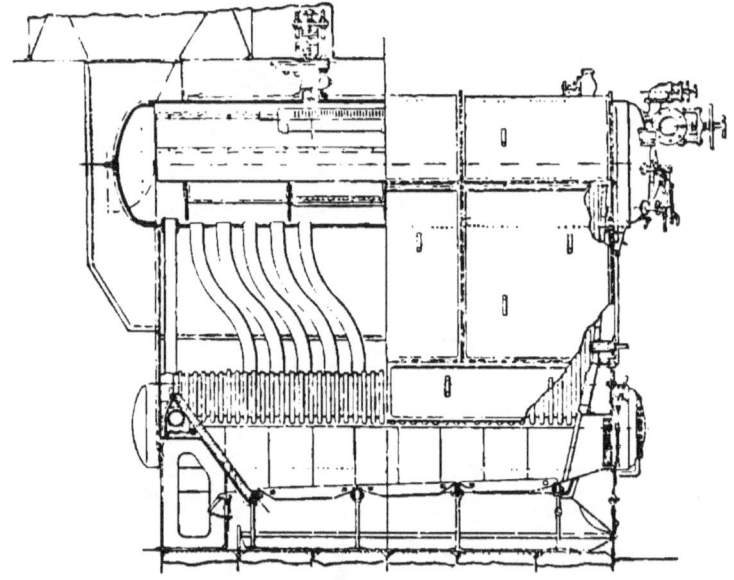

Fig. 41.—Thornycroft Boiler.   "Daring" Type.

each, each group in a separate water-tight compartment,
and the boilers of each group placed back to back, making
four stokeholds for the eight boilers.   The total grate surface is 171 square feet, and the heating surface 12,000.
On trial they supplied steam to twin-screw triple-expansion
engines for 3,157 horse-power.   The inner and outer rows
of tubes in these boilers are of steel, and the intermediate
ones of brass.   The maximum average speed obtained was
17·1 knots.

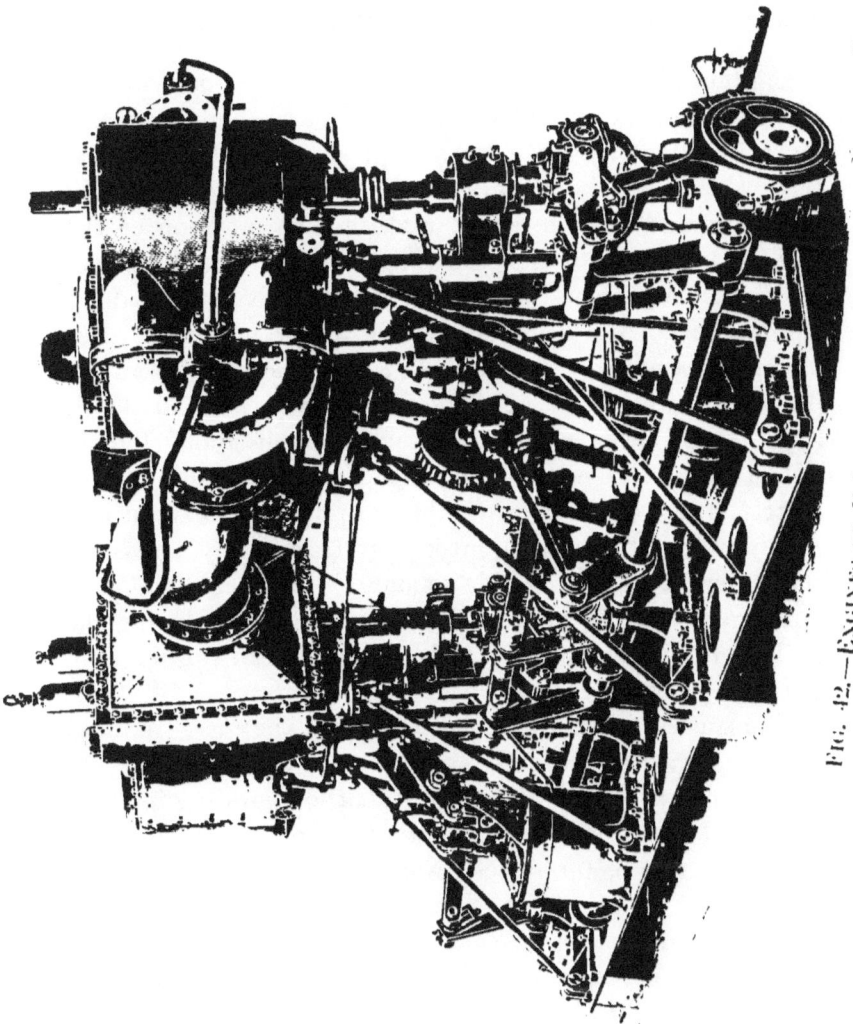

FIG. 42.—ENGINES OF H.M.S. "DARING."

Captain Neilson, Danish Director of Naval Construction, in his report states : " During the trials the boilers worked most excellently; steam was kept up with the greatest ease. The steam-generating power could be regulated nearly immediately to suit the steam consumption of the engines by means of the stop-valves on the steam pipes of the fans. At the end of the sea-speed trials we forced the engines up to 3,157 horse-power in a few moments, after having steamed over seven and a half hours, with an air pressure of about 0·6 inch, and could keep the ship at this high horse-power with an air pressure of about 1 inch. When going full speed we often stopped the ship immediately, and we could bring the ship up to full speed in a few minutes, it not being necessary to pay any regard to the boilers, these being able to stand all sudden changes of temperature. The boilers did not prime either during the highest forcing, or during sudden changes in the working of the engines."

The success of this group of boilers in the *Geiser* induced Mr. Thornycroft to make an offer to the Admiralty to supply one of the first-class gunboats then building in 1893, with boilers of this type, guaranteeing to furnish 4,500 instead of the 3,500 horse-power required with locomotive boilers, and to do it on less weight of boilers, and without occupying any more space. Accordingly the *Speedy* was both built and engined by the Chiswick firm, and was the argest vessel that had been launched so high up the river. The engines were of the same type as those used in similar gunboats, the boilers were very different. In the eight boilers a great saving in weight of water was effected, as the boilers fitted in the *Speedy* when full were some twenty tons lighter than those of other gunboats of the same size. The *Speedy*, on trial, developed a horse-power of 4,674, which gave her a speed of 20 knots an hour by log, against

FIG. 43.—ENGINES OF THE "ARDENT."

a heavy sea ; she is of 810 tons displacement, 230 feet long, and 27 feet beam, while her total cost was £58,927.

In June of the following year took place the trials of the *Daring*, which for a little time held the proud title of " Fastest ship in the world," and was only beaten by successive boats, built and engined at Chiswick by Messrs. Thornycroft. Her engines are peculiar, and show a bold departure from recognized models, if only on account of the slight inclination of the cylinders from the vertical, but the boilers, another type of water-tube, fitted for the first time in the *Daring*, are the real points of interest. They are three in number and are capable of raising steam from cold water in fifteen minutes. The actual records of the three last runs at full speed are :

	Time.	Speed.	Revs. per min.
Against tide . .	2 m. 7·6 sec.	28·214 knots . .	383
With tide. . .	2 m. 6 sec.	28·571 knots . .	385·7
Against tide . .	2 m. 3 sec.	29·268 knots . .	395·1

The horse-power indicated was estimated at 4,700 to 4,800.

In " The Times " of January 26th, 1895, I find the following : " The official trial of the new torpedo-boat destroyer *Boxer*, built and engined by Messrs. Thornycroft and Co., of Chiswick, took place yesterday off the Maplins. Leaving Greenhithe at 10.50 a.m., the vessel proceeded on the trial ground, where six runs were made on the measured mile. The mean speed during three hours' running, as measured by the total number of revolutions made, was 29·17 knots; the total distance covered in that time being 100.6 statute miles. This speed exceeds that ever obtained on an official trial by more than a knot. The four vessels of the class, namely, the *Daring*, *Decoy*, *Ardent*, and *Boxer*, all built by Messrs. Thornycroft and Co., have each beaten the record in turn, and are now the four fastest ships in the world."

The Blechynden boiler, an illustration of which has been kindly furnished me by the Naval Construction and Arma-

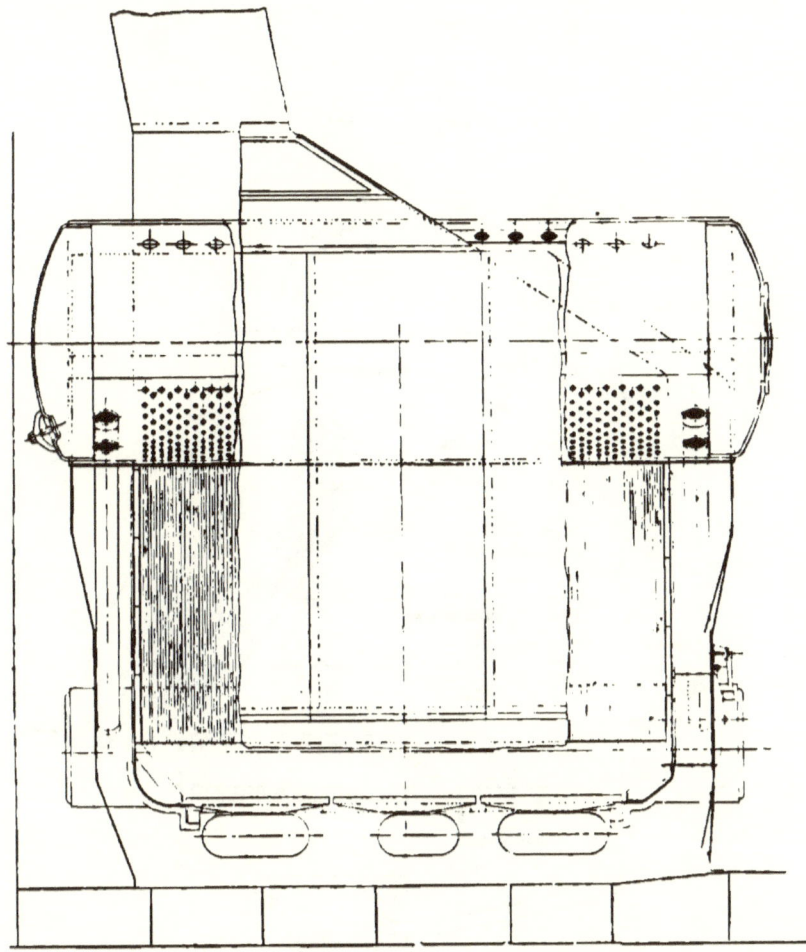

FIG. 44.—BLECHYNDEN BOILER.

ment Company, Barrow-in-Furness, of which its inventor was the engineering manager, differs little in principle from the Yarrow boiler. The construction, however, is different.

Instead of the steam and water drums being made in two
parts, with bolted flanged joints, the two parts of the

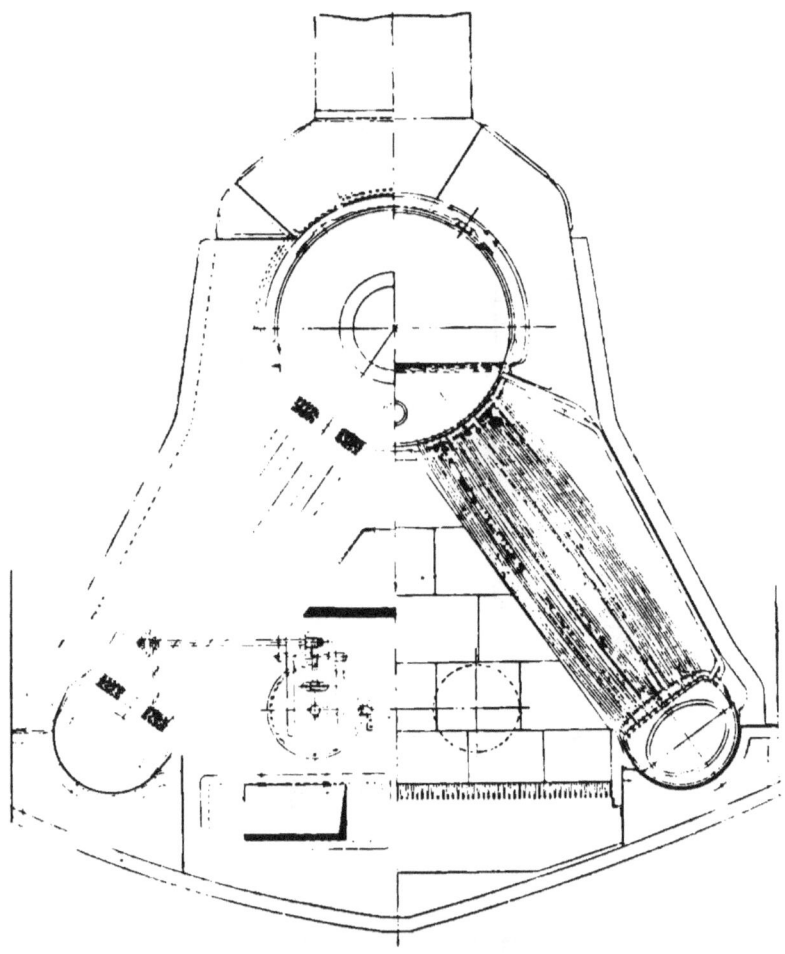

FIG. 45.—BLECHYNDEN BOILER.

lower drums are riveted together, as are also the two parts
of the steam drum.   The latter is made much larger than
in the Yarrow boiler, and is provided with two row of holes

along its upper surface through which any tube may be removed. The tubes are drowned, as in the Yarrow, and are slightly curved, and the two outer rows, which act as downflow tubes, are arranged very much like the outer rows of tubes in the new Thornycroft boiler. Boilers of this type have been fitted in the *Skate*, *Starfish*, and *Sturgeon*, all destroyers with a speed of 27 knots and over.

The Lagrafel-D'Allest boiler is similar in many respects to the Babcock and Wilcox, the headers in the latter being replaced by plate water chambers stayed in the manner usual with the flat water surfaces of cylindrical boilers. The holes in the outer plates are secured by hand hole plates placed inside the boiler, the joint being made with a thin asbestos washer and a ring of thin copper wire.

Mr. Milton, from whose paper the illustration is taken, says of this boiler that the feature distinguishing it from all others is the arrangement made for the circulation of the products of combustion amongst the tubes. The boilers are usually arranged in pairs, each part having its own feeding and water circulation independent of the other; but a combustion chamber is common to the fires of both parts, being arranged between the two nests of tubes. The interior of the tubes and water chambers can be readily examined or cleaned through the numerous small doors, and the removal of any tube in case of necessity can be made in a short time, the tube being either replaced or the holes plugged.

These boilers have been fitted in a number of French fighting ships, the *Bouvines*, *Jemmapes*, and *Valmy* each having twelve of 8,300 horse-power, *Carnot* twenty-four of 14,000 horse-power, and the *Jauréguiberry* twenty-four of 13,000. The tubes are from 3 to 3·25 inches in diameter.

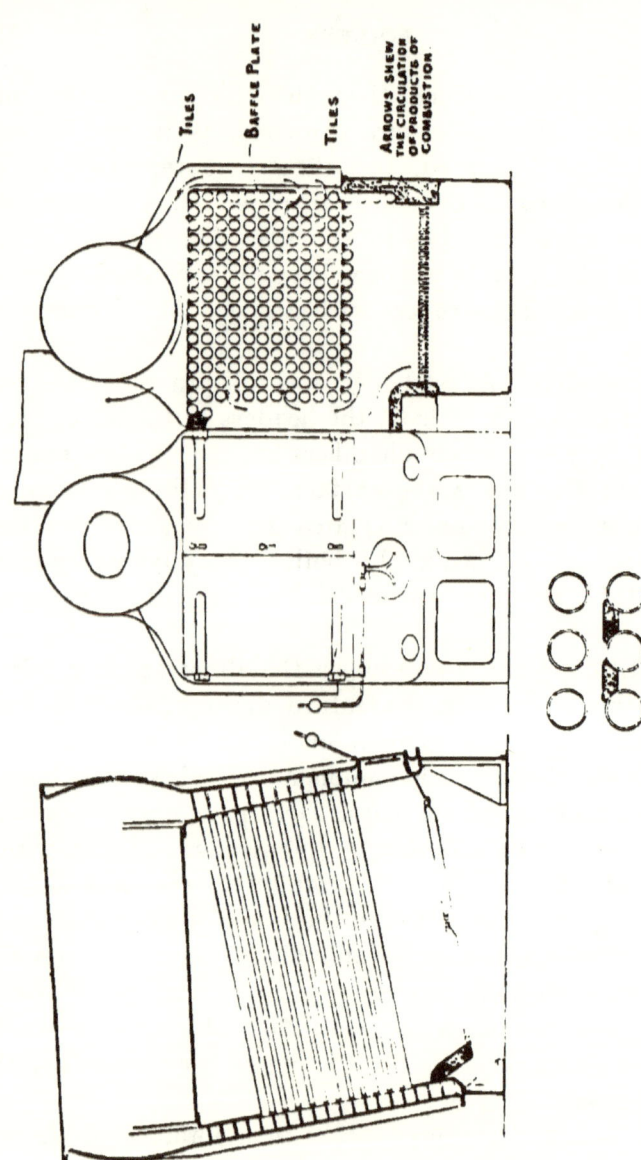

Enlarged view of tubes and tiles.

Fig. 46.—Lagrafel-d'Allest Boiler.

TILES

BAFFLE PLATE

TILES

ARROWS SHEW
THE CIRCULATION
OF PRODUCTS OF
COMBUSTION

They have been successively fitted in the *Bombe*, where two
of them of 2,000 horse-power replaced the locomotive
boilers of that vessel, which had been a constant source
of trouble from the day they were put in. With these
boilers the *Bombe* is said to have made 19·2 knots, her

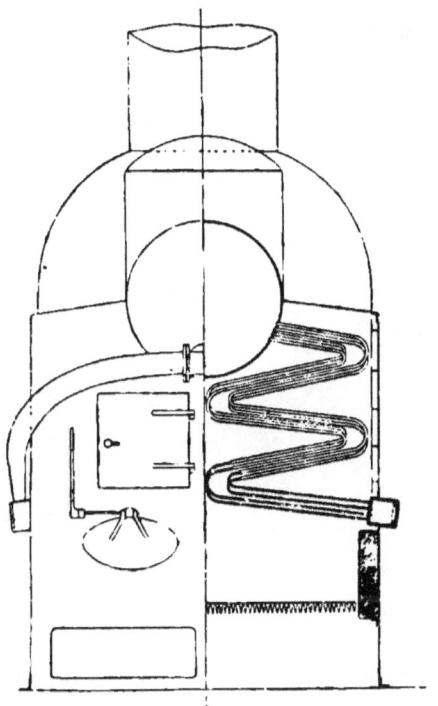

FIG. 47.—DU TEMPLE BOILER.

speed with the locomotive boilers having been from 17·5 to
18 knots.

The boilers of the *Jauréguiberry* contain 1,085 square
feet of grate and 35,092 square feet of heating surface, and
are intended to work under a pressure of 213 lb., which will
be reduced to 170 at the engine. The tubes are 3·15 inches
in diameter and 8 feet long. The weight of the boilers

alone is 235 tons; of the smoke-boxes, 99; feed pumps, pipes, and floors, 138; and water, 80 tons.

The Du Temple boiler is one of a type that has been fitted in a number of French torpedo boats. The tubes are each of two diameters, the lower end connecting with the water chamber at the side being smaller than the upper. The upper ends deliver near the water line. It has been fitted to the torpedo-boat destroyer, *Spanker*, and, at the

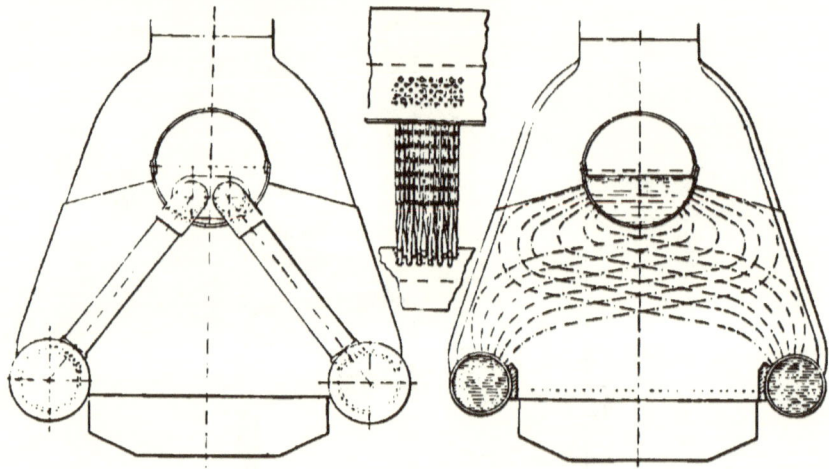

Fig. 48.—DU TEMPLE BOILER.

moment of writing, experiments as to its efficacy are being carried out.

Two boilers of this type have been fitted in the French torpedo boat, *Chevalier*, built by Normand. On trial with a displacement of 119 tons, she made a speed of 27·22 knots. The power was not indicated, but was estimated at from 2,700 to 2,800, the coal burned per square foot of grate being upwards of 62 lb. per hour. Each boiler has 43 square feet of grate, and 1,644 of heating surface.

The Normand boiler is so much like the Thornycroft as almost to render a description unnecessary. It has outside circulating pipes, as in the old Thornycroft, but differs from it in having all the tubes drowned, resembling the Yarrow in this respect, except that the tubes are not

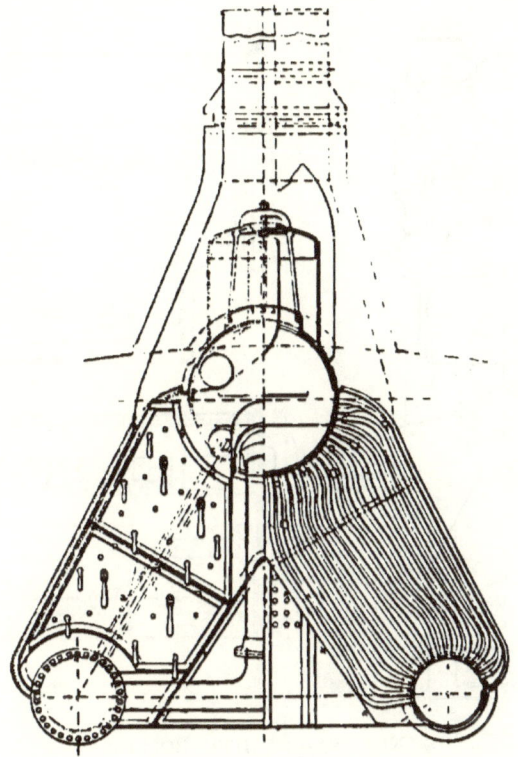

FIG. 49.—NORMAND BOILER.

straight. Boilers of this type have been put in the French torpedo boat, *Forban*. As a result of the experience with brass tubes, no more will be used in the Normand boiler, steel being substituted. The arrangement of the tubes is such, that the gases go the full length of the boiler, and

then return amongst the tubes to the funnel at the front
end. The British Admiralty evidently have a high opinion
of this boiler, as they have ordered it for the destroyers,
Ferret, Banshee, Contest, Dragon, Lynx, Rocket, Shark, and
Surly.

The White boiler, as will be seen from the illustration,

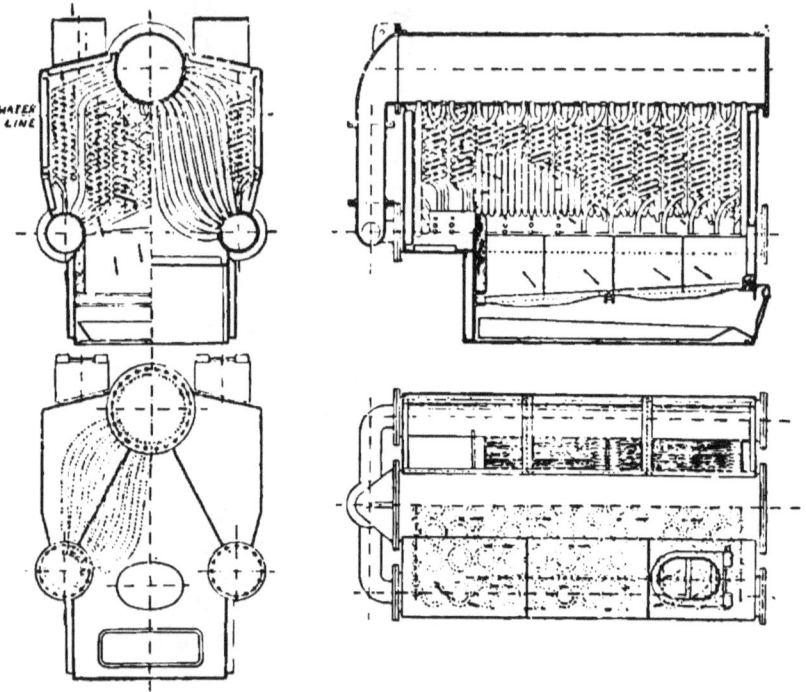

FIG. 50.—WHITE BOILER.

has the usual upper steam and water drum, and a water
drum on each side of the furnace connected to the upper
drum by a series of coils, so arranged that the products of
combustion have to pass down the furnace and back
between the coils to the funnels, which are at the front
of the boiler. There are outside circulating pipes as in the

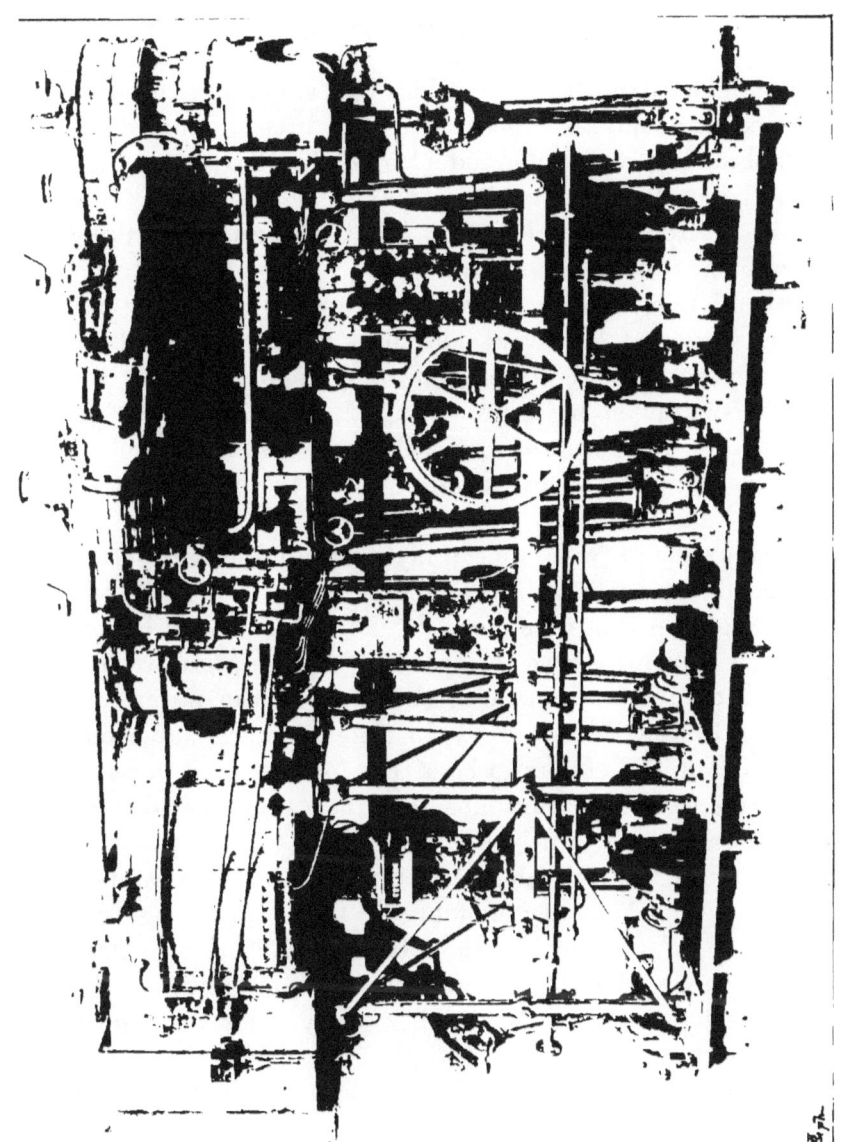

FIG. 51.—ENGINES OF TORPEDO BOAT 94.

original Thornycroft boiler. This boiler, manufactured by Messrs. Maudslay, has been fitted to three of our recent first-class torpedo boats, and also to the destroyers, *Conflict*, *Teazer*, *Wizard*, and *Zebra*.

The Seaton boiler bears in many respects a striking resemblance to the Lagrafel-D'Allest. The most important points of difference are that there are no stays for the water spaces at the front and back, and that the back water space, instead of being directly connected with the drum, is supplied by a circulating pipe at the back of it. The covers of the front and back water spaces are ribbed, and are arranged to be removed so as to reach the tube ends.

I have very grave doubts in my own mind as to whether the combination of cylindrical with water-tube boilers in the same ship is a wise one. If the old-fashioned boilers are to be generally used for cruising purposes, how are the stokers to get familiar with the ways of the water-tube ones? In the British Navy, in time of peace, supposing one-third of the boilers to be of the former class, those of the latter would certainly not have their fires lighted more than four times a year—on the occasion of their quarterly steam trials. I consider that the Admiralty were perfectly right when they announced that, after long consideration of the matter, they thought it better to have nothing to do with the "combined" system. If the water-tube boilers are good at all, surely they are good altogether.

A small objection to having two kinds of boilers in the same ship is also to be found in the necessity which is entailed of two descriptions of spare gear and two descriptions of many kinds of tools. One of the greatest grievances of the gunnery officer in a large man-of-war is the variety of ammunition made necessary by the many kinds of

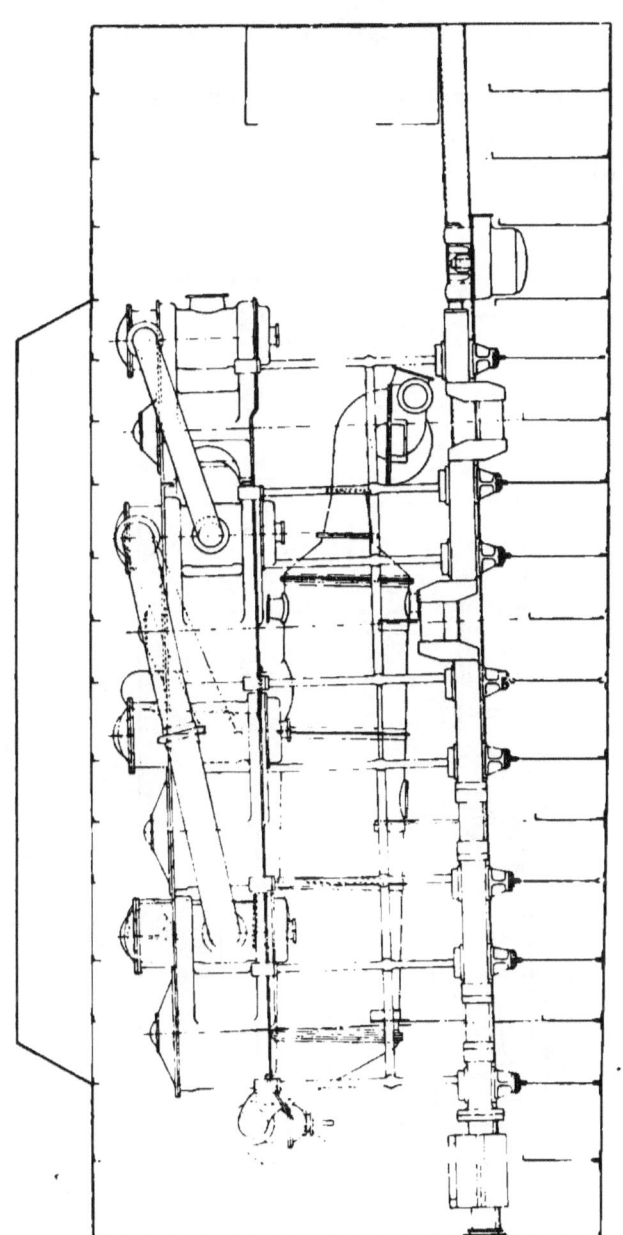

FIG. 52.—ENGINES OF "CONFLICT."

ordnance now provided, and the difficulty of correctly supplying himself with the fresh stores he requires. This, in a lesser degree, would be the fate of the chief engineer whose ship was fitted with two entirely different kinds of boilers.

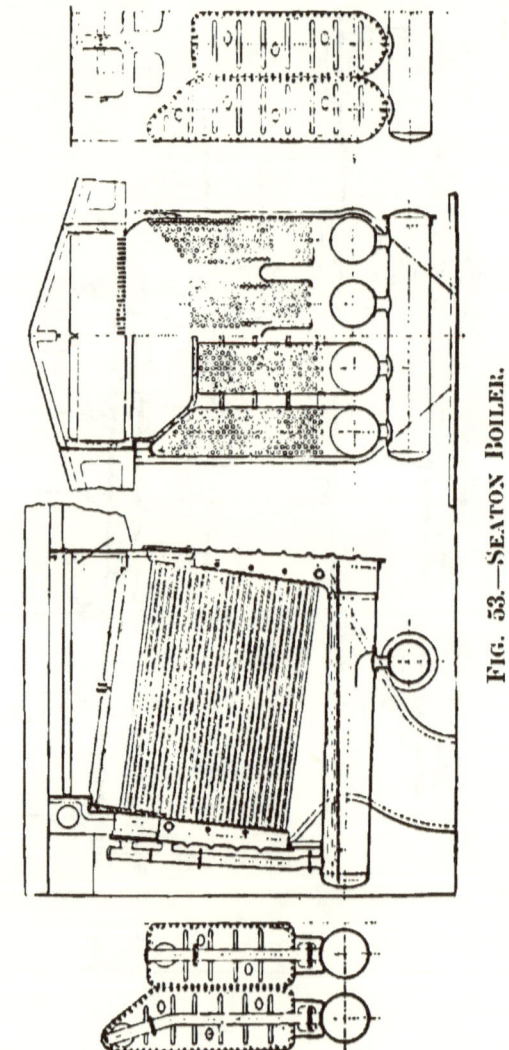

FIG. 53.—SEATON BOILER.

CHAPTER IX.

PROBABLY never in the history of engineering has there been such a controversy as has, during the past year, been carried on between the supporters and opponents of water-tube boilers. Never were two parties to a discussion more diametrically opposed to each other, and never was the question at issue of more importance. It is very likely that, soon after this book is published, one side or the other will have to own themselves practically vanquished, for the steam trials of the *Terrible* will then have taken place, and the experience gained from them will settle the point for ever. Mr. Maudslay, indeed, says, " We cannot stand still, and there must be experiments made ; but the Belleville boiler is far beyond any experimental stage, being a thoroughly well-tried and successful boiler, and fitting her Majesty's ships, *Powerful* and *Terrible*, with them cannot be looked upon as an experiment"—but Mr. Maudslay is an interested witness, while I write, at all events.

On the evening of March 11th, 1895, Mr. Allan, the member for Gateshead, who is himself a manufacturing engineer, made a strong attack on the policy of the Admiralty in deciding to fit the two largest cruisers in the world with Belleville boilers. He especially blamed them, and here I

do not know that he was particularly unwise, for adopting
a new form of boiler—new at least to our Navy—on such
an extensive scale. On March 14th of the same year there
appeared in the columns of "The Times" a long letter
from Mr. Maudslay, chairman of the firm which possesses
the sole right of manufacturing Belleville boilers, followed
by many more, some of equal or greater length, to which
I may refer hereafter, to all of which "The Times"
willingly allowed space. Of course the writers of these
letters took up opposite sides of the question in dispute.
On April 16th there appeared a large-type article, headed
"Navy Boilers," which, with the permission of "The
Times," I here transcribe *en bloc*.

"At the present time the marine boiler is attracting an
amount of attention not usually given to a subject of so
technical a character. The discussion upon the merits of
various types of steam generator, which has been carried
on with great animation in engineering circles for some
time past, has overflowed professional barriers, and has
extended to the public. The correspondence which has
lately appeared in 'The Times' is evidence of this general
interest, which arises, doubtless, from the fact that the
efficiency of the ships of the Royal Navy is deeply involved
in the question.

"Mr. W. Allan, the member for Gateshead, who is himself an engineer, made a vigorous attack in the House of
Commons upon the Admiralty for placing the Belleville
water-tube boiler in the two large cruisers, *Powerful* and
Terrible, now in course of construction. No doubt this was
a bold step on the part of the Whitehall engineers, but
that they consider there is no cause to repent is shown by
the statement of the First Lord of the Admiralty, that it is
proposed to fit all the vessels of the new programme of
which the design has been settled with water-tube boilers.

Never before in the engineering history of the Royal Navy has so radical a change been carried out.

"The Belleville boiler, which is now raising so much controversy, is no new thing, having been fitted into a number of foreign vessels of large size both in the naval and the mercantile marines. In design it consists substantially of a series of steam-generating pipes, arranged within a casing and above a furnace. The pipes are in short lengths, but are attached to each other at their ends. A group of these pipes forms what is known as an element, there being several elements in each boiler. The lengths of pipe in the elements are slightly inclined from the horizontal, returning on each other and sloping alternately in opposite directions. In this way each element forms an ascending zigzag passage through which the water circulates. The elements, say to the number of eight or ten, are placed side by side in the casing, the hot gases from the furnace surrounding them. Water for evaporation passes from a suitable receptacle into the bottom ends of the elements, and through them ascends into a steam-drum above, which is common to all the elements. The water in its ascent is partly evaporated, and the steam is taken from the drum to the engine.

"As far as our description has gone, we have a pipe-boiler which would be, at any rate for marine purposes, a dangerous and inefficient steam generator, and one closely analogous to some early forms which failed disastrously over thirty years ago. We have not yet, however, thoroughly described the design, and it will render matters clearer if, before doing so, we explain why the boiler, as above imperfectly described, would be inefficient. Suppose we take a long pipe, fill it with water, and place it vertically, or at a steep inclination, over a fire. In the lower part, nearer the fire, evaporation will take place first. If the fire be very fierce, steam will be formed in this lower part with great rapidity, even with a quickness almost approaching explosive force. The water above will thus be driven forward into the steam-drum. If steam were generated very slowly it might have time to disengage itself from the water, the bubbles floating up gently to the surface, but such a condition would require very sluggish evaporation, quite unsuitable for a marine boiler. In order to overcome the difficulty, the water-circulating arrangement which distinguishes the modern water-tube boiler, is fitted. It is a very simple device, and in the Belleville boiler takes the form of a vertical tube, placed outside the casing and connecting the steam-drum with the receptacle from which the elements are supplied with water. Taking the whole design of the boiler as described, we have, therefore, a continuous passage or thoroughfare round which the water constantly circulates. Thus, feed-water is pumped into the steam-drum, from which it descends through the vertical pipe to the receptacle which supplies the elements. The water then passes into the elements (in an ideal case each element would afford a passage to its equal share), and is through them discharged into the steam-drum, some water, of course, being evaporated in the ascent. In this way, though water may be driven upwards, owing to evaporation of steam below it, its place is continuously supplied by a fresh body of water. Thus the tubes are not denuded of water for any appreciable time, and therefore they do not become overheated. It will be evident that this race of water and steam through the whole system of the boiler is due to the difference in specific gravity between the colder water in the exterior or 'down-comer' pipe, and that of the mixture of hotter water and steam in the steam-generating pipes of the elements.

" In the Belleville boiler the steam-generating tubes are from 3 inches to $5\frac{1}{4}$ inches in diameter, varying according to the purpose for which the boiler is required. In the Thornycroft and Yarrow water-tube boilers the tubes are from 1 inch to $1\frac{1}{4}$ inch in diameter.

" It would be impossible here to describe all the various forms of water-tube boilers of which the engineering brain has been so prolific of late, and we propose to refer only to the three forms which have been lately most prominently before the public, namely, the Belleville, Thornycroft, and Yarrow types. Doubtless, many of the newer designs possess special features which will bring them to the front in the near future, if it is to be, as some predict, an era of water-tube boilers.

" In the designs of the Thornycroft and Yarrow boilers there are certain important differences, but they may be taken together here, as they both are what are known as ' express ' boilers; that is to say, they are very rapid steamers, bearing extreme forcing by fan blast, and evaporating large volumes of water whilst making small demands upon weight and space. In place of the few and comparatively long zigzag pipes of the Belleville boiler, the evaporative element is formed by a far larger number of shorter pipes which communicate between the steam drum at the top and the receptacles through which the water is supplied to the pipes. In the Thornycroft boiler there are two large pipes, external to the casing, which provide for the circulation of water. In the Yarrow boiler these external pipes have been abandoned, circulation being obtained by some of the internal pipes acting as ' downcomers.'

" There are certain qualities which it is desirable a marine boiler should possess, and among them lightness. compactness, economy of fuel, durability, safety, and accessibility

may be described as cardinal virtues. Cheapness is a
purely commercial question, which we need not touch
upon. It is evident that some of these qualities are antagonistic to others; for instance, lightness and compactness
are opposed to economy. Like the warship, the marine
boiler is a compromise. The question the naval engineer
has to decide is which design gives the balance of advantages, for it is evident no one boiler can possess all virtues
to a paramount degree.

"In a comparison between the Belleville boiler and the
ordinary marine type it would appear that with regard to
weight there is not much difference between the two so far
as the actual boilers are concerned, but, as the Belleville
boiler contains much less water than the return-tube type,
there is a gain on the total weight devoted to steam generation. It is claimed that this amounts to from a quarter to
a third of the total weight. It has been stated that trials
made with the *Sharpshooter* showed that at moderate rates
of combustion the gain in weight for approximately equal
fuel economy was no less than 50 per cent. in favour of the
Belleville boiler. The evidence on this point is, however,
somewhat bare, and a gain of 50 per cent. is certainly far
in excess of the most sanguine expectations of the Admiralty engineers. In regard to space occupied it may
be sufficient to state that responsible engineering contractors
were willing to supply ordinary boilers of equal power to
the Belleville boilers to be placed in the *Powerful* and
Terrible without asking for more space. Fuel economy is
a vexed question, upon which very divergent views are
held. Perhaps those who believe that at moderate rates of
combustion the Belleville boiler is equal to the return-tube
boiler, but at higher rates the economy will fall below the
return-tube boiler, will be found to be right; but, as already
stated, lightness and fuel economy are antagonistic qualities,

and one can nearly always be increased at the expense of the other. Ample heating surface, in terms of coal burnt, means fuel economy and a heavy boiler; scant heating surface, an extravagant but light boiler. Durability depends largely upon the rate at which a boiler is driven. For instance, the boilers in some of Her Majesty's ships were practically useless after running a trial at forced draught, whereas they would have lasted for years had they been less hardly pressed. It is on this point that those who advocate the Belleville boiler base their strongest claim. They say if it be granted that there is no gain in weight and space— granted also that fuel consumption is greater with forced draught—yet with forced draught the Belleville boiler can be worked for a long time, whereas an ordinary return-tube navy boiler would be ruined by being subjected to the same ordeal. The point engineers would like to have information upon is the extent to which the water circulation in the Belleville boiler will permit it to be forced. The question of safety may be included in what has been said above, excepting as regards damage from projectiles, the smaller quantity of water contained giving the water-tube boiler an advantage. The Belleville boiler is doubtless very accessible, and tubes can be readily replaced. On the other hand, a leaky tube in an ordinary boiler can be still more easily plugged. Generally speaking, all water-tube boilers have an immense advantage in quickness of raising steam. That is an important tactical advantage.

" Turning now to the express boilers with small tubes of the Yarrow or Thornycroft type, we find they possess the virtue of lightness to an eminent degree. They occupy less space than the return-tube boiler, and probably less space than even the loco-marine boiler, with which they may be more aptly compared. Very complete trials made by a high authority with a Thornycroft boiler prove it to be

remarkably economical in fuel consumption. In the matter
of safety these boilers undoubtedly stand very high. As
regards durability, the chief point that has to be decided is
that of corrosion. The small thin tubes are inaccessible for
cleaning, but when fresh water is used and zinc plates are
inserted the evidence available seems to point to the conclusion that steel tubes will last a reasonable time. These
express boilers are undoubtedly lighter than the Belleville
boiler, but they are less accessible.

"The water-tube boiler has conclusively proved its superiority as a rapid and light steam generator in small swift
vessels such as torpedo boat destroyers. The *Havock*, the
first of her class, was fitted with locomotive boilers, and was
looked on as the highest exemplification of what could be
done in this class of construction. Her performance has
been surpassed by the aid of the water-tube boilers, not
only by vessels launched from the same yard, but by those
of other builders—indeed, Messrs. Yarrow and Co. themselves in their letter to 'The Times' recently, recognize
the superiority of the water-tube boiler. The fact is sig-
nificant, as this firm has been eminently successful in the
past with its locomotive boilers. In the *Speedy*, built and
engined by Messrs. Thornycroft, we have an example of a
vessel of 800 tons, which has, by aid of her water-tube
boilers, given a better result than any other vessel of her
class. Although these facts are promising, they do not
bear immediately on the case of the *Powerful* and *Terrible*,
as the boilers of these vessels are of a different class; but
in the case of the Belleville boiler we have the example of
the French navy, and the Admiralty engineers have had
the advantage of the experience gained by French mercantile vessels. They have also their own not very extended
experience with the *Sharpshooter*. In spite of these things
the fitting of water-tube boilers in two vessels, each of

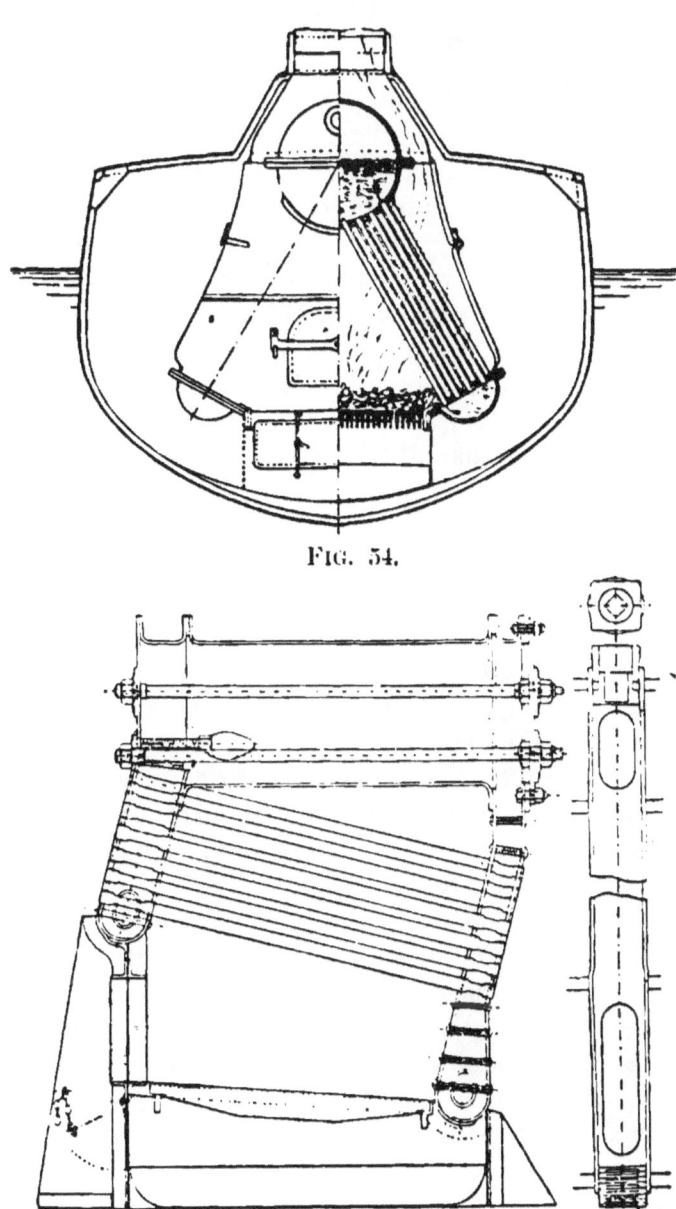

FIG. 54.

FIG. 55.—YARROW BOILER.[1]

[1] See also p. 180.

25,000 horse-power, is an extremely bold undertaking. Whether the Admiralty authorities would have been better advised in following mercantile marine practice and fitting return-tube boilers resembling those of our ocean liners, or whether they will be justified by success in the steps they have taken, we may well wait for events to prove, as the work is now too far advanced for change to be made."

It will be seen that the opinion of this writer, though decidedly favourable to the Belleville boiler, is not decisively made up. It is rather that of an engineer of advanced and enlightened views than of " The Times " itself. However, on the following day, April 17th, " The Times " published a leading article on the subject, portions of which are well worth quoting, as indicating the current of public thought on this important matter, and really forming an impartial summing up of what was said on both sides of the controversy. Says " The Times," " The change is only in the experimental stage. It is possible the experiment may fail. But a successful application of water-tube boilers to the vessels in which they are now about to be tried would undoubtedly cause a wide extension of their use and would probably lead to their adoption as the marine boiler of the future, at any rate for war vessels. Whether the same prediction can be made with regard to mercantile steamships is a question on which expert opinion still differs very widely and very vehemently. Mr. Allan, who during the debate on the Navy Estimates made a sensational and rather intemperate attack on the policy of the Admiralty in adopting water-tube boilers for the Navy, declared that he was supported by all those members of Parliament who knew what a marine boiler was and what it ought to be. Mr. Charles Wilson, however, who claims that for the last forty years he has had to consider the best form of marine boiler, declared a few days later in our columns that he is a convert to the water-tube type, and that ' if improved Atlantic greyhounds are wanted, water-tube boilers will have to be used.' He accordingly congratulated the Admiralty on their setting the example to some of our engineering firms. Another correspondent, on the other hand, has affirmed that nothing more unjustifiable has ever been attempted since we have had a steam Navy than the adoption by the Admiralty of the water-tube type of boiler for several warships of the largest size now building, These views have been vigorously combated by other correspondents, and the particular type of water-tube boiler known as the Belleville has found its natural and very capable advocates in Mr. Walter H. Maudslay and Mr. John Sampson, two representatives of the firm which holds the Belleville patents in this country."

" The Times " goes on to say that it does not feel called upon to take a side in this important controversy at this stage in the matter. It should, however, be noted by outsiders that self-interest is a factor common to both sides of the controversy. That is, that the makers of the new boilers are anxious to get a market for their wares, and the constructors of the old type naturally look with dismay upon any chance of the expensive plant they have established becoming valueless, or next door to it. The essential question is not whether the water-tube boiler is likely to become the marine boiler of all steamships, but whether the Admiralty were well advised in adopting a particular type of water-tube boiler for the large warships now building and projected.

"Now, it is claimed by those who advocate the employment of water-tube boilers for large sea-going steamers, that it is by their use alone that further advance can be looked for in the reduction of boiler-weight per unit of power, and in the safe increase of steam-pressures and consequent increase of ocean speeds; that they raise steam far more quickly than cylindrical boilers of equivalent power; that they are capable of being fitted and taken to pieces in detail without interfering with the structure of the ship wherein they are placed; that they are more easily and largely susceptible of minor repairs *in situ* and even at sea; that they are far less liable to serious injury from projectiles large or small; and that, owing to the subdivision of their water-heating elements, they are practically inexplosible, or that in any case the explosion of one or more of their tubes would not and could not be so disastrous in material and moral effect, as the explosion of a boiler of the cylindrical type. It must be manifest to every one that, if these advantages are found to belong to any water-tube boiler adopted for use in large sea-going ships, such advantages are precisely those which, as was ably argued by Captain Charles Johnstone, R.N., in our columns, would be regarded by every naval officer as almost ideally desirable. The cylindrical boiler lacks every one of these advantages in greater or less degree. It may be that for a given horse-power some types of water-tube boiler weigh more and require more space than the cylindrical, and in coal consumption are somewhat less economical.

" That may be a very good reason for not adopting them in the mercantile marine, though, as our columns have shown, many high authorities maintain the superiority of the water-tube boiler in these respects also. But this is in itself no reason for not adopting the water-tube boiler in warships. The advantages above enumerated, if attainable, far outweigh the alleged but by no means established disadvantages of increased size, weight, and consumption of fuel. . . . We have no experience of the performance of water-tube boilers in large warships in our own or other navies. . . . The adoption of the Belleville boiler for large warships is, therefore, if not a leap in the dark, a leap only in the light of theory and of experience limited to conditions very different from those of warship efficiency. We do not say that it is an unwise leap on that account. After all, it is a question of confidence in the technical advisers of the Admiralty. They, at any rate, are not influenced, consciously or unconsciously, by self-interest in the matter. Their responsibility is heavy, and it has been openly and deliberately assumed. If the boilers of the *Powerful* and the *Terrible* should prove failures, the country will hold them to a proportionately heavy reckoning. We must assume that they have weighed the technical and practical objections urged against water-tube boilers, and found them wanting. We must assume that, like the French and Russian naval authorities, they have thoroughly satisfied themselves of the special and unique advantages of water-tube boilers for use in warships—so thoroughly, indeed, as to have no misgivings as to the wisdom of the experiment they have recommended. On this hypothesis they have deserved well of the Navy and the country. On any other it will have to be said of them hereafter, as one of our correspondents has already said quite prematurely, that 'nothing more unjustifiable has ever been attempted since we have had a steam Navy.'"

This is the opinion of "The Times" as a journal, which, no doubt, soon became that of the general public who thought about the matter at all. I, however, go further than the anonymous writer in "The Times," further than "The Times" itself. I do not believe it possible that any mischance can occur from the use of water-tube boilers, especially considering the rough treatment they so frequently receive with impunity. A contributor to the "Globe" in June, 1895, wrote: "A naval officer who has had better opportunities of forming an opinion than most of his fellows

is quite enthusiastic in his praise of the Belleville boiler.
He says he never wishes to be shipmates with the old type
again.   They will stand very rough usage, such as would
make one's hair stand on end if applied to boilers of the
usual kind.   For instance, stop after a full power trial, put
out the fires with the fire extinguisher, clean out the furnaces, blow out the boiler, sweep tubes, fill up again with
fresh water, and lay fires and light up again, all these
operations being done as quickly as possible, with no sus-
picion of a leak anywhere.   Again, with the automatic
feed apparatus, a detail, such as a broken gauge-glass, may
be utterly neglected."   And this, from such a witness, is
very valuable testimony.   Briefly summarized, the contents of the more important letters which appeared in
"The Times," other than those noticed in its leading
article, were as follows.   Mr. Maudslay, who began the
fray, wrote, on March 14th, that, roughly speaking, about
sixty ships have been fitted with water-tube boilers, driving
engines of a total power of 350,000 horses, and in no case
have we ever heard of an accident of any sort; and yet Mr.
Allan speaks of the Admiralty as using untried boilers of
a most dangerous character, and states that dreadful accidents have taken place with them.   Mr. Maudslay alleges
that Belleville boilers have been in use for a great number
of years, and have been gradually improved upon until
they have become as nearly perfect as boilers can be.   Here
follows a list of thirteen French warships, of powers varying from 6,600 to 14,000, that have been fitted with
Belleville boilers.   Surely, to imitate these examples, even
in the case of our largest and most important cruisers, can
hardly be called a leap in the dark.   The Russian Government have, during some years, fitted their most important
vessels with Belleville boilers.   For instance, the new
Rurik and the *Standard*, the new yacht of 14,000 horse-

power, are the latest. Water-tube boilers are easily repaired. A Belleville boiler can be readily taken up or down any hatch without disturbing the vessel; there is no necessity to drag up the decks to remove a boiler, as is the case with cylindrical ones.

On March 19th, Mr. Charles H. Wilson, M.P., considers that Mr. Walter Mandslay fully explained how water-tube boilers have advantages in every single point over the old boiler type. He also brings forward a new element into the dispute. He says, " I believe there are reasons why there should be this outcry. It has been found necessary to get heavy hydraulic machinery, in order to press the plates together and drive home the rivets; this machinery will be useless. The great advantage to the Navy is in economizing weight, and facility for quickly raising steam."

On the following day, Mr. John D. Ellis, chairman of John Brown and Co., of Sheffield, wrote that for large war, passenger, and cargo ships the makers of the Belleville and similar boilers are not likely to find the cylindrical boiler dead, as they apparently wish every one to believe. As far as warships are concerned, I believe firmly that it *is* nearly dead, but its precarious existence may be prolonged for a little by the strenuous efforts of the owners of the expensive plant required for its production, as pointed out by Mr. Wilson above. Mr. Ellis says the London, Brighton, and South Coast Railway has two new steamers running between Newhaven and Dieppe. The *Seaford*, since lost by collision, built by Messrs. Denny, had cylindrical boilers, ordinary " serve " tubes, plain stay tubes, and closed stoke-hold forced draught, which is the least economical of mechanical draughts, because it does not utilize the waste heat of the gases after they leave the boiler. The sister ship, *La Tamise*, was built in France, and fitted with

Belleville boilers. They both develop the same indicated horse-power and have the same speed, but the *Seaford* averages 27 tons of coal per trip, and the *Tamise* 37 tons. If this be the case, there is doubtless some other cause than the difference in the type of boiler to account for it.

But one of the most interesting and important letters is that from Captain Charles Johnstone, R.N., which was mentioned in " The Times " leading article. He says that he has no right to speak for anyone but himself, but he cannot help thinking that his own view agrees with the sense of the service generally, viz., that they rejoice at the introduction of these boilers into men-of-war. As a sea officer, he believes the introduction of these boilers to be a step as advantageous as it is important. He looks at the question from a man-of-war's-man's point of view, and considers that if these boilers will stand wear and tear, and give the required speed, we may make the advocates of cylindrical boilers a present of all the advantages they claim. " Are the water-tube boilers, taken generally, more expensive of coal ? Do they occupy more space ? Be it so, we will accept that; but what we want in the Navy is boilers which :

" 1. Will raise steam quickly.

" 2. Can be renewed without pulling important parts of the ship to pieces.

" 3. Will not suffer much from small projectiles.

" 4. Will not explode with most disastrous effects.

" All these needs, I understand, the water-tube boiler supplies. This has not reference to any particular make— to this boiler or that boiler—but to the type of boiler which contains its water in small spaces.

" The Belleville boiler seems to have been very thoroughly tried ; but even supposing it is not good, then let us have for our largest ships a water-tube boiler which is good."

It will be seen from what I have written that the balance of opinion expressed by engineers, shipowners, and naval officers has been very much in favour of water-tube boilers. No doubt most of us were somewhat startled at the news that the Admiralty had decided, on the advice of their engineering staff, to fit them in such important vessels as the *Powerful*, *Terrible*, *et seq.*, but the time had fully come for such a step, and we may feel pretty confident that when they counselled its adoption, the Engineer-in-Chief of the Navy and his assistants knew perfectly well the extent of the responsibility they were undertaking. They probably knew more about the matter than anybody else in the world, for they had unequalled opportunities for obtaining knowledge, and so far from Mr. Gaudin being a French engineer, as Mr. Allan called him, he is an English naval engineer officer, born in Guernsey, with a knowledge of French acquired in his childhood. He is also a most accomplished officer from a professional point of view, and was, therefore, very naturally selected to make two voyages to Australia and back in vessels belonging to the Messageries Maritimes, which are fitted with Belleville boilers. He has been a commissioned officer for about ten years, and is now the engineer overseer of torpedo-boat machinery, building on the Thames. His testimony was, of course, of great value, but it must not be considered that it did more than add a little weight to the enormous amount of evidence which had already been accumulated in favour of the Belleville boiler.

We shall see what we shall see. But I shall be utterly discomfited if we see anything else but the two largest cruisers in the navy of any maritime power steaming at a faster rate and with greater ease than any of their competitors. I confess that, had I been in their place, I should not have had the courage to make such an experiment on so large a scale as the Admiralty engineers have done, but I believe they were perfectly justified, and admire and applaud them for it.

A writer in the "Russian Naval Magazine" for July, 1890, who had been afforded unusual opportunities in France for forming an opinion, draws the following conclusions from his experiences. "The Belleville boilers, with their appliances, cannot, in any case, occupy less space along the vessel than the ordinary cylindrical boilers; on the contrary, the Belleville boilers, with their appliances, if arranged in the most advantageous manner, will occupy about 6 per cent. more space than ordinary boilers along the line of the vessel. If Belleville boilers are used, the saving of space along the width of the vessel will enable the coal supply in the bunkers to be increased by not more than 10 per cent., and this increased supply will be only apparent, for Belleville boilers expend 10 per cent. more coal than ordinary boilers per indicated horse-power. The weight of the Belleville boilers, with water appliances and spare parts, will be from 36 to 42 per cent. less than the weight of cylindrical boilers for larger vessels, and their working and management present no difficulties, even with voyages of thirty days' uninterrupted steaming. All the automatic appliances of these boilers act in a thoroughly satisfactory manner, independently of the condition of the sea.

"The quantity of distilled water required for making good the inevitable waste of water in the boilers does not exceed three tons in the twenty-four hours for each thousand indicated horse-power, even on voyages of thirty days' continuous steaming. The Belleville boilers should not be fed with sea-water, except in cases of the most urgent necessity, which could only happen under most exceptional circumstances. If fed with distilled water, these boilers do not require to be cleaned until after thirty days' steaming, but if they are fed with salt water the tubes will inevitably burn through, even after eight days' steaming, as is conclusively shown by the trips of the steamer *Ortegal* from Marseilles to London and back. Belleville boilers, if vessels are sent on a three or four years' cruise, should be supplied with spare gear, including the working parts of the donkeys, to about 12 per cent.

" Replacing unserviceable tubes by spare ones can be easily carried out, and the boilers, with tubes replaced gradually during the course of the five or six years' service of the boiler, can serve for another four to six years, but at the expiration of from ten to twelve years' service the remaining portions of the boilers, viz., separators, the external casings of the boilers, the smoke-boxes, funnels, and other parts, will become unserviceable, and new boilers, with all their appliances, will have to be put in. In the course of ten to twelve years' service of Belleville boilers the cost of their repairs will be about 50 per cent. of their original cost, and when repairs are going on the deck will not have to be broken up. In the course of ten to twelve years' service of Belleville boilers, the steam pressure will not have to be reduced. They contain ten times less water than ordinary boilers of the same horse-power, and accordingly the danger in case of the explosion of a Belleville boiler will be less than with the explosion of an ordinary boiler. If a Belleville boiler bursts, there is no reason to fear the loss of the vessel. In the construction of Belleville boilers, it is necessary to be most exacting as to the quality of the material employed, and also as regards the perfection of manufacture of each detail of the boilers and their appliances, because it is only by the accurate observance of these conditions that the boilers can do their work successfully."

For most of the foregoing I am indebted to the translation by Major Wolfe Murray, R.A., which appeared in the number for January, 1891, of the "Journal of the Royal United Service Institution." Although this is now nearly five years old, it must be remembered that Belleville boilers had then been in use for close upon twelve years.

CHAPTER X.

In an interesting article in the "Naval Annual" for this year, by Commander C. N. Robinson, R.N., I find: "As regards dockyard-built ships, the machinery for which is supplied by contract, it will be instructive to give particulars of a typical case, because thereby it can be shown how the money paid by the country and the work done is practically spread over a very wide area, although this may not appear on the face of the contract, and indeed is not so well known as it should be. Moreover, *mutatis mutandis*, an exactly similar state of things occurs in regard to the construction and equipment of contract-built ships; for, as it will be explained later on, it is not every contract shipbuilder that supplies his own vessel with machinery. None supply it all, and this is particularly the case with that intended for auxiliary and not for propelling purposes.

"The example selected is that of the *Renown*, building at Pembroke; first, because she is a ship now under construction, and, therefore, exemplifying the practice as it is; and, secondly, because the contract for her machinery has been placed with a firm which is pre-eminently noted as manufacturing on its own premises more articles than perhaps any other engineering establishment in the kingdom. That is to say, that in other instances the work would probably be spread over a still wider area. The contract for the whole of the propelling and auxiliary machinery of the *Renown* was placed in the hands of Messrs. Maudslay, Sons, and Field, and the following statement shows how this firm is more or less the medium through which the greater part of the contract money finds its way to the various manufactories engaged in the production of special items connected with this class of work.

" The propelling machinery and boilers are manufactured by the contracting firm; the steering engines by Messrs. Caldwell and Co., Glasgow; the air-compressing machinery by the contractors; the electric-light dynamos by Messrs. Siemens Bros. and Co., Limited, Erith; the electric-light engines by the contractors; the evaporators and distilling condensers by Messrs. Caird and Raydor, London; the capstan engines are supplied by the dockyard; the pumps are manufactured by the contractors; the hydraulic machinery by Sir William Armstrong, Mitchell and Co., Limited, Elswick; the boat hoists by Messrs. Clarke, Chapman and Co., Gateshead; the coal hoists and ash hoists by the contractors; the indicators (Richards's Patent) by Messrs. Elliot Bros., Limited, London; and the telegraphs, revolution indicators, and voice pipes, by the contractors.

" So much for machinery. Now to turn to material. The crank shafts are manufactured by Sir Joseph Whitworth and Co., Limited, Manchester; the intermediate and stern shafts by Messrs. W. Beardmore and Co., Glasgow; the piston rods by Mr. W. Somers, Halesowen; the connecting rods by Messrs. John Spencer and Sons, Limited, Newcastle; the crossheads by Messrs. T. Firth and Sons, Limited, Sheffield; the cast steel cylinder-covers by Messrs. Spencer of Newcastle; the cast steel crank bearing frames by Messrs. W. Jessop and Sons, Sheffield; the cast steel pistons by Messrs. Firth, of Sheffield; the steel springs by Messrs. George Salter and Co., West Bromwich; the brass condenser tubes by Messrs. Grice, Grice and Sons, Limited, West Bromwich; the copper steam pipes by the Broughton Copper Company, Limited, Manchester; the boiler plates by Messrs. W. Beardmore and Co., Glasgow; the boiler furnaces by the Leeds Forge Company, Limited; and the boiler tubes by Messrs. Howell and Co., Sheffield.

"The following firms were also engaged in the production of material for this contract: Messrs. John Bibby, Sons and Co., Manchester, rolled brass plates; Messrs. Ridley and Co., Limited, Newcastle-on-Tyne, small steel castings; Messrs. Steward and Clydesdale, Limited, Glasgow, steel tubes; Messrs. J. Russel and Co., Walsall, steel tubes; Messrs. Dewrance and Co., London, water gauges, etc.; Messrs. P. R. Jackson and Co., Limited, Manchester, and Messrs. Applegarth and Co., London, sundry articles; the Elliott Metal Company, Limited, Birmingham, rolled brass tubes; Messrs. W. and J. Galloway and Sons, Manchester, steel steam pipes: Messrs. J. Stone and Co., Deptford, brass forgings; the Weardale Iron and Steel Company, Limited, London, light steel platings; and Messrs Harper and Co., Willenhall, sundries. The boilers are put together and finished, and the screw propellers are also manufactured by the contractors.

"It will be seen from this example that no less than thirty firms, whose establishments are situated in fifteen towns, were engaged in supplying various portions of machinery and material under a contract made by Messrs. Maudslay, Sons, and Field, for a single ship, and no account has been taken of those who supply the crude material, such as the coal, iron, etc., used in the production of the various articles. A similar list of firms, directly or indirectly employed by the Government for the supply of materials in the construction of the ship herself would be still more lengthy. It is obvious that if we multiply this number by that of the

Q

vessels built under the Naval Defence Act, we enormously increase the area affected by a large Government order for shipbuilding, and see how widespread would be the stimulation if the Admiralty demands were made on an emergency scale.

"In dealing with the subject of the machinery supply for contract-built ships, it may simplify matters if it is explained that it is the Admiralty practice to make one firm responsible for the contract for both hull and machinery, even when the second firm is recognized as the sub-contractor for the machinery. That is to say, that the Admiralty retain their right to associate engineers and shipbuilders, but put upon the latter the onus of principal contractors and the responsibility for completion, etc. It is, moreover, frequently the case that the Admiralty name certain specified patterns or patented articles to be supplied, and certain firms to be dealt with, while other portions of the vessel's equipment, such as capstans, are either ordered by the ship-builder, and inspected by the Admiralty engineers, or are supplied from the dockyards. As a rule, however, contracts are given for ships to be made in most respects ready for sea, but not including the putting in place of the armament, which is done after the ship arrives at the dockyard. This rule might of course be modified in an emergency in the case of contractors who supply guns. The armour is usually bought by the Admiralty and supplied to the contractor, and the armament is always distinct from the ship and engine contract. The reason for this is obvious, for the Admiralty can thus deal with the supply as a whole for dockyard and contract ships."

Two considerations from the above facts are manifest, namely, how large a subdivision of the money allotted for the construction of a given pair of engines takes place, and how small a share of it can be left in the hands of the original contractors. Every ounce of the materials they need to build up their engines and boilers with they must buy from outside metal merchants, for few indeed are they who are both makers and users of steel and brass. Of the former metal the first important introduction to naval use took place in 1876, when the *Iris* and *Mercury*, in their day the fastest fighting ships in the world, were both built of mild Landore steel, and the same metal was used for their boilers. Since that day, excepting for rare and special purposes, iron, and more especially cast-iron, has been entirely ousted from the constructive arts by the more useful metal, steel.

For use on board ship, however, steel is in its turn now being for many purposes supplanted by two alloys of copper, phosphor bronze and manganese bronze. Ordinary bronze is usually considered as an alloy of copper and tin, but it is difficult to make of it a quite homogeneous compound. When, however, phosphorus is added in the form of metallic phosphides of definite compositions, in proportions to suit the various degrees of hardness aimed at, a very much superior metal is produced. The exact proportions are, of course, trade secrets, but they are very small, varying probably from 0·25 to 3·0 per cent. The cost of phosphor bronze is about six times that of steel. This alloy has been supplied for over twenty years in considerable quantities to the British Navy by the Phosphor Bronze Company, Southwark, but as there are no patent rights the Admiralty now generally make their own metal in their own dockyards. Phosphor bronze is now largely used in the Navy for cast piston rings, bearings of all kinds, pump rods and studs, rolled metallic valves, cast stem and stern frames, propeller shaft brackets, etc., etc. Phosphor-bronze sheet withstands the action of sea-water much longer than does copper. In

a comparative experiment made at Blanckenberghe, lasting
over a period of six months, between the best English
copper and phosphor bronze, the following results were
arrived at : the loss in weight due to the oxidising action
of sea-water averaged for copper 3·058 per cent., while that
of the phosphor bronze was but 1·158 per cent. Propellers,
as will have been noticed in various passages above, are, in
spite of the extra cost, now generally made of bronze. They
give practically no trouble and cause no expense to maintain in order after fixing, while continual patching and paint-
ing is necessary to keep up the efficiency of partly-worn
steel blades above an unreasonable minimum degree.

Though completely differing in its chemical constituents,
manganese bronze has many of the same characteristics as
phosphor bronze. The principal objects to which this alloy
is applied in Her Majesty's ships are as follows : Propeller
blades and propeller bosses which are, of course, cast in sand.
Propeller bolts and studs, which are forged in the forgeable
quality of the bronze. For tubes for hydraulic mains, for
carrying water under heavy pressure to various parts of the
ships. For various castings, such as stop-valves, bends,
branches, valve boxes in connection with the tubes, which are
cast. For all kinds of gun mountings and fittings, such as gun
recoil cylinders, buffer cylinders, holding-down rings, clip
rings, pivot plates, toothed wheels for rotating guns, hydraulic rams for raising and lowering guns and for hoist
fittings, etc. The fuse stampings, which are made from the
forgeable quality of Parsons' bronze, stamped into the
requisite form by putting the material into the steel dies
when red hot and applying pressure. All kinds of pump
rods, air-pump rods, donkey-engine rods, valve spindles,
thrust block screws, etc., all of which are made of the forgeable quality of Parsons' manganese bronze. All these
articles used to be made in gun-metal and ordinary brass,

which have an ultimate tensile strength of about 14 tons per square inch, with an elongation of from 5 to 15 per cent. Parsons' bronze has an ultimate strength of about 35 tons per square inch, with a minimum elongation of 15 per cent., the strength of the rolled material being about the same.

The Manganese Bronze and Brass Company say, "By kind permission of Sir W. G. Armstrong, Mitchell, and Co., we give the following report of the testing of a piece of manganese bronze tube supplied to them by us, and used for conducting water under hydraulic pressure, or working heavy guns on board ship.

"The pipe was 4·9 inches outside diameter, ·3 inch thick, and 18 inches long.

"4,000 lb. per square inch internal pressure was applied without increase of outside diameter.

"5,000 lb. pressure produced an enlargement of ·03 of an inch.

"6,000 lb. pressure produced an enlargement of ·08 of an inch.

"The testing pump would not go beyond this pressure, so the tube was turned down to an outside diameter of 4·55 inches, leaving ·125 of an inch in thickness.

"1,000 lb. pressure produced no alteration in diameter.

"2,000 lb. pressure produced an enlargement of ·1 of an inch.

"2,500 lb. pressure burst the pipe.

"Two longitudinal specimens were taken from the pipe, and tested for tensile strength. They gave an ultimate strength of 31·5 tons per square inch, and a stretch of 27·5 per cent. in 3 inches."

Besides the two above-mentioned bronzes, one formed of another metal has within the last few years been gradually forcing its way to the front. The British Aluminium

Company, Limited, of Milton, Staffordshire, are now the owners of all the valid patents for the production of aluminium by means of the electrolytic process, and they expect to produce some 500 or 600 tons of the metal next year at their new works at Foyers, where they have bought some 8,000 acres, and thereby secured a large water-power. At the same time they have bought extensive banxite mines in Ireland, and their new works at Larne will treat the banxite to produce alumina—under patent—having from 98·5 to 99 per cent. of pure anhydrous alumina. This will then be sent to their Scotch works, and turned into pure aluminium by the electrolytic process. Large orders for the ingot metal will be executed direct from the Scotch works, and to make the combination complete they have a large foundry and rolling-mills at Milton for dealing with castings, sheets, angles, and the like, in aluminium and its various and valuable alloys.

At the present time the price of the pure metal is about £160 a ton, and even at this price it is cheaper bulk for bulk than tin, and a close competitor with copper. The metal has now for several years past been used extensively by both the French and German Governments for both naval and military purposes, and during the last two or three years our own Government have been introducing it in various directions. A number of castings in both aluminium and aluminium-bronze have been made for the last lot of torpedo-boat destroyers. Aluminium, slightly alloyed, is said to be the ideal metal for all castings where great strength is not required, having a tensile strength of about 9 tons per square inch and upwards, and aluminium-bronze is the strongest and toughest bronze known at the present time, as tensile tests well above 35 tons per square inch are obtained for some work. The aluminium bronze, in addition to being stronger and tougher, is also slightly lighter bulk for bulk as against other bronzes, its specific gravity being only 8·0. Aluminium copper alloy plates and angles, as used by Mr. Yarrow in his French torpedo boat, will probably be largely used for similar boats, and also for ships' boats, etc. This plate has a tensile strength of about 15 tons per square inch, and a specific gravity of 2·7 only. It will be perceived from the foregoing that there is an extensive field for the employment of aluminium and its alloys in the Royal Navy.

The French Ministry of Marine were so pleased with their aluminium boat that they have decided to have six more built, but, from patriotic reasons, not in England, although they will have to pay a much higher price to their own countrymen than to Mr. Yarrow. We, in England, have constructed an aluminium torpedo-discharging tube, which, however, was not an unqualified success. The bolts and hinges were broken and destroyed by the concussion of firing the torpedo, but gun-metal fittings have been substituted for those of the lighter metal, it is hoped with satisfactory results.

"The Morning Post," of July, 1895, said that recent experiences in the application of aluminium to the construction of torpedo boats, had tended to prove that many of the disadvantages which have been stated to accompany the employment of that material in sea-water had been very considerably diminished, if not altogether removed. Among the foremost of its foes are heat, and all matters of an alkaline composition. When heated the metal oxydizes very speedily, and when annealed at even a comparatively low temperature it loses an appreciable portion of its strength, although some of it may be restored by urging the process further. It is evidently, therefore, not suitable for the construction of any part of a machine which is exposed to the direct action of a high temperature, or sub-

jected to a large amount of friction, the inevitable pre-
cursor of that frequently dangerous agent. Its liability to
be attacked by alkaline products places it *hors de combat*
for the manufacture of pumps, condensers, and those parts
of gearing and machinery which are, in the course of
repairs and cleaning, brought into contact with soda.
These disadvantages, however, are but small when weighed
against its merits in other respects, and if they restrict its
range of useful action under the special conditions alluded
to, there is still open to it a large area for development
in fields more congenial to the display of its valuable
qualities.

While aluminium has always been regarded as practically unassailable by fresh water, it is known that it does
not enjoy the same immunity when immersed in sea-
water, and at one time fears were entertained that this
susceptibility would prove a bar to its future employment
in that direction. Fortunately, these fears have been dis-
sipated by further experiments, which have established
most conclusively that the corrosion of the metal from the
action of sea-water does not exceed 4 per cent. per annum in
unpainted plates of a thickness not exceeding one-twelfth of
an inch. As plates of aluminium, as well as those of iron
or steel, when used in shipbuilding must be painted, it is
obvious, for reasons already adduced, that a description
of paint must be selected which is deprived of all in-
gredients calculated to react upon the metal. It is also
not advisable, on electrical grounds, to place a boat of
aluminium in direct metallic contact with a copper-bottomed
craft.

In the construction of the aluminium torpedo boat for
the French Government by Mr. Yarrow, the usual alloy of
6 per cent. of copper was added to the pure aluminium
from which the plates were rolled. Their thickness was

one and a half times what would have been considered
sufficient for steel plates rolled for the same purpose. The
joints in the different plates were made by rivets of
aluminium in those parts of the boats which would necessarily be submerged in the water, but in the other parts
rivets of mild wrought iron were used. As far as possible
aluminium bronze was employed in the actual machinery
and engine work, with the exception of the principal
piston. When completed the little craft weighed 10 tons,
and when loaded with an additional 3 tons, ran at a speed
of over 18 knots an hour. A steel boat of the same power
and capacity would have weighed $2\frac{1}{2}$ tons more.

The greatest drawback to the employment of aluminium
for the construction of ships on a large scale is not the
result of external agents, but is inherent in the material
itself. It is its very low range of elasticity in comparison
with that of its rivals, iron and steel. As a material for a
"ram," aluminium would, in its present condition, be a
most unsuitable material, although it is not impossible that
this serious defect may be partially remedied in future by
the aid of the metallurgist, the engineer, and the ship-
builder. It should be kept in view that it is but a very
few years since aluminium or its alloy was first utilized in
the construction of boats. The credit of manufacturing
and launching the first specimens is attributed to the firm
of Escher Wyse, of Zurich. In 1892 that firm turned out
three small petroleum launches, built of aluminium bronze.
During the same year half a dollar per lb. was the price
quoted in the American papers for the purchase of
aluminium in large quantities in the United States.
Aluminium ingots can now be purchased in the English
market for about 1s. 9d. per lb.; but considering that the
weight of aluminium is almost exactly one-third that of
steel and iron, its proportionally equivalent rate would

amount to 7*d.* per lb. The price of the "wrought aluminium alloy" suitable for plates, bars, angle-irons, and other sections used in construction is naturally much higher, exactly in the same manner as wrought iron and steel exceed in cost their own raw material.

CHAPTER XI.

AMONG the most important items of naval expenditure, and about which little indeed is known by the general public, are stores, and these in the engineering department are certainly not of less consequence than in any other. When one considers that a fighting ship must always be to a great extent self-supporting, that she may be stationed for her whole commission where no assistance can be obtained, except of the most trivial kind, from the shore, it is evident that the periodical visit of the store-ship must often be eagerly looked forward to.

But ships can keep themselves efficient while relying wholly on their own resources, without having any recourse to a dockyard. Thus the *Sirius*, a second-class cruiser of 3,600 tons, and 7,000 horse-power, natural draught, arrived home recently from the south-east coast of America, where she had been doing duty as Senior Officer's ship for over three years, and where it had been impossible for her to be docked to undergo the usual yearly examination and repairs, to say nothing of cleaning her bottom, and yet on her passage to England realized a speed of 18·2 knots. Surely this is creditable alike to the engineer officers of the ship and to the construction of the machinery. This speed was in excess of that obtained nearly four years before on the measured mile.

The varieties of stores that have to be supplied

to the engine-room departments of her Majesty's ships amount to some hundreds, while the gunner, boatswain, and carpenter among them absorb almost as many more. Every single article, from a shearing machine to a sail needle, has to be entered in a book and signed for by the officer to whom it is supplied and who is responsible for its expenditure. Fortunately, a wiser and more common-sense view obtains at the Admiralty now as to the expenditure of stores than was the case thirty or forty years ago. In those days an officer was actually as liable to come to grief for having too large a quantity of stores, according to his books, when his ship paid off, as too few, and, as every-body's object during the commission was to economize stores in case of emergency, at the end of the commission, after three or four years, there were large surpluses of different kinds which had to be got rid of. When practicable, these were handed over quietly to the officers of another ship remaining some time longer on the station, but when this could not be done, they were simply secretly thrown overboard, or burnt in the stokehold. Many scores of pounds' worth of stores have thus been wasted, on approaching England, in a single ship. Now, an officer may return and get a receipt for any amount of stores he likes, within reasonable limits. The Admiralty are still, however, very strict in insisting on a proper explanation of all deficient stores.

At the time when so many valuable stores were wilfully got rid of, a 68-pounder gun was missed somehow after the dismantling of a gunboat in China, and the lieutenant in command was kept for many months without his half-pay till the gun turned up in a corner of Shanghai dockyard, although he had no more to do with the loss than the man-in-the-moon, and never heard a word about it till he got home to England.

Many things that one would hardly expect are counted as stores; for instance, new machinery, the estimates for which in 1894-95 were £1,347,315, and in 1895-96 £1,250,135. The accounts do not show the cost of repairing machinery separate from other repairs, nor is the cost of engine stores distinguished from other stores. The cost of coals for steam vessels, as distinct from those used for yard purposes—which are £62,000 and £58,000 respectively—are for 1894-95 £534,000 and for 1895-96 £475,000. The decrease in the latter year is partly due to the abolition of the Indian and other troopships.

Coal is naturally one of the most important articles of naval stores, and its supply is therefore a matter most carefully looked after. It is now only obtained for ships in Great Britain from South Wales, and an experienced fleet engineer always resides there who is responsible for the quality of the coal for which he recommends the Government to conclude contracts. Not so many years ago the law was rigorously enforced that when possible the coal burnt in the ships of the Navy should always consist of a mixture of one-third North Country with two-thirds Welsh, but the smoke which resulted exasperated the admirals in command of squadrons, as naval tactics became very difficult since signals could not be made out. Sir William Dowell, in command of the Channel Fleet, and H.R.H. the Duke of Edinburgh, when later commanding the Mediterranean squadron, both remonstrated so energetically and efficaciously on the subject, that now nothing but Welsh coal is burnt. Of course, this is obtained from many pits and many merchants, who are constantly being changed and whose prices constantly vary. There is no better hand at a bargain than the Admiralty, and right it is that it should be so.

When ships are abroad, and find themselves within hail

of a coaling station, they are usually supplied with the
same coal as they would obtain in England, and when they
have to deal with private merchants they are generally as
well off, only they have to pay the merchant's price, if he
has not a contract, which he generally has, with the British
Government.   At Sydney, however, the native coal is so
good and cheap that none is imported.   There are two
kinds, as in Great Britain, one resembling North Country,
appropriately termed Newcastle, and one more nearly like
Welsh, called Bulli.   This last, when I knew it, was almost
smokeless, but used to cover the deck with showers of tiny
scoriæ which were very unpleasant.   At Esquimalt a coal is
obtained which is quite good enough to obviate the necessity of using English coal, which twenty-five years ago
used to fetch £5 per ton in the Pacific.   Of course, the
coal at Gibraltar, Malta, Singapore, Hong Kong, and many
similar places, is the property of the British Government.
It will be seen from the above what an important article of
stores is coal.

The Mediterranean station affords a good example of the
brands of Welsh coal usually supplied to Malta for the
fleet.   These seem to be Hill's Plymouth Merthyr, Dowlais
Merthyr, Cyfartha Merthyr, Nixon's Navigation, Ferndale,
National Merthyr, and occasionally Powell's Duffryn.
Lately, Cyfartha Merthyr seems to be the principal sort
sent out by the Government.   At other places on the
station Cory's Merthyr and International Merthyr, and at
Port Said, Standard Merthyr.   At this last-named place
the coal is always excellent.   One firm there is never
without some 70,000 to 100,000 tons of Welsh coal in
stock.   In the event of war, supposing the path for supplies
were kept open, Port Said would more than supply the
whole Mediterranean squadron with coal.   It is actually
trimmed there into the bunkers for 19s. per ton.   The

merchants are part proprietors of the mines in Wales, and thus are able to dispense with middlemen and their profit. They shipped 12,000 tons one day last year. Every summer the Admiralty despatch five or six colliers to the Mediterranean, and the ships then fill up with coal in the sheltered harbours of some of the Levant Islands.

From another most trustworthy source I learn that the best coals of South Wales are obtained from the Merthyr and Rhondda Valleys, but the original valuable seam, known as "four foot seam," has become very scarce. The best coals are Penrykyber, Nixon's, Harris' Deep Navigation, and some eight other varieties, but the Aberdare dry coals are the only absolutely smokeless coals—all the others are, more or less, semi-bituminous, and burnt in the naval boilers give off a certain quantity of smoke. The quantity of coal loaded at Cardiff every year under Government contracts is, roughly speaking, 200,000 tons.

There is so much competition at the present time that all the colliery owners endeavour to the best of their ability to ship the coal in the very finest condition with regard to size and screening. At some of the collieries the coal, after being tipped from the trams, is carried along by endless bands, with men stationed to pick out all shale and other rubbish. The width between the bars of the screens is 1½ inches, that being the legal width.

West of the Rhondda Valley the coal is of an anthracite nature, but unfortunately means have not yet been discovered by which it can be burnt in a satisfactory manner in an ordinary furnace. The coal decrepitates to such an extent that the openings between the fire-bars soon become choked, with the result that the bars soon become melted. It is a most valuable coal if this difficulty could once be overcome. It is most peculiar, but the analysis of these coals appears very little different to the analysis of the steam coals; it is supposed that the constituents are combined in some different manner.

Next in importance to coal comes oil, as an article of perpetual use in the engine-room. It may safely be said that without oil engines running at their present speed would be impossible. In the days of slow-moving engines a good deal of oil was used, but the sole internal lubricant employed was tallow. Casks upon casks containing hundred-weights of this evil-smelling substance used to be hoisted inboard whenever the engineer was drawing stores; now it is known no more. It used to be employed every day for soaking "gaskets," as the plaited circles of spunyarn were called, for packing the pistons of cylinders and plungers of air and other pumps, and, under way, the stoker of the watch would be constantly keeping the grease-cups of the engines full with it, but it is never seen now.

The oil used, nevertheless, is much the same, for external use, as was used then. It was always called Gallipoli, in those days, from the town near Tarranto, which is remarkable for its oil-tanks excavated from the solid rock, in which olive oil is deposited for exportation, but, probably because the sources of its supply have been extended, it is now universally known as olive oil.

In India and China local oils are frequently procured, especially castor oil, and though not considered equal to the products of South Italy, they answer well enough. Indeed, the superiority of the workmanship of to-day over that of thirty years ago renders oil of somewhat less importance now than it was then. For internal use, wherever there is a chance of its reaching the boiler, mineral oil is invariably used. On account of its superior cheapness, the Admiralty, many years ago, made an attempt to introduce Rangoon oil as a substitute for Gallipoli, but the outcry against it was too great. Now, a refined mineral oil is found to be of the utmost value. It is generally prepared from petroleum.

With regard to lubrication, a writer in an American periodical, called "Cassier's Magazine," says : " In steam-ship service, for instance, quality of lubrication is known to affect speed. This is so fully recognized by steamship builders, that in tests of certain naval vessels, where extra speed developed would mean large money premiums, oilers were stationed in every possible place, with oil-cans and syringes filled with oil, to squirt at and upon every bearing, to insure full lubrication. That abundance of oil is not, after all, the real essential, is evidenced by the fact that the naval cruiser *Detroit*, in her famous run, was so complete in her automatic oiling appliances that hand oiling was at no time necessary, and in spite of her great speed, her oil consumption was normal."

I have heard a great deal about the automatic system of lubrication, but a naval engineer officer, in whom I can thoroughly trust, writes to me that most of his fellows have found the system of lubrication of bearings by means of a "drop" regulated by a valve to be unsatisfactory, as it is wasteful and requires constant attention, so that he, for one, has gone back to the old system of worsted siphon lubrication, as being by far more trustworthy.

About other stores there is not much to say. Spun-yarn, of which large quantities are still used in naval engine-rooms, is made exclusively in the rope-walks at Chatham and Devonport dockyards. Brown oakum is picked in the prisons of Millbank, Holloway, and others. Cotton waste, the consumption of which never grows less, comes direct from the mills of Lancashire and Yorkshire. Shovels, hammers, chisels, files, and other tools, come from con-tractors all over the kingdom, who are constantly obtaining

R

and ceasing to obtain orders. To these stores may be added paint for the double bottoms, packing for the engines, asbestos sheeting, copper-wire gauze, red and white lead for joints, and india-rubber rings ; yellow ochre for the funnels, thermometers, salinometers, indicators, sheet iron, steel, brass and copper bolts, rivets, angle-irons, lathes, forges, anvils, vices, drilling, punching, and shearing machines, etc., etc., so a large amount of gear is necessary to keep a warship going.

In China and the Mediterranean the *Humber* and *Tyne* respectively have the sole duty of keeping the ships of the squadrons adequately supplied with stores. It may well be imagined that not the least of the duties of the chief engineer of a ship is the seeing that the expenditure of his share of them is properly looked after and accounted for. And yet, nine times out of ten, he cannot afford the time from more important work to trouble about his stores. Very often only a stoker who can write a good hand has the sole control of thousands of pounds' worth of stores, because nobody else's services can be spared.

Before leaving the subject of stores it may be as well to mention that artificial fuel, *briquettes*, has often been tried in the English Navy. The French are very fond of this combustible, and have even used it for trials, but whether theirs is of a better quality than ours, or whatever be the reason, it finds no favour with us. One reason, no doubt, is the extra quantity of smoke it produces. We in England are so accustomed to the use of practically smokeless Welsh coal that a steaming fleet with long black feathers of smoke floating from its funnels would seem a much greater anomaly to us than it does to foreigners. Of the disadvantages of smoke there is no need here to discourse. We have only lately found out how to dispense with the pillar of smoke by day and pillar of fire by night which distinguished our 27-knot torpedo-boat destroyers—the only craft that seemed always doomed to make their presence known by smoke. More careful firing, having light fires at first in the furnaces, both consumed the smoke and burned the gases before they reached the top of the funnel.

Oil has been burned with considerable success in Italy, and even more in Russia, especially upon the Caspian Sea. It has never been tried in the British Navy, but is shortly about to be. Some celebrated engineers look upon it as the fuel of the future, but I think it will be a distant future before we are driven to import petroleum from Russia or the United States as long as we can get coal from South Wales at a reasonable rate. If there were no other objections to the use of liquid fuel, this, I think, would be a fatal one. I am, of course, aware that it has been used in conjunction with coal as a fuel in the locomotives of the Great Eastern Railway, but the fact that so little is heard of it, that no ships are specially built for its use, is a pretty plain indication that British marine engineers of the present day will have none of it.

CHAPTER XII.

At the huge meeting of men-of-war of various nations at the opening of the Baltic Canal at Kiel, there can be no doubt that the ships designed for the British Navy by Sir William White and his able staff well held their own. In the important features of speed, protection for vitals, freeboard, habitability, sea-going and sea-keeping qualities, and cost per ton, our latest battleships showed to advantage, as did also our first-class cruisers. The English fighting ships are the best in the world. But far more than English ships can claim an almost incontestable superiority over all others can English machinery and English engineers. I feel inclined to except both the *matériel* and *personnel* of the American Navy, but it is at present too young to be as yet considered of great importance. In most of the other navies, even where engines by English makers have been fitted, the inferiority of those who have to look after them is, and must be, a certain drawback. This is, perhaps, most manifest in the Russian Navy, of which strange tales are told by the employés of English contractors who are sent out to Cronstadt, or the Black Sea, to look after their machinery.

There is no doubt that the engines of the British Navy have never been in anything like a condition so nearly approaching perfection as they are now. The trials of all the battleships invariably go off without a hitch. Everything works smoothly, and both horse-power and speed come up exactly to expectation—or exceed it. A breakdown is unknown, and there is for many years no record of any mishap in the engine-room department of any battleship after she has been commissioned. The reasons for this happy state of affairs are two. Firstly, that the plans and designs for the propelling engines of large men-of-war have now for a long time been practically unaltered. A detail here, a detail there, may be changed every now and then, but in reality the engines of Penn, Humphrys, Maudslay, of Thomson, Earle, and Barrow-in-Furness are all alike, and there is very little to choose amongst them. A certain standard of excellence, both in design and workmanship, has been attained, and beyond this standard there seems at present neither power nor necessity to go. With boilers, however, the case is altogether different, as we have seen when we came to discuss them. From foreign nations in the matter of machinery we have little or nothing to learn, even from the United States, and all the other nations, except France and Germany, are good customers of ours, though we cannot expect this state of affairs to last for ever.

The second reason for the satisfactory performance of the engines of our battleships, and first-class cruisers as well, is the firm fashion in which these ships are built, so that the foundations on which the machinery rests are practically as solid as if they were on dry land. It is impossible to exaggerate the advantage that this circumstance affords to the engine builder. Vibration is unknown, although by a careful balancing of weight both Messrs. Yarrow and Messrs. Thornycroft have succeeded in abolishing it in even the flimsiest of the hulls they manage to propel at such almost supernatural speed. Shafts once laid true remain so. And here it may be remarked that the fact of the shaft not being exactly in line from the crank to the propeller-box has been the cause of nine-tenths of the accidents and trouble which occur too frequently in the engine-rooms of the mercantile marine.

There is, however, another reason for those breakages of shafts which are quite unknown in the Royal Navy, and that is that merchant vessels invariably proceed at their utmost speed, and the steel gets gradually crystallized and the shaft has to be renewed. Sometimes this condition sets in before it is suspected, and the only warning given of its approach is fracture. Now, I do not remember a single example of a shaft giving way in the Royal Navy for over thirty years, except the unimportant one of the *Satellite*, and probably one reason for this has been because the ships scarcely ever go at full speed, and another was that the chief engineer of the ship, the man who was going to have the whole responsibility of her machinery, always was in the habit of satisfying himself personally—and I daresay he does so still—that the contractors were doing their duty in well and truly laying the main shaft. It might be imagined that things would not go over smoothly between the contractors and the chief engineer, and I believe years ago such was occasionally the case, but I think in these days each party sees the advantage of being on the most friendly terms.

One of the most encouraging circumstances in the present condition of the British Navy is that after a ship has been in commission for a year or more she frequently performs better at natural draught full power than she did on her trials. This at once disposes of the idea that trials are simply meant to get on one occasion only a non-natural speed that will never be either attempted or achieved again. It was so once, no doubt, but now, when the officers and men have got used to their duties, when even the second-class stoker who came from the gutter, the ploughtail, or the brick-field, only, say eighteen months' ago, has thoroughly learned what is expected of him, a forty-eight hours' full-power run often produces results slightly better than those obtained on the official trials before the ship was commissioned.

I do not say this has occurred under forced draught, because it is seldom indeed that forced draught is used, and I am quite sure nothing but the direst necessity would ever induce a captain to order his chief engineer to employ it. But I do say that what will always practically be the full speed of a modern fighting ship, that is, her constant *maximum* sea-going speed under natural draught, has frequently been in excess of what was obtained on her official trials—which is a happy thing to know. It means, at any rate, that if at any time one of our cruisers should suddenly be required on an emergency to steam for a thousand miles to carry dispatches, or perform other important duty, she will do it at a by no means despicable rate.

It now becomes my duty to point out what I consider one of the most grievous blots on our naval administration, I mean the maintaining in commission of so large a number of ships that are utterly obsolete, and, in case of war, would be quite unable either to fight or run away. On looking over the " Navy List " I find no less than forty-five ships of this description, beginning alphabetically with the *Alert*, perhaps one of the best of them because she is new, and ending with the *Wild Swan*, which is undoubtedly one of the worst and oldest. Of these forty-five vessels all but three are actually in commission, and these three are just completed. The *maximum* sea-going speed that can be expected from any of these dummies is 12 knots, the *Wild Swan* would find it difficult to keep up 8, for she was built in 1877 and is yet considered good enough to form one, under a commander's command, of our fleet in the Pacific. The *Hyacinth*, a sloop of 1,420 tons and 950 horse-power, also has an effective speed of 9 knots at most, and is commanded by Captain H. J. May, C.B. The *Caroline*, a sister ship, is also commanded by a post-captain in China. Her *maximum* speed cannot exceed 10 knots.

The ostensible reason for keeping these useless old craft in commission is that the police of the seas is so largely left to Great Britain to maintain by herself, that most of these obsolete vessels can in case of necessity make long passages under sail alone, and that, most important of all, they are in consequence very much cheaper, and, in peace time, as efficient as more modern ships. But fighting ships are not built for use in time of peace alone, and I unhesitatingly declare that, if war were declared, not one of these forty-five vessels would dare to show her nose outside the harbour where she had taken refuge till such time as peace should be declared. Consider what this means. It comes to an average number of more than 4,000 men knocked off the strength of the Navy and hiding away from the enemy. No ship should be commissioned for foreign service that has not a possible sea-going speed of at least 16 knots. Of what use is the *Firebrand* that can barely go 6? Of course, I except the seven surveying ships, to whom speed would never be of any use. What is really wanted for police duties are small ships, of good speed, and fitted with moderate sail power, so arranged that in time of war it could easily be landed, while in seasons of peace any steaming that was found necessary would be carried out at the most economical rate of consumption.

On looking back at what I have written about forced draught, I think I ought at least to give my readers an

opportunity of judging what its friends have to say on its
behalf.   One of the best known and most accomplished
marine engineers in the kingdom, Mr. A. Blechynden, the
late managing engineer of the Naval Construction and
Armaments Company at Barrow-in-Furness, read a valuable
paper called, "A Review of Marine Engineering during
the past Decade," before the Institution of Mechanical
Engineers at Liverpool, July, 1891.   In it he states that
an examination of the records of twenty-eight steamers
showed that in those working under natural draught the
mean consumption of fuel was 1·573 lb. per indicated
horse-power per hour, which, in the case of those using
forced draught, was reduced to 1·336 lb., which is equivalent to an economy of 15 per cent.   Part, however, of this
economy may be due to the other heat-saving appliances
with which the latter steamers are fitted.

But independently of the economy of forced draught in
coal relatively to power, it is like all economies in marine
engineering, simply a question of the comparative cost of
carrying a given freight at a given speed; in other words
it is a question of the total expenses of carrying the freight
—be it corn, wool, guns, and torpedoes, or what not—with
the help of forced draught, as against the total expenses
with natural draught.   It is not a mere matter of coal
consumption, which is only one of the elements that go to
make up the total.   Assuming, indeed, that the consumption of coal per horse-power is not less with forced
than with natural draught, then, since with forced draught
it is possible to develop a given power from a smaller boiler
and consequently with a smaller weight than with natural
draught, here is at once a source of economy, because the
difference in weight may be made up in freight.   Such
evidence as exists, says Mr. Blechynden, shows that not
only is forced draught more economical as regards quantity

of coal, but by its means such classes of coal may be used as would not without it be worth putting on board. I need hardly point out that any economy in this direction, where the saving has perhaps been the greatest in the mercantile marine, is impossible in the Royal Navy, where the use of forced draught is so rare and uncommon.

Thus far the following would appear to be a fair summary of the advantageous points attending the use of forced draught. First, it seems fairly well established that, if the boilers are well constructed and are provided with ample room to insure circulation, their steaming power may without injury be increased to about 30 or 40 per cent. over that obtained on natural draught for continuous working, and may be about doubled for short runs. Secondly, such augmentation is accompanied in normal cases by a decreased consumption per indicated horse-power. But, thirdly, the same, or even greater, power being indicated, it may, with moderate assistance of forced draught, be developed with a smaller expenditure of fuel, the grates, etc., being properly proportioned. Fourthly, forced draught enables an inferior fuel to be used. And fifthly, under certain conditions of weather, when, with normal proportions of boiler it would be impossible to maintain steam for the ordinary speed with natural draught, the normal power may be insured with forced draught. In particular cases any or all of these advantages may be a source of economy; and the first of them may render possible that which would otherwise be impracticable.

As now adopted in the Navy, forced draught is purely an auxiliary intended for use under special circumstances. When a maximum power and speed are required only occasionally, or when the vessel is intended for cruising in hot climates, or under such conditions of weather as to impair the natural draught power, in such cases it is a most important source of economy. Vessels of the cruiser type, which are required in case of necessity to develop, say, over 9,000 horse-power, while the usual cruising speed of about 10 or 12 knots require only from 1,000 to 1,500 horse-power, are rendered possible at a reasonable cost by the adoption of forced draught. Here again, Mr. Blechynden would probably have spoken differently had he had the advantage of the experience of the four years that have passed since he spoke.

The recent troubles with naval machinery in vessels of the *Barracouta* class have done much to unsettle opinions in regard to this problem. But, looked at calmly, it becomes evident that the causes of those troubles are altogether apart from the question of forced draught pure and simple, and are rather questions of boiler design. So long as boilers were designed with ample spaces for internal circulation, ample capacity of furnace and combustion chamber, and so proportioned that the surfaces of the furnaces and combustion chambers were sufficient to absorb a large proportion of the heat before the products of combustion reached the tubes, and, above all, so that the tube-plates were protected from direct impact of the intense radiant heat from the incandescent mass of the fire, no serious trouble ensued. In the recent cruisers built under the Naval Defence Act of 1889, a separate combustion chamber to each furnace has been adopted with perfect success, but I doubt if, since their trials, forced draught has been employed to any extent in any one of them.

Sir William White is not, nor does he ever pretend to be, an engineer, but the twin professions of engineering and naval architecture are becoming every day so much more closely allied, that the opinion of a distinguished

man in either of them is well worth listening to by those
who belong to the other.   In 1878 the French were
already employing the plan of closed stokeholds, which
they had taken up by preference after trying various plans
in large ships : and it was the action of the French which
had led the English Admiralty to go further into the
matter at that time.   The French had gone in at once for
the closed stokeholds.   The first application of assisted
draught in the English Navy had been made in vessels
where, from the arrangement of the armament, there was
great difficulty in getting a sufficient supply of air into the
stokeholds.   The stokeholds were open, but with great
fan-power for supplying air : and in some trials that had
been made in other ships with practically the same boilers
25 per cent. more power had been obtained without any
closing of the stokeholds at all, simply by the improved
supply of air due to assisted draught.   Experiments had
then been made with closed stokeholds, beginning with a
ship of moderate size, and gradually working up to one in
which the horse-power developed exceeded 6,000 ; and so,
gradually all the ships in the Navy had come to be fitted
with appliances for forced draught and with closed
stokeholds.

Forced draught was first employed in the British Navy
in the *Lightning,* our earliest torpedo boat, constructed by
Messrs. Thornycroft in 1877.   The system was adopted,
primarily, if not solely, with the view of obtaining a much
greater power with a given weight of boilers than could be
obtained with natural draught.   Economy of fuel was not
the object sought ; if it had been it would not have been
found.   The *Lightning,* a boat only 84 feet long, of 10 feet
10 inches beam, and 32 tons displacement, attained a
mean speed of over 18 knots more than eighteen years ago.
Her engines, supplied by her builders, were compound,

driving a single screw. The high-pressure cylinder was 12¾ inches in diameter, the low-pressure 21 inches, their stroke was 12 inches. She had a steel boiler of the modified locomotive pattern, working at 120 lb. pressure. Her surface condenser was made of thin sheet copper, and was supplied with a separate engine and centrifugal pump. The machinery of this vessel was very light, steel being largely used, and the workmanship was of the very highest class. She was in her day a complete novelty, both as regards hull and machinery, and was equally a complete success. She is interesting as the pioneer of a very numerous and important flotilla.

In this way it had gradually become possible to get the results described above in the way of a possible increase of speed in a case of emergency. But it had never been intended that the ships furnished with forced draught appliances should be worked continuously at the higher pressures, and it is, therefore, an open question whether it is wise or justifiable to carry so much extra weight at an expenditure of so much extra money, to insure a problematical advantage that may never be made use of during a ship's lifetime.

At an early period it had been laid down that under the ordinary conditions of service the air-pressures in the stokeholds, when closed, should not exceed half an inch of water, which nobody would consider an unreasonably high limit. Going over a considerable period of years, and within this limit of pressure under ordinary working conditions—excluding boilers of the locomotive kind, in which the corresponding limit was about one inch—the experience in the Navy was that, with all except a special type of double-ended boilers, there had been no difficulty whatever; and the fact had been exactly expressed when it was stated that the discredit which had fallen upon forced draught, in consequence of difficulties experienced with boilers, should really be borne not by the forced draught, but by the particular design of boiler used.

In a limited number of ships there were double-ended boilers, in which all the furnaces at both ends of the boilers delivered into a common combustion chamber. This was the kind of boiler in which, not under circumstances of extravagant air-pressure, difficulties had arisen; and these difficulties had, to a great extent, been overcome by reducing the tube surface, by improving the circulation, and by protecting the tube plates from direct impact of the heat. But in these boilers it was not considered advisable to apply the higher or " emergency " air pressure, which, with the ordinary marine boilers in the Admiralty service, had formerly been two inches of water as a maximum.

In the later designs of ships for the Navy the limit of air pressure under circumstances of emergency had been fixed at one inch, which did not exceed the pressure that had been used continuously on Atlantic voyages by some of the finest passenger steamers that ran between Liverpool and the United States. In confirmation of the opinion that the trouble experienced with certain boilers was a question of boiler design and not of forced draught, the further important fact may be mentioned, that in one class of ships where every condition was identical—except that in the earlier vessels a combustion chamber common to all the furnaces was adopted, while in the later each furnace had its own separate combustion chamber—whereas difficulties had arisen in the earlier vessels with the common combustion chamber, no difficulty whatever had arisen in the later vessels with the separate combustion chamber. This difference occurred in boilers of identical dimensions working at the same steam pressure even when the air pressure in the stokeholds of the later vessels had been fully two inches.

It was only right in the interests of progress that these facts should be recognized, because forced draught had in many minds been charged with troubles which were only indirectly associated with it. The question of how best to apply assisted draught was, of course, one largely for experience to answer. In the Navy, closed stokeholds had hitherto been used; and it is an arrangement that the stokers like. Of course there are objections to the several plans. If the stokehold be closed and the air delivered under pressure, air-locks are rendered necessary, with less easy entrance and exit, but then there is no trouble whatever with the stoking. If the under-grate draught be employed, the blast must be shut off when firing. If the induced draught be used it has to be obtained by jets of compressed air or steam discharged into the base of the funnel, or by an exhausting-fan producing suction at the same place. Mr. Martin's contrivance has been alluded to in a previous chapter.

The lightness of the machinery in the Navy is partly due to the circumstance that for the boiler shells of the Navy such thicknesses are not adopted as are common in the merchant service, and so far as experience extending over several years could be taken as a guide, the change to thinner shells has been fully justified by the performances of the boilers. The lightness of the engines themselves is due in a great measure to a circumstance to which sufficient importance has not been attached, but which really exercised a great influence, namely, that in regard to both the ships and the machinery the fullest possible advantage was taken by the Admiralty of whatever could be done in the way of progress at any time by the makers of the materials, and they were prepared to pay more in first cost, if they could

get, either in castings or forgings or in any other way, an
arrangement of material which would give the best combination of strength with lightness. The aim in the Navy
was not to carry any material that was not doing work,
even if its removal had to be paid for.

While it is not an unknown occurrence to have breakdowns in the machinery of the Navy, neither are similar
accidents unknown in the mercantile marine; but to the
latter it is not considered worth while to give the same
prominence which is given as a matter of course to the
former, and which is justified by the interest that the
country takes in the Navy. But over a long period of
years there are not more than one or two cases in which the
accidents in the Navy had been of a serious nature or had
affected the main engines. As a rule they have been confined
to parts of an auxiliary or subordinate kind; and they have
not occurred in parts which are commonly supposed to be
so much lighter than the corresponding parts in the engines
of the mercantile marine. In fairness to those who have
charge of the machinery afloat it should be borne in mind
that great difficulty arises from the engines being so rarely
worked at full power. Reference has been made to vessels
of the cruiser class, which on an emergency could develop
a maximum of over 9,000 horse-power, but as a rule were
developing only from 1,000 to 1,500 horse-power. In
ordinary navigation the latter would be about the range of
power, and only occasional trials were made of the maximum
power. It would readily be understood what must therefore be the difficulty to the engineers in charge of maintaining the same efficiency and readiness in all respects for
developing a high power in ships working so much
below it in ordinary circumstances, as contrasted with the
state of things existing in ships running to cover a fixed
distance with their engines always doing their best. The

conditions are altogether so different that the difficulties
with naval engines are inherently considerable, no matter
what care might be taken.

Sir William White said that the subject of twin screws
was one with which he had been personally concerned now
about seventeen years ago, and at that time he had ventured
to predict that there was coming a period in Atlantic
navigation when the conditions that then existed in the
Navy would be reached in the mercantile marine, and that
twin screws would be adopted as a matter of necessity and
as a distinct advantage. That prediction, which then had
been to some extent a speculation, had now been verified by
experience of twin screws in vessels from the size of torpedo
boats of less than 100 tons, up to vessels of 14,000 tons
displacement, and for speeds varying from 30 to 15 knots;
and so far as could be ascertained under the difficulty of
making exact comparisons with single screws, the balance
of advantage in regard to efficiency of propulsion lay on
the side of the twin screws. The swiftest vessels that had
yet been built, including torpedo boats, had twin screws.
In one instance he remembered such grave doubts had been
entertained of twin screws that the speed for a twin-screw
vessel had been specified 2 knots below what would have
been guaranteed for a single screw, and at the end of the
trial it was found that the speed actually attained was
1 knot above what the single screw would have given.

At the present time the tendency was to subdivide the
power still further in warships. The French had built a
vessel of great size and great power, in which there were three
sets of engines and three screws; and in the United States
the same thing was being done. The matter had been
carefully looked into by the Admiralty many years ago, and
while recognizing the possibility that the time might come
when three screws would have to be substituted for two on

a limited draught of water, he thought the balance of
advantage was not yet sufficiently decided in favour of the
change.   That was one way, however, through which the
French and American designers thought they were going to
get over the inherent difficulty of the great range of power
through which the engines in a warship were required to be
capable of working.   In the *Blake* and *Blenheim*, in which
the power was 20,000 horse-power, there were four sets of
engines, two on each screw-shaft.   This was a plan which
had formerly been devised at the Admiralty, before it had
been applied in any warships that he knew of, but it had
then been set aside as an arrangement that would come in
when much greater powers were required.   Now that these
higher powers had been reached, the plan had been brought
into use.

The problem of working at low speeds by throwing certain cylinders out of action was also one that had by no
means been overlooked.   Eleven or twelve years ago, when
he was not in the Admiralty service, he well remembered
going thoroughly into this matter, with Mr. Marshall, he
believed, to see if it could be contrived to throw one
cylinder out of action, so as to work the engines at the low
powers as a two-cylinder compound instead of a triple expansion.   It was found to be perfectly feasible, and their
experiments at low powers showed that even large engines
when so treated did not indicate quite so much waste as
might be imagined.

The greatest difficulty in a warship was one that had no
connection with engineering, but altogether with tactics;
viz., that, even when the power had been brought down
low, it was still necessary to have a large reserve of power
in readiness for immediate use.   It might be that for the
low power one boiler would give all the steam required and
more; but the possible demands for variations in speed,

necessary for station-keeping and purposes of that kind, compelled the engineers to keep other boilers alight, in order that when the signal was given from the bridge to suddenly increase the revolutions from, say, forty-five to sixty per minute for keeping station, it might be obeyed without hesitation.

In statements as to coal consumption during manœuvres in which the speed of the fleet was, perhaps, only 8 knots, while the possible speed that the ship possessed in order to keep station would be 10 or 11 knots, he had often found that the lower power required only for 8 knots was reported, instead of the higher power which would represent 10 knots. As the expenditure of power varied nearly as the cube of the speed, it followed that when nominally working at only 8 knots, but ready at any moment for the possibility of 10 knots, the boilers must practically be generating twice as much steam as was being actually used except at occasional intervals when a spurt became necessary.

The above expressions of opinion, though more than four years old, are still very valuable, although they would doubtless be modified had their authors to give utterance to them in the light of to-day's experience. I still, however, hold to the views I have already expressed, that forced draught is of very questionable service in the Navy. And that those in authority at the Admiralty are coming round to this opinion is shown by the fact that the *Camperdown*, completed in 1889, a battleship of 10,600 tons, was fitted with engines which gave with natural draught 7,500 horse-power, and with forced draught 11,500; while the *Victorious*, of 14,900 tons, now building at Chatham, is to be of 10,000 horse-power natural draught, and 12,000 forced draught, thus exactly halving the difference established in the elder ship. In this case, as indeed

in most others, the Navy as it is is undoubtedly in a better
state than the Navy as it was.

However, there are signs that things that were in fashion
long ago are now in a fair way of being resuscitated.   It is
generally believed that we are on the verge of a revival
of super-heating, and that it will be successful.   This
means that a plan whereby the steam between the boilers
and the engines was surcharged with an extra dose of heat,
by passing through boxes of tubes situated at the base of
the funnel, is about to be re-introduced.   Theoretical
engineers on shore praised up the system sky-high, but
naval engineers afloat hated it like poison.   It was introduced about 1868, but the way it caused slide-faces to
" seize," and packings to burn, and the universal ill repute
into which it fell throughout the Navy, caused its life to
be short, if not merry.   I do not think myself it was in
use for five years.   There was, however, for about that
period a very determined attempt to use super-heated
steam.   Apparatus was fitted in a large number of instances, and, after trial, was abandoned for several reasons.

First and foremost, there was the difficulty of finding a
lubricant that would not decompose under the influence of
very hot steam.   The introduction of mineral oils and
vaseline has removed that source of failure without any
effort on the part of mechanics.   Then there was the
chance of the super-heater becoming incrusted with salt
carried over from the boiler with priming water.   But salt
in boilers is, or should be, a thing of the past, now that
evaporators are so common, and thus a second source of
failure has disappeared.   The other difficulties were chiefly
mechanical, and individually were not serious.   But, taken
in the aggregate, they are fairly formidable, and it is
certain that they will take some time, and a liberal expenditure of money to entirely overcome.   Attempts, for all

that, are now being made on a practical scale to re-introduce super-heating. They have not, as yet, been tried in the Navy.

In a chapter dealing, however incompetently, with the Navy as it is it would not be proper to leave out all mention of the personnel of the engine-room department. Originating in 1821 as mere working men, recognized as officers in 1847, and equal in rank nowadays to doctors and paymasters, though inferior in pay, there is no doubt that the engineers, dividing as they do the responsibility for the efficiency of the whole of a fighting ship with the executive officers, hold a position the importance of which could not have been surmised thirty years ago. To show the way in which the engineer officers of the Navy have advanced educationally since 1869, it may be mentioned that the *Inconstant*, the fastest man-of-war in the world of her time, carried nine engineer officers and two of the newly-introduced engine-room artificers. Were she to be commissioned now—for her engines are still hale and hearty—she would certainly not have more than two engineers and four engine-room artificers. The complement of such a ship as the *Royal Sovereign*, for instance, of 13,000 horsepower, is one fleet engineer, two engineers, and four assistant engineers; while her engine-room staff of artificers and stokers of all ratings amounts to 138, the total ship's complement being 729. In smaller ships of large power, such as second-class cruisers, the proportion of the engine-room staff is very much larger, amounting to 93 out of a total of 273, or more than one-third.

It is manifest that the entry and training of so large and important a portion of the ship's company, who have such serious duties to perform, ought to be carried out with at least as much care as is bestowed on the seaman part of the crew. With the rank and file of the engine-room such, however, is not the case. As a general rule, more than half the stokers who sail to a foreign station in a man-of-war are not fit to properly perform their duties for from twelve to eighteen months. Instead of being trained from boys, as the seamen are, they are entered usually as striplings of about eighteen, but I am bound to say they generally turn out pretty satisfactorily.

At one time, much more than is the case now, the great cause of anxiety to a chief engineer was what he could do in the way of economizing fuel, and in this matter he was always, to a certain extent, at the mercy of his stokers. Now, however, that the consumption of coal has diminished by one-half, since the universal introduction of triple-expansion engines, it is not quite so serious an affair as formerly. There is one point about coal consumption which, though constantly urged by engineers, is almost as constantly neglected. That is, that with the general use of steam for performing all the ordinary duties on board ship, and the necessarily enormous increase in the auxiliary machinery, a great deal of which has always to be kept going, be the ship in harbour or at sea, the expenditure of coal for other than propelling purposes has become vastly greater. Hence, in Lord Brassey's "Naval Annual," the column of "distance that can be steamed at 10 knots' speed" is often wholly untrustworthy. In some instances no allowance whatever has been made for "auxiliary purposes," which would reduce the distance given by at least a third.

CHAPTER XIII.

SINCE the completion of my chapter on Boilers, Assistant-Engineer John K. Robinson, U.S.N., has contributed a paper to the "Journal of the American Society of Naval Engineers," in which he gives the result of his observations on the working of water-tube boilers in French vessels. He is of opinion that there are only three types which can be said to have any chance of replacing the Scotch boiler; the Belleville, the D'Allest, and the Niclausse. Other types essay to fill the places of these boilers, but, so far as he knows, the three named are the only types that are used in vessels larger than gunboats. Others have been tried with a view to applying them in large vessels, but so far they have not been a success.

He says that the advantages of the Belleville boiler over Scotch boilers most appreciated in France are the great gain on the weight of the steam-producing plant, even with a reduction in the forcing of the boilers, and the ease of raising steam. The pressure allowed for this boiler is practically unlimited by the boiler, on account of the small diameter of the cylinders that contain the steam. The parts are small and can easily be removed from the boiler-rooms without cutting any holes in the decks. In fact, the whole boiler may be removed without troubling the decks at all. All this, however, I have already dealt with.

The Messageries Maritimes, one of the greatest steam-ship companies of France, if not the very greatest, began the use of Belleville boilers six or seven years ago. The officials of the company seem to be fairly well satisfied with the performance of them, but there is a tendency to obtain something that will give better economical results. We in England, during a long and exhaustive series of trials on board the *Sharpshooter*, have succeeded in reducing the expenditure of coal from 2·5 lb. to 1·8 lb. per horse-power per hour, as the stokers got more accustomed to their work.

One of the engineers of the *Australien*, one of the Messageries' vessels, says that the great advantage of the Belleville boilers is the ease with which they can be repaired. A tube can be replaced in two hours, the necessity for which is the most frequent mishap. The tubes are the weakest part. "The reducing valve is very good and always works well. It is rare that there is sufficient priming to interfere with the working of the engines, although it is always considerable. . . . . The great trouble comes from the use of even a small quantity of salt water in the boilers." This French engineer appears to be a little out of date. In any English ships with water-tube boilers, I fancy there will always be a sufficient battery of distilling apparatus and evaporators to render unnecessary the use of even a single drop of salt water. The testimony of this witness is undoubtedly a bit prejudiced. He says the firing is difficult; an ordinary fireman can never succeed here. How, then, have ordinary firemen succeeded so well in the *Sharpshooter*? Are the boilers or the stokers better than the French articles?

The engineer goes on to say that great care has to be exercised with all these delicate machines, and you never can tell which will be the next thing to break down. "If you want Belleville boilers you must have engineers everywhere." In the *Sharpshooter* there have only been two engineers during the whole period of the trials; she is of 3,500 horse-power, and her chief engineer declares that he never wants to be shipmates with better boilers. I hope I have not been tedious in my somewhat lengthy discursus on the Belleville boiler, but I cannot help feeling that it is the most important change in the engineering branch of the Navy since the introduction of the screw-propeller. Nearly one-half of the vessels now being constructed for the French Navy are to be fitted with Belleville boilers.

The D'Allest boilers are not quite so heavy as the Belleville, but the floor space occupied is greater for the same area of grate or heating surface. As, however, the D'Allest boilers are much more capable of being forced than the Belleville—which are uneconomical with over 15 lb. of coal burnt per square foot of grate—it may be said that the space occupied by the D'Allest boilers is not greater for the same power than that required by the Belleville. A great advantage for the D'Allest boilers is that with them it is unnecessary to have more than the ordinary auxiliaries of the Scotch boilers, and the frequency of the repairs required by the Belleville boilers is thus avoided. The amount of water in the D'Allest boilers is not, of course, so great as in Scotch boilers, but it is sufficient to make the use of the automatic feed-regulator unnecessary. The cost of running the D'Allest boilers is far less than the Belleville, and, indeed, it may be said that on this point the D'Allest boiler may be compared with the Scotch. It has an independent combustion chamber, and thus the gases are well mixed before entering the uptake. "The results of steaming with this boiler are in marked contrast with those obtained from the use of the Belleville. While the D'Allest boilers have not required more coal than the Scotch boilers for similar engines, the loss in coal has been with the Belleville boilers as much as 50 per cent."

So says Mr. Robinson, and with the careless firing and imperfect workmanship which not long ago were only too common in France, it is possibly true, but nothing of the kind has been observed in the experiments made in England.

The greatest advantage of the Belleville boilers over the D'Allest lies in the comparative freedom of the tubes of the Belleville boilers to expand when heated, they being fastened at only two points in each element, while those of the D'Allest are fastened the same as the tubes of the Scotch boilers, at each end of each tube. This reduces the danger of leaky tubes in the Belleville below what it is in the D'Allest boilers. Another advantage of the Belleville over the D'Allest lies in the fact that the parts of the former are smaller than those of the latter, and that, therefore, there is less difficulty in removing them from the stokeholds in case of injury beyond repair.

When one considers the fact that the French Government requires reducing valves to be placed between the boilers and the engines whenever water-tube boilers of any type whatever are used, a great reason for the use of the Belleville in preference to the D'Allest boiler may be found. Of course, the question of the advisability of using any type of water-tube boiler is quite apart from the question of the superiority of one water-tube boiler to another.

The Niclausse boiler, an illustration of which is given below, is the only other type that has so far been recognized as possessing the points that are necessary for a man-of-war. These boilers are modifications of the Collet. The differences between the new boiler and the older one lie almost entirely in the details of construction, the main points of the boilers being the same. The boilers are as different from the others as the latter are from each other. They

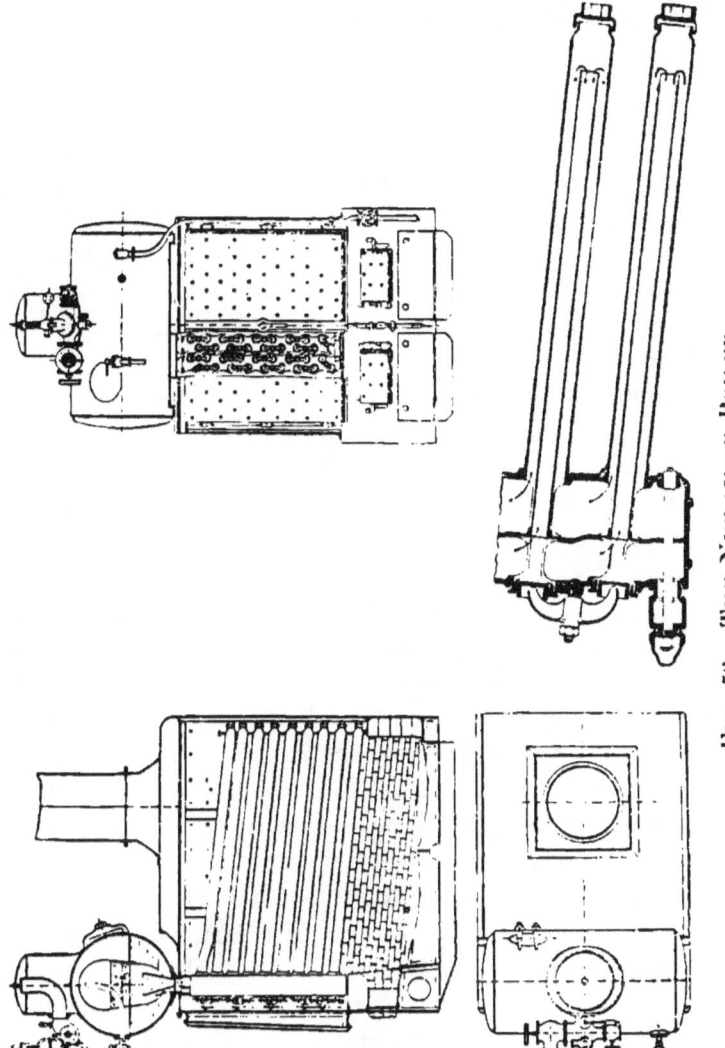

FIG. 56. THE NICLAUSSE BOILER.

are only compared with the D'Allest, as, says Mr. Robinson, the latter are so evidently superior to the Belleville that it would be waste of time to include a second comparison.

It will be seen that this writer's views and my own on this subject differ very considerably, but I have thought it right to give publicity to the opinions of a well-known American engineer, although he has not had the advantage of observing the Belleville boiler as we intend to use it in England.

The amount of water in the Niclausse is less than in the D'Allest, but it is still large enough, so that the water level may be easily maintained without the use of any other than the ordinary check-valves on the boiler. The greater the amount of water in any boiler, however, the better it is for keeping a steady steam pressure ; and some difficulty was experienced in maintaining the pressure of steam constant during the forced draught trials of the French vessel *Friant*, fitted with Niclausse boilers.

The frequency of repairs to one of these boilers is about the same as to the others, and the cost in each case is nearly equal. The joints in the Niclausse boiler are all metallic and conical, and so require more care in the making but are less liable to give trouble when once made. The tubes are all free at one end, and, therefore, the danger of leaky tubes is reduced to a minimum. In fact, during all the trials of the *Friant* there were no leaks in the boiler. It is another point in its favour that all repairs are made from the front of the boiler. It must also be remarked that it is easier to mount and dismount a tube in the Niclausse than in any other type of water-tube boiler. Within Mr. Robinson's observation, the complete operation of removing a tube and replacing it with another took less than two minutes.

In the use of these boilers in the French Navy it is not

to be forgotten that even with the number of spare boilers
—20 per cent. in many cases—and with the small rate of
combustion allowed, never above 31 lb. of coal per square
foot of grate, and with engines that are considerably heavier
than those used for the same power in America, the total
weight of the machinery is not so great.   In no case of a

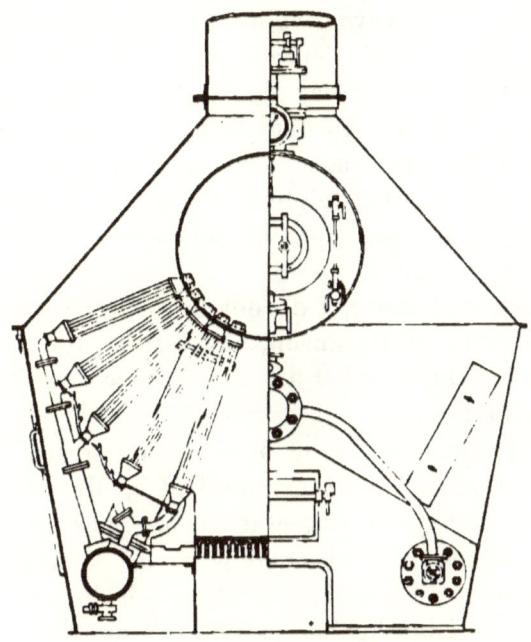

FIG. 57.—THE NICLAUSSE BOILER.

modern French man-of-war fitted with water-tube boilers
has the weight of all the machinery been over 200 lb. per
indicated horse-power: in most cases it is down to 185 lb.
These figures are, of course, for battleships and large
cruisers.   This seems to be the greatest, if not the only,
advantage for water-tube boilers.

The pseudo advantage of quickness in raising steam

is one that is more than counterbalanced by the always attendant greater difficulty in managing the boilers when under pressure. The pertinent points that seem to Mr. Robinson to need attention in the French boilers are that the tubes are always so arranged as to be easily removed or cleaned. This seems to be an absolute requisite for any boiler that can entirely replace the Scotch boiler. Water-tube boilers will always give more trouble to keep in good condition than would Scotch boilers, but they are sure to retain their full efficiency almost indefinitely, as the worn parts are replaced by new ones that are as strong as the old ones were in the first place. There is no shell to deteriorate. The gain in the weight of the boilers may be said to be about equal to the weight of the water in Scotch boilers of equivalent power.

As I have said above, I do not by any means agree with the opinions of Mr. Robinson, but I think it only right to let my readers know what are the American objections to the Belleville boiler.

Since my reference to the *Magnificent* and her system of Martin's induced draught, as supplied by Messrs. Penn, on page 54, contrary to expectation, she has run a most successful series of trials, and is to be commissioned as a flagship in the Channel Squadron within two years of the first plate of her keel being laid down. Opinions were divided as to the advantages of induced over forced draught as applied to marine boilers, so these trials were looked forward to with special interest. They have been so far conclusive as to prove that an increased pressure of steam may be more quickly raised and maintained. There was also a decided gain so far as the health, comfort, and safety of all who are engaged in the stokeholds are concerned.

Shortly after her full speed trials were concluded, the

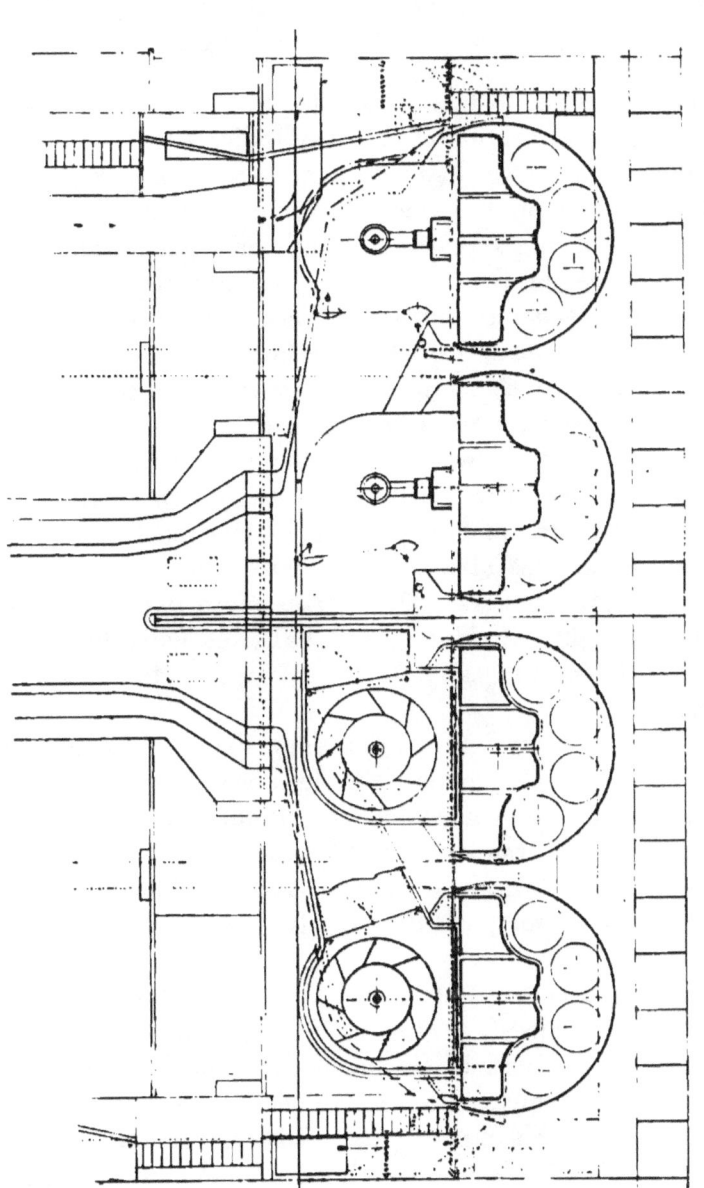

FIG. 58. MARTIN'S INDUCED DRAUGHT APPARATUS, AS APPLIED TO THE BATTLESHIP "MAGNIFICENT" BY MESSRS. PENN.

ship underwent a 30 hours' trial for the purpose of ascertaining the consumption of coal per indicated horse-power per hour. The power had been fixed at 6,000 horses. The results attained on the whole 30 hours' run showed that with a steam pressure of 133 lb. per square inch and 82 revolutions of the engines per minute the indicated horse-power developed by the engines was 6,086 and the consumption of coal, 1·67 lb. per horse-power per hour. This was held to be eminently satisfactory, as the boilers were worked with natural draught only throughout the run, and the engines were never stopped from the beginning to the end of the trial. There was exceptionally fine weather, and the smooth working of the machinery was remarkable, as was also the ease with which steam was kept up in the boilers. Of course, more experience of induced draught will be required, but from what has been seen of it in the *Magnificent* it appears to be quite successful.

The *Circe*, engined also by Messrs. Penn, is one of the latest examples of the first-class gunboats of which the *Rattlesnake* may be considered the prototype. The latter vessel, however, was only of 550 tons and 2,700 horse-power, while the *Circe* is of 810 tons and 3,500 horse-power. She has many sisters, and her type is believed to be a most useful one.

The torpedo boat "destroyers" have lately done wonders in the way of speed. Messrs. Yarrow turned out the *Sokol*, for the Russian Government, which is the first destroyer in the construction of which nickel steel has been employed. Of this metal a detailed description will be found below. She is fitted with eight of Yarrow's patent water-tube boilers, and, carrying a load of 30 tons, she achieved on the Maplins a speed of 30·25 knots—which is equal to nearly 35 statute miles, 34·8, to be rigorously exact

FIG. 59. -ENGINES OF H.M.S. "CIRCE," BY MESSRS. PENN.

T

—per hour. The air pressure in the stokehold was only about one inch of water, which is undoubtedly an evidence of the efficiency of the Yarrow boiler. The *Sokol* is 190 feet long by 18 feet 6 inches beam, and her engines develop upwards of 4,000 horse-power.

Her trials were scarcely over when we heard that the *Forban* at Cherbourg had actually beaten the *Sokol's* record. According to the contract, the *Forban* should have been able to steam at the rate of 29 to 30 knots, keeping up this speed for an hour at a time, but she has done more, as she has travelled at a speed of 31 knots. The *Forban* is 144 feet long, not quite 15 feet in breadth, has a displacement of 135 tons, and her engines are of 3,250 horse-power.

These speeds are well to read about, but it is of more importance to know what one of these destroyers can do in a comparatively long sea voyage. The *Ardent*, built by Messrs. Thornycroft at Chiswick in 1894, now attached as a dispatch boat to the Mediterranean Squadron, is 200 feet long, 19 feet beam, 250 tons displacement, and 4,500 horse-power. She was recently ordered to proceed from Bûdrûm to Malta, a distance of 660 miles, which she easily accomplished in 35 hours, and had some coal left in her bunkers, out of the 60 tons she started with, at the end of her trip. This is, as nearly as possible, 19 knots per hour, which, for a long cruise, is satisfactory enough.

I have omitted to mention that several of our old battleships have been supplied with new triple-expansion engines. Pictures are given of the new machinery of the *Monarch*, third-class battleship, 8,000 horse-power.

*   *   *   *   *   *   *

Nickel steel is manufactured from ordinary steel by the addition of nickel in the proportion of from 3 to $3\frac{1}{2}$ per cent. Ordinary steel consists of carbon and pure iron, the carbon varying from 0·3 to 1·5 per cent., while mild steel,

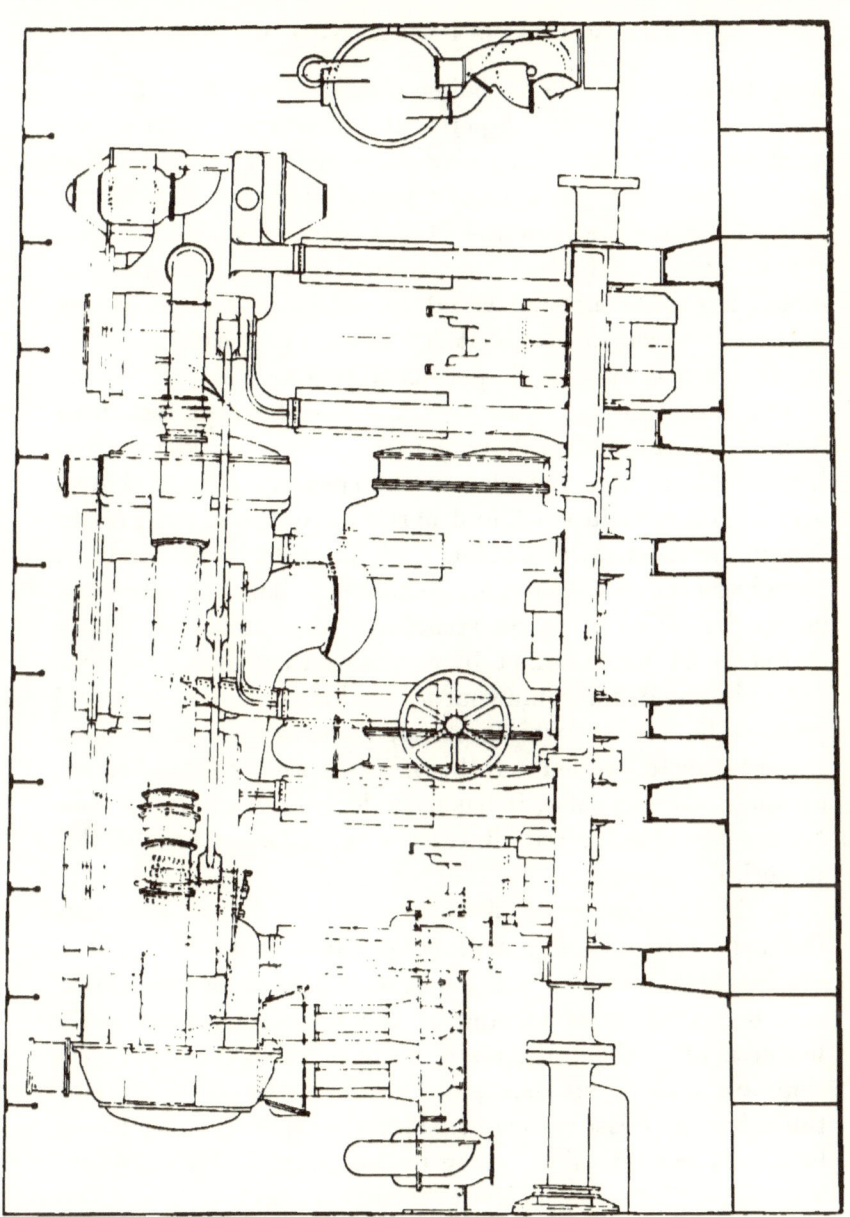

FIG. 60.—ELEVATION OF NEW ENGINES OF H.M.S. "MONARCH," BY MESSRS. MAUDSLAY.

from which ships' plates, boiler plates, angle bars, etc., are made, contains under 0·5 per cent. of carbon. Most of the mild steel used for these purposes is made by the Siemens-Martin process. In a recent paper read by Mr. H. A. Wiggin, before the Iron and Steel Institute at Birmingham, it was stated that steel containing about $3\frac{1}{4}$ per cent. of nickel has an elongation equal to ordinary mild steel, but its tensile strength is about 30 per cent. greater, and its elastic limit is at least 75 per cent. greater.

The material also possesses the merit of perfect uniformity of texture, or homogeneity, and is therefore quite trustworthy. The increase in the strength of nickel steel over ordinary mild steel, and particularly the much greater elastic limit—nearly double that of mild steel—that it possesses render it extremely suitable for building purposes, either for ships or large structures on shore. It is also stated to be less affected by corrosion than ordinary steel, but opinions differ somewhat upon this point, and it would perhaps be wise to await experiments on a scale larger than those hitherto carried out before accepting this statement as final. In any case, it has been decided to construct new boilers for the United States cruiser *Chicago* out of this material.

If the non-corrosive properties of nickel steel are satisfactorily determined, it will be possible to build shells of marine boilers of the same weight as those at present in use, but capable on account of the greater strength of the material of withstanding strains of much higher pressure than are now being used ; or, which is the same thing, if the existing pressures are considered sufficient, there would be a very considerable saving in the weight of the boilers. The very high elastic limit of nickel steel is the determining factor in this case, for in all structures subject to a load the working load is well fixed by the elastic limit, and

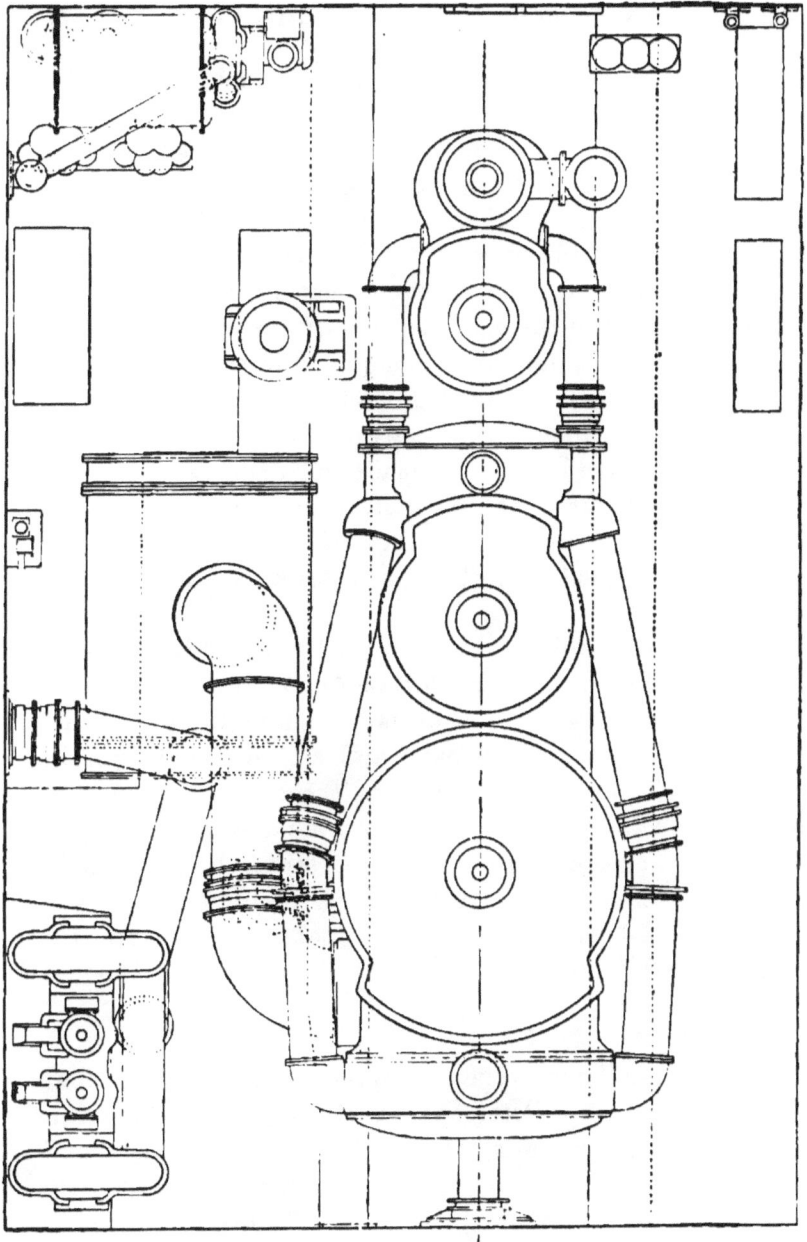

Fig. 61.—Plan of New Engines of H.M.S. "Monarch."

not by the ultimate tensile strength of the material used in the structure.

It is not only in constructions which are subject to either a steady or a slightly fluctuating load, such as a steam boiler, that nickel steel is likely to prove useful. It is much more capable of withstanding sudden shocks than ordinary steel, and it is probable that it will be brought largely into use in the manufacture of guns and of armour plates, and it is being already employed in the construction of various parts of machinery, such as shafts, piston-rods, and the like, which are liable to sudden strains. Some experiments have been lately made in Sweden with armour plates manufactured of nickel steel, in which it was found that plates composed of this material were 54 per cent. stronger than good wrought-iron plates of the same dimensions.

It is also capable of being forged and welded quite as easily as ordinary steel, and although at present it is more expensive to make than this latter material, there is no reason why increased demand and supply should not in time bring it down to the price of the ordinary steel. In any case, in the construction of warships where saving of weight is a matter of so much importance, the small extra cost can count for nothing. It is probable that in a battleship the saving in weight upon the hull and machinery would be from 700 to 800 tons by the use of nickel steel.

* * * * * * *

One of the latest types of water-tube boilers is that patented by Messrs. Petersen and Macdonald, of Fountain Court, E.C., and manufactured by Messrs. John Fraser and Son, Millwall. The boiler in question has been built upon the compound water-tube principle of the inventors, which allows of each nest of tubes, nine in number, being coupled up at each end with the steam drum and circulating system respectively by means of a single opening, thus reducing proportionately the number of holes necessary under other systems, where each tube is secured singly in the plates.

The boiler consists essentially of a steam drum, or receiver, placed axially from front to back at the upper part, and supported at each end by two large pipes, in which the water circulates downwards to supply the compound tubes. These latter are arranged radially on each side of this drum, the fire-grate being between them; thus, the flame and draught divide right and left, and the hot gases pass among the tubes practically at right angles thence round the drum to the funnel.

Each compound set of tubes is interchangeable in its own row, and is quite independent of its neighbours, so that expansion is well provided for; also, each is capable of being turned round on its axis, so as to present another portion of its exterior surface to the action of the fire, thus prolonging its life. The circulation is so active in these tubes that scale does not lodge within them, but it is all swept out into the steam drum, and finally is deposited in the feed drums below. This fact has been actually ascertained.

The boiler which I have been describing is one of 400 horse-power, standing upon a floor-space of about 9 feet by 8 feet, the height being 9 feet. Steam had been raised in it at the beginning of November, 1895, on more than fifty occasions, the time occupied from the moment of starting the fire, with cold water, until the gauge registers 150 lb. per square inch, being from twenty-one to twenty-five minutes. The numerous joints have always remained perfectly tight under this treatment. These joints are made with a soft copper ring between faced flanges, and are so arranged as not to be in the direct draught of the fire, being protected by baffle-plates, provided with projecting ledges on which ashes accumulate, and so form a non-conducting wall, which also keeps the casing cool.

The steam produced is quite dry. A handkerchief dipped in water, wrung out by hand, and then held in the issuing steam being perfectly dried in about a minute.

Not the least advantage of this type of boiler is the ease with which it can be transported over difficult country, and erected at its destination by unskilled labour, and without riveting, in the course of a few hours. The heaviest piece, the steam drum, weighs about 25 cwt., and could, if necessary, be made in sections to suit circumstances; and, for sea transit, most, if not all, of the parts might be packed inside the drum. When the grate area had been properly adjusted it evaporated 13 lb. of water per pound of coal per hour, from and at 212° Fahrenheit.

APPENDIX.

SOME STANDARD WORKS ON PROFESSIONAL SUBJECTS.

"A Manual of Marine Engineering," 1893. By A. E. Seaton, Lecturer on Marine Engineering to the Royal Naval College, Greenwich, etc., etc. Price, 18s. Griffin and Co., The Hard, Portsmouth. Ninth edition, comprising the design, construction, and working of marine machinery, with numerous tables and illustrations reduced from working drawings. This work is considered, with reason, to be the most valuable ever published on this subject.

"The Marine Steam Engine." By Richard Sennett, late Engineer-in-Chief of the Navy, and Managing Director of Messrs. Maudslay, Sons and Field. Price 21s. This book, which has been translated into Italian, and other foreign languages, would undoubtedly have been kept up to date but for the premature demise of its gifted author. As it is, it is probably one of the most practical works on the handling of the modern marine engine.

"The Steam Navy of England, Past, Present, and Future." By Harry Williams, Chief Inspector of Machinery, R.N., 1894. Price 12s. 6d. W. H. Allen and Co., Waterloo Place, London. Third Edition. "A series of essays, clearly written and often highly suggestive, on the still

unsolved or only partially or tentatively solved problems
connected with the manning and organization, and propulsion of our modern warships."—*Times*.

" Steam and the Marine Steam Engine." By John Yeo,
Fleet Engineer, R.N., Instructor in Steam and Marine
Engineering at the Royal Naval College, Greenwich. 1894.
Price 7s. 6d. Macmillan and Co., London. This book has
been prepared from the lecture notes of the author, and
represents, in an abbreviated form, a considerable part of
his course of instruction in Steam for Executive Officers at
the Royal Naval College.

"Elementary Lessons in Steam Machinery and the
Marine Engine." By J. Langmaid, Chief Engineer, R.N.,
and H. Gaisford, Engineer R.N. 1893. Price 6s. This
book was compiled for the use of the Naval Cadets studying
on board H.M.S. *Britannia*, but although of such modest
intentions, it yet contains information of much value,
especially the short description of the construction of a
battleship.

" A Treatise on Steam Boilers ; their Strength, Construction and Economical Working." By Robert Wilson, C.E.
Fifth Edition, 1893. Revised by J. J. Flather.

"Boilers, Marine and Land ; their Construction and
Strength," 1890. By Thomas W. Traill, R.N., C.E.,
Engineer-in-Chief to the Board of Trade, etc. Second
Edition. With Illustrations. London, Charles Griffin and
Co. A Handbook of Rules, Formulæ, Tables, etc., relative
to material, scantlings, and pressures, safety-valves, springs,
fittings and mountings, for the use of engineers, surveyors,
draughtsmen, boiler-makers, and steam users.

" The Marine Steam Engine ; its Construction, Action,
and Management," 1892. By Carl Busley, Professor at
the Imperial German Naval Academy. Two editions,
German and English.

"Fuels, Solid, Liquid, and Gaseous," 1891. By H. J. Phillips, F.C.S., Analytical and Consulting Chemist to the Great Eastern Railway. Lockwood and Sons, London. Their Analysis and Valuation for the use of Chemists and Engineers.

INDEX.

www.ingramcontent.com/pod-product-compliance
Lightning Source LLC
Chambersburg PA
CBHW021037030726
47496CB00006B/1585